Five Therapists and One Client

Five Therapists and One Client

Raymond J. Corsini
and Contributors

F.E. PEACOCK PUBLISHERS, INC.   *Itasca, Illinois*

Copyright © 1991
F. E. Peacock Publishers, Inc.
All rights reserved
Library of Congress
Catalog Card No. 90-62760
ISBN 0-87581-345-3
Printed in the U.S.A.
Printing 10 9 8 7 6 5 4 3 2 1
Year 95 94 93 92 91

To my friend and publisher
F. Edward Peacock

Contents

Preface xi

Chapter 1	**FIRST INTERVIEW WITH DONALD GREEN**	1
Chapter 2	**ADLERIAN PSYCHOTHERAPY** *editor:* Harold H. Mosak *therapist:* Raymond J. Corsini	13
Chapter 3	**PERSON-CENTERED THERAPY** *editor:* Nathaniel J. Raskin *therapist:* Fred Zimring	59
Chapter 4	**RATIONAL-EMOTIVE THERAPY** *editor:* Albert Ellis *therapist:* Leonor Lega	103
Chapter 5	**BEHAVIOR THERAPY** *editor:* G. Terence Wilson *therapist:* Barbara McCrady	141
Chapter 6	**ECLECTIC THERAPY** *editor:* Allen E. Bergin *therapist:* Sol Garfield	195

Figures

2.1	Protocol for establishing Adlerian life style	24
2.2	Donald Green's comparison of himself and his sister	25
4.1	RET Self-Help Form	113
4.2	Client's three-month goal form	130
5.1	Self-recording form for daily routine	155
5.2	Example of Donald Green's self-recording form for daily routine	157
5.3	Problem list for Donald Green	164
5.4	DSM-III-R Axes for diagnosis of mental disorders	165
5.5	Initial treatment contract for Donald Green with Barbara McCrady	169
5.6	Graph of lateness and discomfort ratings for Donald Green	174
5.7	Definitions of cognitive distortions	178

Contributors

Allen E. Bergin, *Brigham Young University, Provo, Utah*
Raymond J. Corsini, *private practice, Honolulu, Hawaii*
Albert Ellis, *Institute for Rational-Emotive Therapy, New York, New York*
Sol Garfield, *Washington University, St. Louis, Missouri*
Leonor Lega, *St. Peter's College, Jersey City, New Jersey*
Barbara McCrady, *Rutgers University, Piscataway, New Jersey*
Harold H. Mosak, *private practice, Chicago, Illinois*
Nathaniel J. Raskin, *Northwestern University Medical School, Chicago, Illinois*
G. Terence Wilson, *Rutgers University, Piscataway, New Jersey*
Fred Zimring, *Case Western Reserve University, Cleveland, Ohio*

Consulting Editor: **Danny Wedding, Ph.D.**

Preface

Although the vast literature in psychotherapy covers practically all aspects of this complex field, there is still an important lack with theoretical and practical consequences. Simply stated, what is missing is an answer to the question: How would therapists using different systems handle the very same client?

Five Therapists and One Client is intended to provide a preliminary, partial answer by demonstrating as precisely and as completely as possible how five therapists working within the structures of five different major theoretical orientations would have treated the same person. One way this can be done is by having real therapists do imaginary therapy with a fictitious client.

In developing this book, my first task was to invent a relatively normal person with relatively minor but unusual and persistent problems—what generally occurs in the private practice of psychotherapy. A second task was to select contemporary systems of psychotherapy, each different from the others in theory and practice. With the assistance of Dr. Danny Wedding, my collaborator in *Current Psychotherapies,* four clear-cut systems of therapy were selected: Alfred Adler's Individual Therapy, Carl Rogers's Client-Centered Therapy, Albert Ellis's Rational-Emotive Therapy, and the Behavior Therapy of a number of innovators, among them G. Terence Wilson. Finally, after a considerable amount of discussion I decided to add Eclectic Therapy, on the grounds that most psychotherapists are really eclectics, and eclecticism is probably the wave of the future.

The next problem was to enlist experts as chapter editors. They were asked to write short introductions about their systems, to select the therapists to write the case histories, and to write critiques of the therapies provided. Editors and authors received "The First Interview with Donald Green" (Chapter 1) and an instruction manual to ensure uniformity in the writing and to provide readers with a disciplined comparison among the systems.

I had three roles: as overall editor, as author of "The First Interview with Donald Green," and as one of the therapists. The reason for the last role is that the first therapist recruited by Harold Mosak did not meet production standards, and the second one missed two deadlines. And so, at Dr. Mosak's suggestion, I became the therapist of my own imaginary client. I imagine this to be a literary curiosity, but I believe the purpose of the book is not compromised; all others involved in the book approved this innovation, and my chapter was edited and critiqued just as the others.

I was pleased to discover that the concept of *Five Therapists and One Client* made sense to all in this book. The editors and authors met my highest expectations. I personally learned a good deal about each of the other systems, even though I knew a good deal about them already.

A close reading of this book should affect every therapist's thinking and procedures to some extent, and I hope this book will advance the science and art of psychotherapy to some degree. Reading these caricatures of real therapy by people who are passionate adherents of the various points of view should be a real learning experience, not only for therapists. Students, people in need of therapy, and all who have curiosity about vagaries of the human condition and how others attempt to alleviate human psychological suffering should also learn from it.

Finally, I wish to express my most earnest thanks to Ted Peacock, president of the publishing firm which bears his name, to whom I dedicate this book—perhaps another literary curiosity.

Honolulu, Hawaii   Raymond J. Corsini
Spring, 1990

First Interview with Donald Green

After my one o'clock client left, I looked at my schedule and noted that I would be seeing a new client at 2:00. His name, carefully written with an underline under the last name to indicate that this was exactly how it was spelled, was Donald Green. I had no other information about him.

When Donald Green arrived, I saw he was a bit shorter than average and somewhat pudgy. He was wearing a brown suit and glasses. We shook hands, and I noticed that he had a firm, warm, dry grip. I waved him to the chairs and couch in the room and walked over to my chair. He took the seat farthest away from me, and we looked at one another a while, sizing each other up. I got the impression he was a bit more uncomfortable than the typical first-time client.

I said, "I'm pleased to meet you," and waited to see what he would say in reply.

Mr. Green took an envelope out of his inside coat pocket and offered it to me. "I have here a psychological report done on me which you may want to see," he said.

I reached over, took it, and put it on my desk. "I'll look at this a bit later," I said, "but right now I'd like us to talk a bit. Will you tell me the reason for this appointment?"

He answered, "I've been having problems on my job, so my supervisor suggested that I see a doctor. I went to my regular physician, and he ordered all kinds of tests. When he got the results he told me he could find nothing physically wrong, and he thought I should see a shrink. So I looked in the telephone directory, and I selected you."

"Tell me something about yourself," I said.

"Well, my problem is that I come in late to work practically every morning. I am an engineer for (mentioning a large industrial manufacturing company). I'm in charge of waste disposal systems and controls for emissions from smokestacks, pollution, things like that. I've been with this company since I graduated from engineering school 17 years ago, and I've had this particular job for 6 years. I work on my own and report to the chief engineer, but I hardly ever see him or bother him. Every evaluation I have had has been very good. In recent years, though, there has been one black mark on my job ratings—being late for work."

"Can you tell me more about that?"

"As I said, I'm late almost every morning. I always was sort of a sound sleeper. In college I had an alarm clock. Now, I have three alarm clocks, two electric and a windup model. I set them at five-minute intervals, and every night I hide them in different places, one in the bathroom, one in my living room, and one in my bedroom. I also have an arrangement with a neighbor to call me on the phone and keep ringing until I get up and answer—the phone is in the living room. And finally, the paperboy comes and I pay him to keep knocking at my door until I open it and get the newspaper from him. And after all that, I still get in late."

"I see. Can you tell me any more?" I asked.

"I like my job, and I have always been punctual about almost everything. This coming in late started about three years ago and has been steadily getting worse. It's not at all like me. I usually stay after regular hours to make up for coming in late, and sometimes I go to the office on weekends and do not ask for overtime pay, though I live out in the suburbs. I don't think my job is in real jeopardy, but people are talking about me. My supervisor likes me and is worried. He thinks I should do something about the problem, and that's why I'm here."

"Well," I said, "I want to ask you some questions. But first, do you have any questions to ask me?"

"Just how confidential is this therapy?" Mr. Green asked.

"According to the ethics of my profession, I am obligated to give no information about you to anyone unless you give me permission to do so, unless I learn something I clearly believe would be dangerous to you or to other people."

"Oh, there will be nothing of that sort, I assure you."

"Good. Let me ask you this: Have you ever had any personal counseling or psychotherapy before, or have you ever thought of having any? And if so, for what reasons?"

"I guess everyone has problems or thinks of discussing matters with therapists. I *have* thought about it, but I never really considered it seriously. No, I've never seen any professional person about personal problems, but I'm sure I have some, just like anyone else. I suppose the reason I have such trouble getting up in the morning has some psychological basis, but I can't figure what it might be."

I said, "Now I'd like to ask you some personal questions." When he nodded his agreement, I asked, "What is your present family situation?"

"I'm not married, never have been," Mr. Green replied. "I have one sister but I have not seen or heard of her for ten years. I don't even know where she lives or if she is married. We never got along and never liked one another. She is eight years older than I am, just 50 years old now, and I'm 42. My parents are dead. There are some uncles and aunts but I have never really had anything to do with them. I live alone."

"How about your social life?"

"I have two pretty good friends, Jim, an artist about 20 years older than I am, and Mary, his wife, who is a bit younger. I have dinner at their home every Thursday night. I usually bring some of the fixings, like a steak, and she cooks while Jim and I play chess. Then we eat, talk, and I walk home."

"Is that your entire social life?"

"Practically all. We have a company picnic and a Christmas party that I go to, but I usually go alone. I just don't do much socializing. I even eat at the company cafeteria by myself, but usually I brown-bag it, bring my own lunch and eat it in my office. I guess you could call me a loner."

"Do you date?"

"No, I've never dated. Look, you will ask me this eventually, but I am not a homosexual. Just never dated—well, once, at the senior prom in high school. I like women, but I just am shy with them, I guess."

"Ever have sex? With anyone?"

"Never."

"Tell me about the family you grew up in."

"I more or less grew up as an only child, since my sister was so much older, and she didn't like me. My father was 15 years older than my mother; he was 40 and she was 25 when they got married. I was a so-called change-of-life baby, born when my mother was 41 and my father was 56. He was a strange man, liked to be by himself a lot. I saw very little of him. He worked as a bookkeeper, and he would come home for dinner, go into his room—he had a separate bedroom—and that was that. Our family hardly ever did anything together. My sister was usually with her friends—she had lots of them. My mother used to try to get her to take me along but she wouldn't. She was mean to me."

"What can you tell me about your mother?"

"She was a saint. Quiet, always working. If she had nothing else to do, she would knit. She had a few friends who would come to the house, but not when my father was home. He did not like strangers coming into the house. She was loving but not affectionate."

"How did your parents get along with each other?"

"They rarely talked to one another. I never saw them even hold hands or anything. When I learned the facts of life I could not believe that they had ever slept together—you know what I mean?"

"Yes, of course. So, essentially, they ignored each other?"

"More or less. I know my mother liked to talk and socialize, but not my father. She was a kind of martyr, but I think she loved him."

"What was your relationship with your father?"

"Distant. We practically never talked or did anything together. He just avoided me—but then, he avoided everyone."

"And what was your relationship with your mother?"

"She took good care of me, like nursed me when I was sick. But she was not really affectionate. I don't think she ever hugged me or kissed me."

"Are you more like your mother or your father?"

Mr. Green looked up to the ceiling and thought for a moment. "I guess I am a bit like both of them—solitary like my father and a hard worker like my mother. I'm always busy. Besides my job, I have a paying hobby fixing up used cars."

"I'll want to know more about that a bit later," I said. "First, tell me something about your sister."

"Oh, Diana. She was wild, rebellious, sociable, just as different from me as possible. I was obedient, tried to please my parents. Neither of them could do anything with *her*. And, as I mentioned, she ignored me. I was good in school and she was not. My mother wanted my sister to take me out so I could be with her and her friends, but she never wanted to. There used to be a lot of arguing about that. I didn't want to go with her, anyway. She had lots of friends, but I usually had just one."

"Can you tell me more about yourself as a child?"

"I played a lot by myself. I did my chores. I did my homework. I didn't want to go to summer camp after the first time. I was a Boy Scout for a while, and I always did a lot of reading—I still do. I did well in school, better than my sister. And I helped a lot around the house, while Diana went out a lot. She got yelled at and punished often, but not me. She was very competitive with me and jealous of me."

"Is there anything about you that you might want to change, besides this matter of not getting up in the morning?"

"Well," Mr. Green said, "yes and no. I realize that I am different from other people, and I wish I were more sociable. Still, I feel I am a success and get along OK. I sometimes feel lonely and depressed and wish I had more friends. Sometimes I think I would even like to get married and have children." He paused, took a breath, and then continued. "Actually, I feel trapped in my life-style—the way I live—and I don't know how to break out of it. Sometimes I feel like screaming. I've even had thoughts of suicide. Deep down, I'm lonely. I've never talked so much about myself to anyone else in my life as I'm doing now with you. I don't really have any confidants. Even Jim and Mary, my friends, they really don't know much about me, and I don't know much about them, either."

"So there is more that concerns you than just getting to work on time?"

"That's right. I don't know much about therapy, but is it too late for me to start being more—well, like other people, more normal, in the statistical sense? Or am I doomed to be a loner all my life?"

"I can't answer that," I said.

"I suppose it *is* kind of a dumb question. I really want to know what makes me tick. Do you think you could help me?"

"That really is a judgment you must make yourself," I replied. "I can assure you of only two things: What you tell me will be confidential, and I will try my best to be of real help."

Mr. Green smiled. "I do feel comfortable with you," he said, "and I have confidence in you. When I took your name out of the telephone book I figured I would see maybe a half dozen or so people and take the best one I could find. But now I think I will not see anyone else. What do you think of that?"

"I think that's up to you, of course, but I appreciate it that you feel comfortable with me."

Mr. Green looked me in the eye and asked, "How about you? Do you like me?"

"As of this moment, I simply want to get to know more about you," I replied. "I want to keep any feelings out of the situation. We are now more or less sizing each other up to see whether we can work together, and I am only interested in getting more information from you. Is there anything else I should know about you?"

"Well, my sexual impulses are toward women. I subscribe to a couple of men's magazines. I take care of myself sexually. You know what I mean?"

"Of course. We can go into that in greater depth if you wish later. Anything else?"

"Yes, there is. I am ashamed to tell you about it."

Mr. Green looked up to the ceiling, contemplating this confession. I wondered what it could be. When he began to talk, it was evident that whatever he was going to say, it bothered him a great deal.

"You will think I'm crazy," he began. "Every once in a while I go into a kind of panic about something, and then it turns out that there was no need for the panic. But these things I imagine are so real, so real . . . ." He seemed to be struggling for self-control. For a long time he was silent, while I waited to hear what was bothering him.

Finally he said, "I fantasize catastrophes. They become real, and I act in weird ways. And I do it again and again and again. I don't learn from my experiences; it happens over and over. I imagine something, always terrible. I exaggerate whatever it is. It keeps me from sleeping sometimes, I get so worried." And again he was silent for a long time. I waited patiently to see whether he would tell me more.

When Mr. Green started talking again, he said, "Let me give you an example. I buy cars, fix them up, and then sell them at a profit. I live in a small house, but it has a large heated garage that can take four cars. I have a lot of machinery, a metal lathe and other equipment. I look up ads for cars for sale by owner, and if I find a model I like I call the person up and make arrangements to see it. If I like it I buy it, take it to my garage, and fix it up. Then I resell it. So, as I told you, I have a paying hobby.

"About a year ago I saw one of the cars I had sold in front of a garage. I began to think that the woman who bought it from me had taken it to the garage because it wasn't working. I decided she was angry with me; maybe she was going to sue me or have someone beat me up for selling her a lemon—that sort of thing.

"So I began to keep away from the part of town she lived in. It got so I avoided going to town at all, afraid of meeting her. This went on for months. I couldn't sleep, was in constant fear. I even thought of giving up my job, changing my name, moving to another state. One evening I was in line to go to a movie, and someone tapped me on the shoulder. I turned around. *It was her!* I wanted to faint, scream, run away, but I controlled myself. She just started talking about the movie, and then I asked her about the car. She said she was happy with it and it ran fine.

"I then mentioned, as casually as I could, that I had seen the car in front of a garage. She said she had never had to take the car in to be fixed—she drove it all over, and nothing had ever gone wrong with it. I was so relieved, I can't tell you. But then I started concocting another and even worse imaginary catastrophe. I hope you can understand that they become more real to me than reality."

"I can certainly understand fantasizing of this kind," I said. "But you said you had another fantasy?"

"Yes, one right after another; it's been like that for many years. Here's another example. One year I did not send in my income tax return on time. I kept delaying and started to think that if I did send it in I would be penalized or even jailed. The longer I waited, the more I became certain that I would be sent to jail. One day or night the FBI would break into my house, arrest me, and send me to prison. For months I agonized about this. Finally I told Jim, my friend, about it. First he laughed at me and told me there was nothing wrong with what I had done. He said lots of people miss the deadline, and the IRS simply fines them for being late. But I would not believe him. Finally he practically dragged me to the IRS office; I wouldn't go alone. I was positive I would be put in handcuffs."

"What happened?"

"The woman I talked to at the tax office was very nice. She told me a lot of people for one reason or other did not send in their returns on time, and there might be a small penalty, a fine or something. But you know what happened? Actually, I had a refund coming. Instead of being fined or going to prison, I got money back. The company had taken more money out of my checks than necessary. Can you beat that?"

"So, you scare yourself about things that are not real?"

"I guess that's so, but they sure are real to me at the time. Very real, very, very real. Does this sound crazy?"

"No more than children being afraid of ghosts and hobgoblins living in closets. Well, I think I have a good deal of information about you. Is there anything else you want to tell me or ask me?"

"I already feel better having told you all this," Mr. Green said. "I think you should read the report I gave you, however."

"We'll get to that," I said. "But first, I'd like to know if there is anything else about you that you think I should know."

"My job calls for me to give directions to foremen and mechanics about pollution and manufacturing to specifications. If they start to argue with me, I usually don't make a fuss over it or stand up to them. I feel that they are more powerful than I am, even though I have authority over them in these matters. I'm afraid of them; I even have done work myself rather than make a fuss about it. I guess I'm kind of a coward. At times like these I feel worthless. Deep down, I have a fear of other people."

"Is there any fear of anything right now?" I asked.

"No," he replied. "I'm between these crazy fantasies right now. When I finally find out how nutty I have been, like seeing that woman on the movie line or the IRS agent, then I feel OK. But I wonder about my imagination, my growing fear, my inability to tell anyone about it, my unwillingness to do anything about it. Like, it seems I just want to stew about it."

"Anything else?"

"I do have a strange phobia—fear of dogs. No, not of dogs, but the barking of dogs. Even a little puppy, if it starts to bark, I get all upset. I will be walking down the street and sure enough, if I hear a dog barking—even if I can see it and know it's tied up or behind a fence—I will either cross the street or turn around."

"How about dreams? Do you dream often, do you have a recurring dream?"

"There are two dreams that I have over and over. One is that I have just failed a crucial examination and will not get my degree. It is so real that when I wake up I have to assure myself that it is not true. The other one is that I am somewhere with no money and no place to go; sometimes I'm even naked. I'm just lost.

"Oh, some years ago I had absolutely the most unusual dream of my life. To understand it, you have to know that I am not at all musical. I like music, but I have never been able to learn to play any instrument. In this dream I was in an opera house. I think I was alone. And—here's the unusual part—I could hear the beautiful music and when I woke up I was angry because I wanted to hear more of it. What's funny about this dream is that I never dream sound, and certainly not music."

"We may go into dreams later, but now I'd like to ask you about your first memory."

"My first memory? . . . Well, yes, there is one I think about once in a while. I think I was about three years old. I was standing on the roof of an apartment building we lived in, looking down to the street. I was with my mother, who was waiting for my father to show up. Finally she saw him, and she pointed him out to me, saying he was carrying something, and she hoped it was ice cream."

"Can you tell me more about that first memory?"

"Well, I could not see my father, and I guess the reason is that I'm shortsighted. You can see I wear glasses. I remember thinking how wonderful it was that she could see him, and I remember hoping that my father would be bringing ice cream, since she wanted it."

"Yes, that is an interesting first memory," I said. "I'm writing it down, and we may discuss it later. Anything else?"

Looking as though he were about to cry, Mr. Green said, "I came here because my supervisor suggested I see a doctor and then the doctor suggested I see a psychotherapist. This was about my getting to work late, but there are a lot of things that bother me. I feel I have been a failure in life—living like a hermit—no real friends—no women—no possibility of ever settling down, getting married, having children—being scared of dogs barking—the fantasies that become so real. I am even worse off than my father was. At least he got married and had children. Do you think there's any hope for me?"

"Yes," I said, "there is always hope. People *can* change. And psychotherapy can make a difference. Whether it will in your case, I certainly don't know at this time. But let's look at what's in this envelope you gave me. I've heard of this industrial psychology firm. They have a very good reputation. How did they come to evaluate you?"

"Well, my company decided to have every person in the organizational structure at certain salary levels evaluated for managerial potential. The way it worked was like this: First, all who were eligible had to volunteer to be evaluated. It was only suggested, not required, that you have this evaluation, whether or not you wanted to become a manager. The evaluation was to go to us personally and not to the company. The only thing the company would know would be whether or not we were considered to have potential as managers, so the company could decide which employees should be sent to a training course. I did not want to be a manager but I wanted the evaluation, so I went through the three-day program. They gave us all kinds of tests, and we had stress interviews, role-playing, sensitivity sessions, that sort of thing. I finally got this confidential report, which they promised went only to me. I wish you would read it. We were told that if we went to any therapist, like I'm doing now, the psychology firm would give you fuller information—exact scores on tests, that sort of thing."

I took out two sheets of paper imprinted with the name of the industrial psychology firm and noted the name of the psychologist who had written the report. I read it quickly, while Mr. Green waited.

CONFIDENTIAL REPORT ON DBG

This report is written at the request of an industrial organization which will be given a recommendation of Yes or No relative to our estimate of the managerial potential of the above employee, identified by initials only. No other information on the employee will be given to the employer. This report is given to DBG, the person evaluated. No other copies are made or kept. As a matter of company policy, we will not discuss the report with DBG or provide him with any further information about our evaluation procedure. However, any professional licensed in this state to practice a helping profession may be given, with DBG's written permission, copies of documents relating to the report, including objective test scores, projective materials, etc., within one year of the above date. After this date, all such materials will be destroyed.

At the time of this evaluation, DBG is an adult male who states that he is in good physical health, takes no medication, and is a moderate drinker and a nonsmoker. He has a B.S. degree in engineering and has taken additional courses in his specialty. He graduated from elementary school, high school, and college at the usual times and went to work for his present employer immediately after graduation from college. He obtained his job through his father, who had worked for that company for many years.

He has moved upward within his specialty and is considered a good employee who can be depended on. His direct supervisor states that DBG frequently is late coming to work, but in view of the nature of his work, and his tendency to work overtime without compensation, this is no problem. Nevertheless this supervisor, who is planning to retire soon, believes that DBG may have difficulty with a new supervisor because of his lateness. We have not explored the reasons for this behavior.

DBG states he has no interest in becoming a manager. He has taken this evaluation mostly for the purpose of knowing more about himself. We find that he is relatively unambitious, at least as far as further advancement in this company is concerned. He intends to remain with the company, in which he has been employed 17 years, until retirement.

In discussions with others about DBG, a part of our usual procedure, we find that he is thought to be peculiar. From all we can learn, this opinion is based primarily on the facts that he has no close associates in the company; usually eats lunch alone, frequently brown-bagging it from home; does not participate much in company parties or picnics; and does not engage in social relations with anyone in the company, either on or off the job.

He has never been officially reprimanded (except advised relative to his lateness) and maintains a kind of protective shield about himself. In talking with this evaluator, DBG answered all questions completely, volunteered little, and did not appear to be hostile or anxious. He seems to have a lot of self-control. In a word, his relationship with the evaluator was formal and neutral. I did not get to know him very well.

Test Results

Intelligence. Two tests of general mental ability, a group and an individual test, put him in the top decile of adult males. He functions well in both verbal and nonverbal areas.

Interests. A test of vocational interests shows a preference for person-centered activities, especially sales. Because this finding is in decided contrast with both his training and his stated preferences, a second test of vocational interests was also administered, with the same results. There is a secondary interest in mechanical work.

Personality. On the basis of a questionnaire, multichoice test of personality, nothing significant stands out, and the same is true for a projective test. He falls well within the limits of normality, showing a considerable degree of creativity and imagination on the projective test. In discussions, he states that he has no artistic or creativity capacity and does not do any writing or painting.

Leisure-time activities. He spends most of his free time repairing and refinishing automobiles. He purchases cars and then resells them. He does some fishing and a great deal of walking. He takes walking tours on his vacations and has taken some cruises.

Summary

Overall, DBG is a self-contained individual, of above-average intelligence, but within the expected limits for his profession, a person with creative capacities and social potentialities, who seems to have established himself comfortably in a position for which he has been trained. He seems to have no desire to move either horizontally or vertically in this company or to seek employment elsewhere.

This writer would say that DBG has found his niche and seems content on the job and is well suited for his work. He may benefit by having some personal counseling in view of his solitary habits. He is not recommended for managerial training.

Neil T. Pinckney, Ph.D.

I put the report down and said, "Seems rather complete and well done. What about it? Anything you want to discuss?"

"I thought it all fit in quite well, but I wonder about the item that says I have an interest in selling. I've never sold anything in my life, and I don't particularly like the idea of selling."

"All I can say about that is that apparently you replied to the questions in the vocational-interest tests in the same way successful salespersons do. This may be worth examining in greater detail later on. Anything else before we discuss whether you want to start therapy with me?"

"Yes . . . can you tell me anything about the therapy?"

"I will, but not today; we just don't have time. So let's get a schedule established, days and hours we can meet, how often you would like to meet with me, and we will discuss whether you have insurance, the payment schedule for my time, and so on. OK?"

"Fine," said Mr. Green. "Let's get the business part of this over with."

Adlerian Psychotherapy is based on the personality theory of Individual Psychology originally developed by Alfred Adler. This theory represents a psychology of growth (rather than instincts or drives), in which each person strives for maximal competence to achieve personal goals, which often are not conscious. The individual attempts to reach these goals in a unique, creative manner, within limits established by heredity and environment. Taking a holistic approach, each person establishes a unique life-style which becomes normal and useful when it is in accord with the needs of others.

The Adlerian therapist is not a curer of sicknesses but rather a teacher. Clients are seen not as ill but as mistaken, discouraged, defeated, pursuing wrong goals, having incorrect views, moving in useless directions. The therapist's task is to listen to clients to achieve a deep understanding and then to redirect them and encourage them to change their concepts, perceptions, and behaviors. In this way, the therapist helps them to move in the direction of social interest.

The concept of *Gemeinschaftsgefühl* (social interest) is the single most unique and most important element of Adlerian psychology. This philosophical notion that success (in the total sense of being an optimally functioning human being) is a function of caring for others is a distinct break from the notion that psychology should be neutral and free of philosophical values.

Harold H. Mosak

Adlerian Psychotherapy

SOMETHING ABOUT THE THERAPIST • *Raymond J. Corsini*

When I received the master's degree from City College of New York in educational psychology in 1941, the only course that concerned any kind of human interaction was one in which we learned to administer individual intelligence tests. Nothing in the curriculum had anything to do with psychotherapy, which at that time we understood as a medical procedure limited to psychiatrists who had had years of personal analysis. Psychologists were supposed to be specialists in testing, though they might do low-level counseling such as vocational guidance. I took my first course in psychotherapy 14 years later, after I had done more than 1,000 hours of individual and group psychotherapy.

My bachelor's and master's grades were always well below average, though I tried my best to earn good grades. In contrast to my miserable academic career was my performance on objective tests. I had received a scholarship to CCNY based on my scores on the New York State Regents scholastic examinations, and on entering college I scored in the top percentile, 1 of 20 out of 2,000 entering students. Later, while enrolled in the master's program, I competed in a state civil service test for junior psychologist. Even though I had the poorest grades of my academic cohort of 25 students,

I scored No. 1 in my class on this test, and this led to an appointment as junior psychologist at Auburn Prison in New York.

While working at Auburn I was accepted in the Ph.D. program at Syracuse University. After five years of attending classes evenings, weekends, and summers, I was flunked out. At age 34, while working at the California state prison at San Quentin as senior psychologist, I enrolled in the Ph.D. program at the University of California at Berkeley. Three years later, I again was flunked out. I finally earned the Ph.D. from the University of Chicago in 1955, at age 41. I mention my unusual academic history because it has meaning relative to my own psychotherapy.

At Auburn Prison I moved up from junior psychologist to associate psychologist and then was raised to the highest grade, senior psychologist. After a temporary transfer to the newly opened reception center at Elmira Reformatory, I was appointed as the chief psychologist at San Quentin. Three years later I became the supervising psychologist of the Wisconsin Department of Corrections, then the most prestigious and best-paid position in the field of prison psychology. After three years there, I left Wisconsin to study for the Ph.D. with Carl Rogers at the University of Chicago.

Once I had the Ph.D., I worked at the University of Chicago as a psychometric expert, became a partner in an industrial consulting firm for the next five years, and then taught for a year at the Illinois Institute of Technology and for another year at Berkeley (where I had flunked out some ten years earlier). At age 50 I moved to Hawaii and established a private practice, from which I retired in 1988 at the age of 73. Along the way, in addition to my various jobs, I was always busy doing research and writing and editing books, several of which are devoted to psychotherapy.

Professional Experiences

At Auburn Prison one of my duties was to make sure every inmate's prison record included an IQ score. Since Auburn was a transfer prison, with most inmates coming from Sing Sing, where they had been tested by another psychologist, my main task was to interview inmates and write preparole reports. (Over the years, I wrote about 2,000 such reports in the three state correctional departments that employed me.)

Eventually I established what amounted to a private vocational counseling practice at Auburn Prison. After two years of this practice, I decided to see how my clients had done relative to my vocational advice. I was able to get 100 percent follow-up with 50 inmates—after all, this *was* a prison. To my surprise, not a single prisoner I had counseled had followed my advice. I later published an article about this experience, with a postnote written by Carl Rogers (Corsini, 1947).

I had read Rogers's book *Counseling and Psychotherapy* in 1943 and, intrigued, had been looking for an opportunity to try his nondirective procedure. When an inmate in his 20s who had come to see me for vocational guidance indicated he would also be interested in personal guidance, I attempted to do formal psychotherapy in a nondirective manner for the first time. By the third session this client was in tears, wanting me to tell him whether he was a homosexual. I could only reply endlessly, à la Rogers, that he was *worried* that he was a homosexual. He was in love with another inmate to whom he had never even spoken, and for this reason he had concluded that he was gay. I wanted to give him reassurance that even if he was a homosexual, this was not necessarily bad, and at the same time I wanted to stay true to Rogers's method, so I suppressed my humanistic impulse and would not give him the answer he was asking for. I wrote to Rogers, taking a long chance that I could get his opinion on how to handle this client. To my surprise Rogers replied, and for several months he supervised me by mail.

While taking graduate courses at Syracuse University, I sat in on one taught by a Professor Wells whose specialty was hypnosis. Fascinated by his demonstrations, and with no other training, I decided to try hypnosis at the first opportunity. What happened was so traumatic that I did not "fool around" with hypnosis again for many years. A prisoner who had come to me for counseling about getting a divorce had an unusual criminal history. He was in prison for his first crime. At the age of about 30, he had assisted another man in an armed robbery, driving a stolen car to and from the scene, and then he had refused to accept his half of the stolen money. He had told his wife about the crime and his plan to confess it, leaving her in hysterics. He had gone to a police station, confessed, and pleaded guilty. He had been found guilty and sentenced to 15 to 30 years. Now, he told me, he wanted to give his wife a divorce so she could remarry.

Intrigued by the unusual circumstances of the crime, I asked him whether he might want to know the real reason for participating in a robbery and then giving himself up. He agreed to hypnosis and I began the procedure, imitating the professor I had seen. To my surprise, within minutes the client was in a deep trance. For over three hours I had him in and out of hypnosis, suggesting he would have amnesia when he came out of it. I tried all kinds of tests to make certain he was in a trance, since I could hardly believe that my first attempt had been so successful. When I asked him, while he was hypnotized, why he had committed the crime, he said it was because he wanted to go to prison—which he later indignantly denied in his normal state. Finally I informed him that on coming out of the trance he would have a complete memory of all that he had told me. I gave him the signal to come to his normal state and, to my surprise and then to my horror, he got up from the chair, got on his knees, and started banging his head on the concrete floor, in an evident attempt to kill himself in this manner. I jumped on his back and put my hands between his face and the floor, and for minutes we struggled. When he stopped he went into a fetal position and sobbed "Eight more years, eight more years," the time he still had to serve before he could see the parole board.

Since that time I have seldom used hypnosis except in private practice to help clients stop smoking. I believe that all psychotherapists should learn how to use hypnosis, but no psychotherapist should ever attempt what I did—using this powerful and mysterious technique without adequate training and safeguards.

At San Quentin, where I supervised four other psychologists, I was expected to do individual and group therapy as well as diagnostic work, including the certification of inmates on death row as sane or insane. As part of my assignment, I taught psychiatrists participating in rotating residencies how to do group therapy. I also maintained the equivalent of a private practice of psychotherapy in this prison, using the client-centered method for individual therapy and psychodrama for group therapy. Later, as the supervising psychologist in the Department of Corrections for Wisconsin, I supervised seven psychologists in five institutions and taught junior psychologists how to do group therapy.

When I took my first course in psychotherapy at the University of Chicago with Tom Gordon, I was older than he and had had more clinical experience, and I had already published more than the typical professor at the counseling center. But I was eager to learn as much as I could from the distinguished faculty that Carl Rogers had assembled, including, in addition to Gordon, John Butler, John Schlein, Jules Seeman, Rosalind Dymond, and Elias Porter. I asked Rogers for personal counseling soon after I arrived, but he informed me his counseling schedule was full. He said that when his schedule permitted he would see me, but meantime I might consider participating in a therapy group with one of his graduate students. This turned out to have unexpected benefits.

This group consisted of a student-therapist and six students, all younger than I. Within a few sessions our group was reduced to three: the therapist, another student, and myself. One day while I was talking, I suddenly, inexplicably experienced a sharp pain or constriction in my throat, and I could no longer speak. Tears were running down my face. I grabbed the arms of the chair in an attempt to gain control, but it was no use. I vaguely could see the other two men in the therapy room looking at me in wonder. I could hear my mother's voice saying *"Sono contento che e morto senno sono* **sicuro** *che ti massavo"* (I am glad that he is dead, otherwise I am *sure* he would have killed you). She was referring to my father.

Embarrassed to be acting this way in front of the other students, I experienced the single most important moment of my life. I suddenly completely understood the reason for my miserable academic history.

My mother had borne twins in her first pregnancy. Both died in infancy. Then I was born. Then came another brother, who died in 1918 during the influenza epidemic. Another brother also died, a crib death. So, of my mother's first five children, I was the only survivor. Imagine her feelings when she saw her husband, my father, hitting her only child with enough force to knock him unconscious. Two of my early memories are of him knocking me out—and he died when I was six.

In this moment of insight I realized that I had strung together a complex series of "logical" connections that went as follows: *(a)* I had been a bad boy, and *(b)* because I was bad, my father tried to kill me, and *(c)* because he tried to kill me, my mother wished him dead, and *(d)* he did in fact die because of her wish, but this was because of my being bad, and *(e)* since I was guilty of being the primary cause of my father's death, I should not succeed in academics.

As a result of this insight, I was finally freed of my unwarranted guilt. I had no further need to sabotage myself academically and got my Ph.D. degree without any difficulty. Among the side benefits of this incident was my conviction, which continues to this day, that psychotherapy is a genuine phenomenon and therapy often is an *Aha!* experience in which the beneficial insight comes suddenly, unexpectedly, and completely. My life changed sharply and for the better from that moment on in other respects, too. I saw Rogers later in therapy, but actually I had already had my real therapy.

It may be of interest that I am an Adlerian after having had a successful personal, Rogerian, nondirective therapy, and that the cause of my problem had Freudian overtones. But life is complex and things are just not that simple, nor am I.

Adlerian History

I heard Alfred Adler speak before the Psychology Club at the City College of New York in 1935 and have written about my memory of that experience (Corsini, 1977). Nine years later, in Auburn, New York, I met my first

Adlerian: Regine Seidler, a former teacher in Vienna who had participated in Adler's group parenting sessions. The director of a settlement house, she was taking graduate courses at Syracuse University at the same time I was. While commuting, we discussed psychology—I, Rogers; she, Adler. Then in 1953, when I gave a talk to the Chicago Group Therapy Association, I met in a single weekend three people to whom I was later to dedicate *Current Psychotherapies:* Carl Rogers, J. L. Moreno, and Rudolf Dreikurs. At this convention I also met Harold Mosak, who was then working in Dreikurs's private practice.

After my talk in Chicago, a small, fat, bald-headed man came over to me and said, in a thick Austrian accent, "My name is Rudolf Dreikurs. Have you ever heard of me? Your speech was excellent. Who are you?" On learning that I was planning to start studying for the Ph.D. at the University of Chicago, he offered me a scholarship at the Alfred Adler Institute, which I accepted.

The years 1953 to 1955 were busy ones. I was studying for the Ph.D., taking evening courses at the Alfred Adler Institute, and on weekends, whenever Moreno came to town, I would be on stage with him as an auxiliary ego. In addition, I was doing part-time teaching at a local college.

My first course on Adlerian personality theory was taught by Dreikurs and Mosak. Finally, after having examined a number of personality theories, having directly experienced Rogers's and Moreno's procedures, and having read their books, I had found something that really made sense to me. I was impressed by the concept that Adler's Individual Psychology is one of *use* rather than *possession,* and even more impressed by his notion of *Gemeinschaftsgefühl,* which has subsequently served as a philosophical guide to my personal behavior.

I became an Adlerian as the result of an incident during a course I took at the Alfred Adler Institute which consisted of demonstrations of family counseling, Dreikurs's specialty. Dreikurs announced that he would be seeing for the first time a family about whom he had absolutely no information. Into the classroom came a woman and a man carrying in his arms a child about 6 years of age, emaciated, with a huge head, big, blank, blue eyes, and arms and legs like bare bones. The child was hanging limply in his father's arms, staring with open mouth, evidently mentally and physically retarded. He was put on a chair and stayed there like a rag doll, with his head at an angle. He never moved during the entire interview. My immediate diagnosis of congenital mental retardation was confirmed by the parents' account of his history.

The father was an attorney, the mother an accountant. They were about to put their son in a state institution for the retarded, and Dreikurs was the last professional they were going to see. The boy was their only child. When he was a baby they thought he was not developing normally, but their pediatrician reassured them that they were worrying unnecessarily. They consulted a pediatric neurologist when the child was unable to talk, feed himself, or walk by his first birthday. This doctor confirmed their fears that the child was developmentally retarded, and they began a series of visits to prestigious clinics, including the Mayo Clinic, and consultations with a number of neurologists, psychiatrists, and psychologists. All agreed that the boy was developmentally retarded, and they had concluded that nothing could be done to help him. One physician suggested trying electric shock, another suggested exploratory brain surgery, but all had concluded—as I had—that this was one of nature's mistakes due to a genetic dysfunction, and the best solution was to put the child in an institution for the mentally retarded.

After hearing this account, Dreikurs, to my surprise, got on his knees, faced the child, and began asking him questions. From where I was seated I could see only the back of the boy's head. Dreikurs asked the child the same four questions over and over, changing the order of the questions. This went on for perhaps five minutes. It seemed evident to me that this child, who never even moved his head or said anything, could not understand the questions put to him by this man who spoke with a thick accent. Finally Dreikurs stood up and stated, "There is nothing wrong with your son. He is normal." And then he began to give the parents explicit advice on what to do about their son.

My first impulse was to leave the room, to get away from this charlatan. Who did this arrogant psychiatrist think he was? A dozen experts had agreed that the child was mentally retarded and developmentally disabled, and there was no hope that he could ever be normal. I had come to the same conclusion myself. Period. Put the child away. Warehouse him.

Some six weeks later, when I saw this boy walk into the same room, albeit shakily, and heard him begin to talk, albeit haltingly, I felt electric shocks run up and down my back. In effect, I would have condemned this child to death. I was wrong and so were all the other experts. Dreikurs was right! There must be something special in Adlerian theory and practice!

After the parents left, I demanded to know how Dreikurs had known that the child was normal and exactly what to advise. With a smile he explained how he had discovered, by means of his four questions, that this child was malingering, pretending to be incapacitated. Dreikurs then justified the logic of the advice he had given the parents, which I had thought at the time was criminally reckless.

This one incident, together with my personal comfort with Adlerian theory and philosophy, later led me to join Dreikurs's clinic and become an Adlerian. I worked for several years alongside Mosak and a number of other Adlerian psychologists and psychiatrists at this clinic, served for two years as Dreikurs's assistant at family education centers, and ran several parent education groups in Chicago. Later I started the Family Education Centers of Hawaii and served as senior counselor for 25 years, doing the kind of Adlerian parenting counseling that I had learned from Dreikurs. Eventually I became the editor of the *Journal of Individual Psychology*. I attend annual meetings of the North American Society of Adlerian Psychology and have written and edited a number of books based on Adlerian psychology, including a basic text (Manaster & Corsini, 1982).

The Setting for Therapy

I work in my home. My office consists of three rooms: a therapy room, a combined bathroom and storage room, and a room where I write and edit. The therapy room has easy chairs, built-in bookshelves, and several paintings of marine subjects. There is no desk, and no diplomas or other indications of my training and experience are in sight.

Most of my clients come from referrals. Ordinarily they call to make an appointment, and I interview them over the phone to find out why they want to see me. They usually have one of three major problems: marital discord, difficulties with children, or self-improvement issues. I refuse to see some people for a variety of reasons. I will not see a client if an agency expects a report from me. I will not even report how many sessions I see a client. I make notes, but after the client terminates I destroy them, a practice some agencies have questioned when they ask me for information. I reply that I work like a Catholic priest, keeping no records. If I have a former client's written permission to give information to a professional or an agency, I will do so, but only after I have read the report to my client for the client's approval. However, my procedure may be illegal in some states. Practitioners of psychotherapy would do well to know existing local and state laws as well as the recommendations of professional organizations in regard to record keeping.

Generally, the first and last time I see a client we shake hands, and if a client wants to hug me, which sometimes happens, especially at our last session, I permit this. Mostly we talk; I vary my approach depending on the client. As a therapist I am "on the level," presenting an attitude of equality rather than acting like an expert. Sometimes, as a counselor, especially when dealing with parents who have problems with children or adolescents, I will be highly directive.

I usually refuse to see children alone or even with their parents, even though a good deal of my private practice involves parent-child problems. I believe it often does harm to such families to have an outsider intrude into their lives. I believe that the most ethical and successful method of dealing with parent-child problems is to train parents how to handle their children. I am a passionate advocate of nonpunitive methods of dealing with children, and for the past quarter century I have been teaching parents to use only logical and natural consequences. I have also developed a novel educational system which is Adlerian in its concepts, the Corsini Four-R School System of Individual Education, currently being used in 12 schools around the world.

THE THERAPY FOR DONALD GREEN

Session 2

When Donald Green left following the first interview, I began to ruminate about him—my usual custom, almost a habit. *Why does he continue to come to work late—his stated main reason for seeking therapy?* The answer is obvious: According to Adler, all behavior is purposeful, and for Mr. Green, coming to work late has a hidden goal. But what could that goal be? The most likely consequence of continuing this behavior, especially with a new supervisor once his present supervisor has retired, is that he would be fired from his job. And why does he go through all those futile attempts to get to work on time? Doubtless it is because he wants to impress himself with his earnestness. Everything he has told me adds up to the conclusion that he is playing games with himself. He seems on the surface to be open and aboveboard, but he is probably a closed person who plays mind games. He might well defeat me with a variety of ways to resist therapy. As a rule engineers are bright, and he might use numerous tactics to continue his behavior if I attempt to direct or control him. I will use my general Adlerian procedures, but I will have to watch myself that I do not give him reason to try to play tricks on me.

I am thinking along these lines while I wait for Donald Green to arrive for our second session. In response to a soft knock on the door, I call out

"Come in," and he enters, right on time. I smile at him; he looks about the room and finally sits down and looks at me. It is evident that he wants me to begin.

CORSINI. How are you?

GREEN. Fine.

> (Evidently, Donald is not going to take any initiative. On the one hand, I do not want to generate the impression that he is to act like a schoolchild, and on the other hand I do not want to ask him to take over. I decide to ask a more or less neutral question.)

CORSINI. Been doing any thinking about our first session?

GREEN. Yes. Actually, I'm pleased I came to see you. I have been wanting to talk to a shrink for a long time, but you know how it is. Sometimes you keep on waiting, just letting things go . . . . By the way, how do you work? How does this therapy go? Are you a Jungian or something like that?

> (This is a reasonable question. Often, especially if asked, I take the opportunity to explain my procedures. I decide to do this right now.)

CORSINI. I am an Adlerian, and I follow a systematic way of operating developed by Rudolf Dreikurs, my teacher. Today we'll start with some personal history about yourself and your family. At the next session we'll use what is known as a projective technique. Then, at our fourth session, everything will be summarized. This will result in what we call a Life Style Analysis—a kind of overall summary of yourself in terms of your past and your present situation.

> (Notice that I use the words "we" and "our." I want to convey that I operate on the basis of equality. He is not expected to be passive, like someone coming in for a haircut.)

GREEN. I guess that is like a diagnosis? (I nod.) Makes sense. I thought you would have me lie down and just talk. Will you be asking questions?

CORSINI. Yes. I have a form here from which I'll ask you questions, and with your permission I'll write down your answers.

GREEN. OK, fire away.

> (Getting a Life Style has several advantages: [a] a good deal of important historical material is obtained, [b] the client begins to think of himself or herself objectively, [c] the therapy proper, which takes place after the Life Style has been obtained, can be focused on areas of greatest concern, which [d] can shorten the therapy.)

CORSINI. Are you ready? Any questions before I start?

GREEN. No, no questions. I'm ready.

CORSINI. I want to explain something about what we will be doing. When you go to a doctor or a dentist they may have X rays taken to diagnose what is wrong. This is the same sort of thing we will be doing, except our diagnosis will be a collaboration. You are the expert on your life; you know yourself far better than I will ever know you. So we are like a couple of puzzle-solvers, trying to figure out why you have this work problem and other things, and then we may be able to figure out what to do about them. That is the purpose of all this preliminary material.

I take out my notebook and begin the formal questionnaire (see Figure 2.1).

CORSINI. As I recall, you mentioned you had an older sister. Is that right?
GREEN. Yes—eight years older than me. Just her and then me in the family. Because of the eight years' difference I used to wonder whether I was an accident....
> (A therapist using a different system might want to stop at this point to discuss Donald's thinking that he perhaps was unwanted. I write on the side of the sheet "Unwanted?" to remind me to possibly explore that issue later.)

CORSINI. In what ways were you and your sister different?
GREEN. Like day and night.... completely different.
CORSINI. Could you explain a bit more?
GREEN. She was social, had hundreds of friends. Everybody liked her. She was talented in everything: art, music. We had nothing to do with each other. She resented me.
CORSINI. Were you alike in any way?
GREEN. Nothing that I can think of.
> (I am starting to have some ideas about Donald. Living with a popular older sister who rejected and resented him and who was [at least in his mind] superior to him may be a partial explanation for his asocial behavior.)

CORSINI. What kind of kid were you?
GREEN. Quiet, invisible. I never volunteered for anything. Wanted to be by myself mostly. I did pretty good in school. I was in the Boy Scouts, but even there I didn't make any friends. I had a lot of hobbies; saved stamps, and I liked to make model cars. I guess you would have called me a good kid.
CORSINI. How about your sister? Can you tell me more about her?
GREEN. She was always with her friends—always singing, dancing, that

Family constellation

List all in family by dates of birth, including parents and dead siblings.

Self and sibling descriptions

Ask, if multiple siblings, who is most like and who is most different from client and in what ways. If only one sibling, ask how alike and how different. Then ask client to describe self and siblings as children. If only child, describe self as child.

Self and other ratings

Ratings desired in some manner, such as from 0 to 5, etc., or in rank order (who was the most critical?)

Brightness	Conforming
Energy	School grades
Helping around house	Rebelliousness
Pleasing others	Critical
Considerateness	Selfishness
Sensitivity	Self-satisfied
Adjustment	Friendliness
Sports	Good-humored
Idealism	Ambitious
Morality	Getting own way

(Add any others that seem meaningful for client)

Sibling relationships

Ask which sibs paired off, which fought with each other, which ones did not like others, etc.

Parent-children relationship

Who was father's favorite? Mother's favorite? Who got punished most? For what and by whom?

Parent descriptions

Describe both parents, what their personalities were like, parental occupations, social attitudes, degree of harmony in the family, who was the boss and in what situations? Did they fight, and if so, who did the client think was right? Were the parents ambitious for the children? In what ways? Any close relatives, especially those who lived in home, or had effect on client?

FIGURE 2.1 Protocol for establishing Adlerian life style. (Adapted from Rudolf Dreikers's, "The Psychological Interview in Medicine," *American Journal of Individual Psychology*, vol. 10 (1954) pp. 99–122.)

sort of thing. She didn't want me around. Sometimes when my parents wanted her to babysit for me, she made a big fuss. She never wanted to be seen with me. I don't know why she was ashamed to be seen with me. Maybe because I was fat—an ugly kid.

I make a note, "Ugly as a child?" As Donald continues to talk about his sister and his parents, I list the ways he compares himself to her as they were growing up (see Figure 2.2).

Donald says he believes that neither he nor his sister had a sense of humor; in fact, there was no humor in the family. From the next set of questions I learn that Diana was more athletic, taller, attractive, and quite feminine. She was spoiled by their father but was punished more often by both parents, mostly by being confined to her room. She was popular and tended to be a leader in her social group. A frequent problem, according to the parents, especially the father, was that she wanted to be with her friends too much.

Donald was rarely punished, but when he was, it was often because his sister lied about him. He was stronger than Diana, but he did not feel very masculine. His mother, whom he saw as weak, tried, usually without success, to protect him from his sister and his father. The father generally ignored Donald.

A childhood friend, Marcel, who was four years older than Donald, moved across the street when Donald was about 9. They maintained their friendship until Marcel's family moved while Donald was in high school. Neither of them had any other friends. Mostly they talked, shared stamps, and played games such as checkers.

DONALD	DIANA
More intelligent	More rebellious
Harder worker	More critical of others
Better grades in school	More selfish
Helped more around the house	Had her own way more
More conforming	Temper tantrums
Tried to please parents	More materialistic
High standards	
More considerate	
More sensitive, easily hurt	
More idealistic	

FIGURE 2.2
Donald Green's comparison of himself and his sister

I then go into sibling relationships, but there is little new to be learned. The sister resented taking care of him. They rarely played games together and when they did, she usually won. She often made fun of him. She was Father's favorite, while Mother had no favorites.

Both parents were dead, Mother at 58, Father at 73. Father had been a quiet, solitary man, a hard worker, without humor. He had some friends at work but never brought them home. Mother was described as a hard worker, self-contained. She always spoke in a low voice, never lost her temper, and maintained her distance. The parents never showed any signs of affection to each other, and only Father showed affection to Diana. Donald thought that he was more like his father, but Diana was not like either parent.

Father was the boss in the house, but Mother sometimes could get him to change his ideas. Donald did not know whether they disagreed about bringing up the children. He saw his mother as a peacemaker, unwilling to fight openly about anything. The parents rarely quarreled; indeed, they rarely even spoke to each other. Donald was inclined to be on his mother's side if there was a conflict, because he thought she was more sensible, but he did not dare speak out. When Donald's father did punish him physically, using a razor strop, he did it silently, mechanically. His mother was ambitious for him and wanted him to go to college. Since he liked to make things and was good in mathematics, he decided to study engineering. No one else ever lived with them, but his father's mother visited the family a number of times. He was always happy to see his grandmother because she gave him attention and affection, which he never got from either of his parents.

CORSINI. Anything else I should know about your early life? Anything else important?

GREEN. I don't think so. My life has always been low-key. I always was—and I still am—a spectator on the sidelines rather than a player out on the field.

CORSINI. If I were only able to help you get yourself to work on time, would that be enough for you? Is that all you want from therapy?

GREEN. I was wondering about all these questions you ask me. I don't see how they relate to my job problem. You have not even asked me one question or made one statement about my getting to work on time. I'd like to know why you ask me all these questions.

CORSINI. That's part of the diagnosis I talked about earlier. If you went to a doctor with a cut on your hand, the treatment might just be to bandage it. But if you had some sort of pain that couldn't be explained, the doctor would most likely order X rays and blood tests to get a diagnosis. Your major concern is to get to work on time in the morning, but this may be a symptom of something else. I don't know at this point if there is something else and, if so, what it is. So I am trying to get an overall understanding of you which should lead to changes in your life, including getting to work on time.

GREEN. Actually I am pretty well satisfied with my life. I don't know if I would want any drastic change, like becoming a playboy or something. Perhaps giving up those crazy ideas I have about other people having it in for me would be important. I know the fears I have are silly after I get over them, but at the time they seem real.

CORSINI. I take a holistic view of my clients. I want to help them become happier and more successful, both objectively and subjectively. This often means not only clearing up their specific complaints but also helping them get a new view of themselves and of life. For example, how would you rate yourself, on a scale of 10, on your job, family, and friends? First, how satisfied are you about your job?

GREEN. On a scale of 10, with 10 being highest? (I nod.) Well, I would say about a 7 for my job.

CORSINI. How would you rate your family life? I know you are not married and have no children and only one sister, but how satisfied are you about being single?

GREEN. Oh, I guess I would put that at about 5. I am used to being alone, and I kind of accept it.

CORSINI. How about if you lived with someone, a wife or a lover, would that be better?

GREEN. That would depend on who it was. I suppose you want to know if I would prefer living with someone. I don't know, I really don't.

CORSINI. Well, let's keep your rating at 5 for family. How about a rating for friends?

GREEN. That would be low. I only have these two friends, and yet they are not really friends. More acquaintances, even though I have known them for many years. We have never really confided in each other. I guess I would give friends a rating of 2.

CORSINI. So it's 7 for job, 5 for family, and 2 for friends. Oh, I see our time is up. I'll see you next week at the same time.

GREEN. Right. See you then.

(At this point in the process of getting the Life Style, I try to keep an open mind, but I do have some preliminary hypotheses. Donald was a conformist in his youth, accepting his parents' views of reality, while his sister Diana was a rebel. A serious, humorless man, he appears to

have taken on the values and behaviors of his father. He seems to be a passive-aggressive type. I wonder about his lack of a social life and the fact that in his early forties he is still a virgin. I have a feeling he has not really joined the human race. He should be an interesting client to work with.)

Session 3

As we begin our third session, Donald sits down, expressionless, avoiding looking at me. I decide to check his present mental status instead of immediately asking for his early recollections, the projective technique I use. I wait to see if he will say something, but he does not.

CORSINI. Is something bothering you?

GREEN (turning to face me). Yes . . . I came here just so I could be able to wake up and get to work on time. But it looks to me that coming here is just like if I go to a garage to have a new tire put on, and they want to repaint my car and put in a new clutch. That's what you are trying to do—make me over.

(This is a common reaction—I have run into this kind of thing before. I know how to react.)

CORSINI. You are right, of course. The reason for the Life Style interview is my concern with you as a whole person. If you simply want to solve this one problem, there are some therapists who may do that for you. A hypnotist perhaps . . . would you want me to refer you to someone else? We can cancel this session and I will only bill you for the two sessions that I've seen you.

GREEN. I didn't mean it that way. It's just that you haven't said a word about my sleep problem. All you've asked about is my family, my parents and my sister. What do they have to do with my problem at work?

CORSINI. I thought we discussed this at the last session. I am much aware of your job situation. But my concern is with the total you.

GREEN. I suppose you are going to say . . . you know best; you are the therapist.

CORSINI. No, not quite. Remember, I said that we are cooperating, trying to figure out a puzzle. From your point of view the puzzle is your inability to come to work on time. But from my viewpoint the puzzle is not only why you are getting to work late but what other problems you may have experienced. I hope we can clear up a lot of things, including the job situation.

GREEN. I really don't know if I want a complete psychoanalysis.

CORSINI. As I mentioned last time, this is the way I operate....

GREEN. OK, then, let's get on with it. Is today some kind of a test? Do I have to write anything?

> (I see Donald's concern about the Life Style procedure as evidence of anxiety. Perhaps he wants reassurance from me. Perhaps this is an attempt to sabotage the therapy, or perhaps this is a way of testing me. In any case, I will stay the course.)

CORSINI. No, I will write down your replies. The first thing I'll ask about is your early memories. In our first interview you told me one of them, where you were on a roof with your mother, and she could see your father while you could not. What I would like now is some more early memories.

GREEN. My earliest memory is that my parents and I used to go the beach every Sunday....

CORSINI (interrupting). Sorry. That is not what I mean by a memory. We call that a report. For us a memory is something specific. Something that happened once. What is the earliest single, specific memory you can recall?

GREEN. The first thing I remember was that I was in the house with my mother and someone knocked on the door. I ran behind my mother. She went to the door to open it. I ran out of the room. Then she was talking to this man, and I was in the other room wanting to look in to see who it was, but I didn't go in. I could hear her talking to him.

CORSINI. How old were you?

GREEN. Maybe two years old.

CORSINI. Can you give me any details about the memory?

GREEN. Just wondering whether I should look in....

CORSINI. Anything else in the memory?

GREEN. Just that...me, on the outside looking in.

CORSINI. Are there any feelings associated with the memory?

GREEN. Scared and wondering. Feeling alone....

CORSINI. How about another memory?

GREEN. It was in 1952. We were in New York City. There was a parade for someone, maybe President Eisenhower. I was about 4. My father put me on his shoulders so I could see better.

CORSINI. What do you remember? What is clearest in the memory?

GREEN. The feeling of my father's clothes. His suit jacket against my bare legs. Like rough wool. It was such a feeling of...togetherness...intimacy. For once I was really close to him. I could feel his body.

CORSINI. It was a strong feeling—a pleasant one?

GREEN. More than pleasant. It was like he was real.
CORSINI. May I have a third memory?
GREEN. It's a sad one. I had been in the first grade for maybe a month. I'm seated on a bench-type chair with another child—a boy. Suddenly, he puts his arm over my shoulder and I put my arm over his shoulder, and I know we are friends. At just this moment, a strange boy comes into the classroom and talks to the teacher. The teacher calls my name. I go up front and she tells me I have to go home because my mother is dying.
CORSINI. What is clearest about this memory?
GREEN. Touching him. I never saw him again.
CORSINI. What feelings were there in this memory?
GREEN. How good it was to be so close. And my shock at being separated from him.
CORSINI. Did your mother die?
GREEN. No, but they thought she was going to. She was very sick. Later, someone told me she had taken poison. We moved away, and I never went back to that school.
CORSINI. How about another memory?
GREEN. I walked over to a park across from the new house we moved to, and some kids were playing there. They tied me to a tree and left me. They just ran away. They made fun of me, called me "four eyes"—I was wearing glasses even then.
CORSINI. Any feelings about this memory?
GREEN. Anger, unfairness. What's the use? Sadness.

I will not go into all ten of the early recollections I obtained in this interview. Essentially, they all have more or less the same pattern. The early recollection process takes about an hour.

CORSINI. Between now and the next session, I will be going over everything you have told me. I will go over your Life Style Analysis with you at the next session.
GREEN. Explain that again, please.
CORSINI. The Life Style Analysis is a tentative summary of you as an individual from a psychological point of view. It becomes the starting point of the therapy proper.
GREEN. I thought this was the therapy we're in. . . .
CORSINI. I said "therapy proper" because I want to separate the diagnostic part, which we have just finished, from the treatment part. Actually, everything we do is therapy. Is that clear?

GREEN. Yes, it's like an engineering problem. Diagnose why some piece of machinery doesn't work, and then fix it.
CORSINI. Something like that. The analogy is not complete, though, since a person is a whole and not just a collection of parts. That's what is meant by holism. People are much more complicated than machines. Well, that is all we have time for today.

Session 4

Donald Green seems anxious at the beginning of this session. This is usual for people who begin Adlerian psychotherapy of the Dreikurs type, since they know they are coming in for a diagnosis. I have written out the Life Style Analysis, and now I intend to read it to Donald. I'll go back to it and refer to it from time to time during the therapy.

CORSINI. Before we begin on the Life Style Analysis, is there anything you want to tell me?
GREEN. Yes! This past week I came to work on time every day! I had no trouble waking up. I am even thinking of telling my neighbor he doesn't have to call me; I know it is a bother to him. And I decided to use only one alarm clock, and I'm going to tell the paperboy not to knock at the door.
CORSINI (laughing). And you were concerned that we would not work on that problem! And here it got cured, as it were, all by itself. How do you feel about that?
GREEN. What did you do to make it go away?
CORSINI. Nothing. I take no credit. You did it all.
GREEN. It makes no sense. Is the therapy actually working?
CORSINI. What do you think therapy is?
GREEN. I really don't know.
CORSINI. I'll tell you a secret; I don't know either. No one knows; it's a kind of mystery. Starting to wake up on time and getting to work on time tells me that you really want to change, even though, as you point out, we have not begun to work on that problem. So the fact that this happened to you is a kind of mystery—why are you making it happen?
>   (*At this point I am optimistic about the chances for successful therapy. Donald's attitude now is quite different from what it was in the last session. Is it because he is now getting up on time? Is this an example of flight into health? He may be trying to escape from therapy, saying in effect: "Thanks, Doc, you cured me. How much do I owe you?" and*

> then he'll disappear. But later the symptoms may come back, and then he can take the attitude that therapy just does not work. Another explanation is that we had formed some kind of bond, what psychoanalysts call transference, and this change was a gift to show me he liked me and wanted me to know he was a good client. This too would be a kind of trick. A further explanation is that he really wants to change, and this was a first attempt.)

CORSINI. Now, suppose we get to the Life Style. May I call you by your first name?

GREEN. Sure—and can I call you by your first name too?

CORSINI. If you wish. Call me Ray.

GREEN. Naw, I'll call you Doc. That's how I think of you.

> (I am pleased by this apparently minor exchange. For the first time Donald is acting on the same level as I am, and he has injected a bit of humor into our relationship. It is a kind of test of me. I will continue with the Life Style Analysis, but perhaps he wants to avoid it. I will check this out.)

I take out Donald's Life Style Analysis and start to leaf through it. Donald looks at me and I can feel that he is frightened, as though he is going to hear bad news. This pleases me because I interpret it to mean that he will be paying attention to what he will hear. I begin reading from my prepared text.

> Mr. Donald Green, a 42-year-old, unmarried engineer, referred to therapy by his supervisor and also by an industrial psychologist, complains that he has difficulty getting to his job on time and says he would like treatment for this specific problem. He mentions that from time to time he fantasizes catastrophic situations that turn out to have no foundation. He presents a report on himself from an industrial psychologist which suggests that he seek counseling due to his asocial behavior. Apparently, practically his entire social life consists of a weekly dinner with a couple some 20 years his senior. He has never dated or had sex with anyone.
>
> He appears to be in good health, states that he has regular medical examinations, and there appear to be no biological causes for either the sleep problem or the social situation. He appears to be generally satisfied with himself and his life, and his main stated concern is getting to work on time.

I pause and look at Donald with a quizzical expression, as though asking him what he thinks. When he says, "You put it quite right; no comment," I continue reading.

> He is the younger of two children, with a sister, Diana, eight years older. She

ignored him as a child and apparently resented him. In the family he played the role of Good Boy while she played Bad Girl. Diana, a rebel, was punished more than he was. While Donald did well in school and was cooperative in the family, nevertheless his father appreciated the sister more and ignored Donald. Mother was supportive of Donald but she and her husband both were distant people. Father was dominant in the family. Apparently, Diana made an independent social life for herself and escaped from the narrow boundaries of the family, while Donald conformed more or less to the parents' expectations.

At this point I pause again and look at Donald, inviting his comments.

GREEN. Right on! She had courage to go on her own. I didn't. I tried to please my parents, and I didn't succeed. I can now see it from Diana's point of view. Maybe she wanted me to be a rebel too, be on her side. Maybe she felt that there were three against her—Father, Mother, and me. Maybe that's why she was angry with me. I never gave that any thought.

Before I continue reading, I note that I am pleased that Donald has been able to empathize with his sister and see things from her point of view. This appears to be a new insight for him.

> As an adult, Donald continued his childhood pattern of behavior and became an amalgam of his father and his mother's more overt personality. Were they alive, they probably would approve of his life-style, in that he is a hard worker, conforming, a pleaser, with high standards. They might also approve of his being, like themselves, solitary.

Again I stop to look at Donald, inviting comments.

GREEN. You are right on the money. I keep thinking: "The child is the father of the man." I can see the picture clearly. They were role models for me. I am now the person they made me become. I kind of sold out. Perhaps it was to gain their love...and I didn't succeed....

After a pause, I continue reading the Life Style Analysis.

> And suddenly, something unusual has happened. Donald, the conformist, the good boy, starts to do something bad. He does not come to work on time! This seemingly minor variation from his whole life history of being a conformist, doing what others expect of him, is a puzzle to him, and now he states that he wants to be "cured" of this problem. He follows the advice of two authorities, a supervisor and a psychologist, to consult me about this problem. When I ven-

ture to discuss the possibility and perhaps the necessity of examining his whole life, it upsets him.

> (I have a bit of concern about reading this last statement, since it seems to be unwarranted criticism. It was a judgment call, and perhaps I was wrong. But I did write it, and so I shared it with my client.)

GREEN. You're right about that, though. I know that getting to work late has a larger meaning.

After this comment from Donald I continue with my reading.

> In his early recollections, five themes appear which are basic mistakes:
> 1. *He believes he is unwanted and unlovable.* This is an error. He is an intelligent, attractive, and successful person, and were he to give others the opportunity to know him, some people would like him.
> 2. *He enjoys contact with others but believes he can only get it in superficial or unimportant ways; he believes relationships are transitory and will not last.* This is also an error. Were he to open himself to others, he would be accepted.
> 3. *He believes he is not capable.* This is another mistaken concept. He is a capable and successful individual.
> 4. *He is unnecessarily fearful, reminding himself of the dangers of life by fantasizing.* This is a curious and totally unnecessary safeguarding mechanism.
> 5. *He does not face people problems directly. He is afraid of confrontations.* This is an error. He has the strength to meet and solve problems directly.

After reading the list, I note Donald's facial expression. He seems to be in deep thought.

GREEN. Would you read all of that again?
CORSINI. I have just a bit more to read, and then if you want I will repeat these themes. But first I want to discuss what strengths I think you have. So far, everything has been more or less negative. OK?
GREEN. *That* will be a relief!

> Donald Green is an intelligent person, willing to learn, successful, in a good profession, and certainly someone others would like if he gave them the opportunity to know him.

After reading this final paragraph, I tell Donald that our time is almost up and I have someone else waiting. I promise to review everything next week. When I do a summary session I try to finish near the end of the hour, since I want the client to be left alone to ruminate on what he or she has heard.

Part of my technique is to find out at the next session how much is remembered of what I said.

Session 5

At the fifth session, Donald opens the interview.

GREEN. I wonder, how accurate is the Life Style? And where did you get it?
> *(He is now taking charge.)*

CORSINI. The Life Style statement comes from two major sources, what you have told me and the interpretations I make based on my training and experience. Another therapist might have come to different conclusions. Remember that it is a tentative statement and open to modification.

GREEN. I just wanted to make sure it wasn't engraved in granite. I have been doing a lot of thinking about what you said.

CORSINI. Good. What do you remember about the analysis?
> *(This is an important question. What I am most interested in is which of the basic mistakes did he remember, and which did he forget? Those that are forgotten are most likely to be difficult to deal with.)*

GREEN. You said I did not have courage to confront others—that I deal with life in a cowardly way.
> *(This was the last of the basic mistakes, and possibly the least important. This is an example of unconscious purposeful forgetting, a common phenomenon, a protective safeguarding process.)*

CORSINI. Do you remember any of the other basic mistakes?

GREEN. You said that I was intelligent.

CORSINI (laughing). That sure does not sound like a basic mistake.

GREEN. Let me see . . . something about intimacy, that I didn't know how to be intimate. (He thinks for a minute.) That's funny, I thought I remembered them all when I left. There were four, weren't there?
> *(Note that he has missed the essence of the second basic mistake, which emphasizes that he gets intimacy only from unimportant or superficial contacts, and he does not expect relationships to last. The discussion above is the reason for my writing down the five basic mistakes in summarizing the Life Style Analysis.)*

CORSINI. There were five. Now, Donald, I have to explain something important. It has to do with psychological theory. Do you play chess?

GREEN. Yes, I used to, but I haven't played for some years.

CORSINI. Say that you and I are having a match. And say that you see me move a knight and you think it is a bad move, and you can't figure out why I moved it. Suppose you consider me to be a pretty good player. Then what would you think?

GREEN. Maybe you saw a better move, one that I cannot figure out.

CORSINI. Right! You would try to figure out why I moved that knight. You assume I had some reason for making the move. You try to figure out what I have in mind. Every move we make in chess has a purpose, and the purpose is to win the game. Now, when I examine your life situation, I wonder what is the reason for it. For example, you live like a hermit. You are fearful of other employees. You have practically no friends. You frighten yourself with all kinds of horror stories. You don't have someone to love or to love you, not even a pet.

I ask myself, why does a man with good intelligence, who is in good health and fairly attractive physically, act as you do? He must be acting this way for some purpose, or a series of purposes. What can that be? My only answer is that you are attempting to achieve some kind of goal, you want to obtain something, but I don't know what that can be.

Some psychologists go about figuring out a client by trying to understand the past. So they may say: Donald had a family that really did not accept him; his father was cold, his mother was weak, and his sister didn't like him. Therefore he is now a loner.

DONALD. Well that's true, isn't it?

CORSINI. Yes, but for an Adlerian, as I am, it does not explain your behavior. Your sister Diana had a similar heredity and environment, yet she went a different direction.

GREEN. Now you've got me confused. First you ask me a lot of questions about my past, and then you say that my personality does not come out of the past.

CORSINI. Bear with me a bit. Most psychologists take the position that the past determines behavior. Adlerians take a different point of view— that the future determines behavior. Your expectations about what will happen, as in chess, determine behavior, what you expect to achieve. Does that make sense?

GREEN. I don't know.... Let me think.... Yes, I think I see what you are saying. What I do, like being by myself, can't be explained by the fact that my family was full of loners, since my sister was always a social butterfly. I just took a different road.

CORSINI. Ah, but why did you do that, and what is the reason for continuing to do so?

GREEN. Beats me. I can't think why . . . .
CORSINI. OK, fair enough. Let us leave that. Maybe the answer will come to you. But let me ask you why you now have started to get up mornings? What in the past led to that? As you said yourself, I did not even mention your sleep problem, but apparently you have conquered it, all on your own.
GREEN. But why did I do that? You tell me. Like you say, I must have had some goal, some reason for being late, but I can't figure it out.
CORSINI. I can only guess. Could it be that you gave up being late for some reason that has to do with me?

> (*My thinking at this point goes something like this: He has suddenly, dramatically changed the very reason for coming to see me in the first place. What of any consequence has happened in his life just before this unexpected change? The only thing has been meeting me. I watch him carefully, hoping that he might react with what Dreikurs called a recognition reflex [which is how Dreikurs knew that six-year-old boy was playing his life-and-death game right from infancy]. I am gratified to see Donald's startle reaction, so I know that I am probably right in my assumption.*)

GREEN. I can't see where you are going, but it sounds OK to me. I'm still confused, though.
CORSINI. I am going to confuse you still more. I believe that one of the few healthy things you have done was *not* getting up in the morning. Isn't that ironic? The very symptom that led your supervisor to suggest you see a therapist, and that you hoped I would cure you of, was probably a *healthy thing!* Had I tried to deal with it, you would have defeated me. As it was, you cleared it up on your own.
GREEN. Whoa there! Do you mean that my getting up late was good?
CORSINI. I think so. But let us see if you can find some explanation, no matter how fantastic, for first, not getting to work on time in the morning, and then for curing yourself.

Donald shakes his head and then looks up at the ceiling, remaining silent for a while. I wait patiently, hoping he will be able to generate some insight into this apparently confused situation.

GREEN. When I was a kid I used to pretend I was sick when I didn't want to go to school. My mother would let me stay home in bed. My father would be furious with her and say that I was shamming. Are you telling me that I am using the same technique?

CORSINI. I didn't tell you anything. All I did was guess that you had some secret goal to achieve by going to work late. But a good boy does not say, "Hey, I don't want to go to school," or "I don't want to work." What does a good boy do? He plays sick. What do you think?

GREEN. Makes sense. I'm still acting like a kid.

CORSINI. See you next week.

Session 6

GREEN. I want to tell you something strange I have been doing on the job. I usually eat lunch in my office. Sometimes, though, if I forget to bring my lunch, I go to the company cafeteria. At the door I look in to see if one of the small tables for two is vacant. If there is one, I then get in line at the counter, get my food, and sit down at an empty table. But if someone else takes the only empty table before I get to it, I leave the cafeteria and get a candy bar from a machine. Isn't that stupid?

CORSINI. What would happen if you went and sat at a table with others?

GREEN. They would fall off their chairs in surprise.

CORSINI. No they wouldn't.

GREEN. You don't know them.

CORSINI. Want to bet?

GREEN. You serious?

CORSINI. Absolutely serious. I'll bet you $2 that if you do just that, nothing of the sort will happen.

GREEN. I've never done anything like that in my life.

CORSINI. Do you really want to change your life?

Donald does not answer for a while. Then he looks at me in a pleading way. I wait, holding my breath. This is a crisis point. I have struck suddenly with a challenge, surprising him.

GREEN. Why $2?

CORSINI. That's what Dr. Dreikurs taught me to bet—never more, never less. Here is the bet. You will do exactly what we said: go to the cafeteria, look for a table where there is an empty seat, and ask if you can sit down. If they fall off their chairs I will pay you $2. If they don't, then you pay me.

GREEN. But why should I do it?

CORSINI. Why did you mention the cafeteria?

GREEN. I suppose because I feel so stupid looking in and acting that way.

CORSINI. Well, then, there are two possible ways of solving that problem. One might be to keep talking about it. The other would be to take action and do something.
GREEN. I'll take the bet.
CORSINI. Good! But to help ensure that I will win my bet, I want to role-play something.
GREEN. I'm no good at playacting.
CORSINI. Even more reason to do it. Make believe that I am at a table and there is an empty chair at the same table. (I arrange a chair near me.) Now get up and come over and ask me if you can sit at my table. Let's see how it will work out.

After some initial hesitation and a number of questions, we role-play the same scene several times. At first, acting the role of a person at the table, I welcome Donald and initiate the conversation to make him feel comfortable. I vary this role several times until he begins to react in a relatively smooth and comfortable manner. Then I take a less friendly attitude and say the chair is reserved for someone else. He is now stymied. Next I change roles with him and have him be the one at the table. He is to treat me the same way I treated him, and I try to handle the situation as best I can. Then we change places, and we keep shifting roles for about a half hour.

GREEN. That was interesting! I began to feel it was real, and after a while I was enjoying it. I'm looking forward to actually doing it tomorrow.
CORSINI. OK. I'm fairly sure that you will do it, and you will succeed. But if you do succeed, what will you have learned?
GREEN. I suppose, knowing how to do things with others.
CORSINI. But is that important?
GREEN. For me, most important. Most important.
CORSINI. What do you imagine *I* think is more important?
GREEN. I have given up trying to figure you out. What? You tell me.
CORSINI. What was your first basic mistake, the most important one of all?
GREEN. Not feeling lovable, not being acceptable.
CORSINI. Ha! You remembered! Does it explain why you accepted my bet? Forget whether you will actually go through with it. Suppose the absolutely worst thing you can imagine happens when you ask for a seat at a table. Say that the people there make fun of you, laugh at you, ridicule you, throw a glass of water in your face. Suppose it is the most horrible experience of your life. From my point of view, while I would

regret that this would happen to you and would also regret losing my $2 bet, nevertheless I would think you have made remarkable progress. You are actually willing to do something new *and* different *and* scary. I'm impressed.

GREEN. I think you are saying that I think I'm OK, that I'm lovable.

CORSINI. I think your taking my challenge means that you think so.

GREEN. As a matter of fact, I do. I *am* OK.

> (From my point of view as a cognitive therapist, the therapy has passed another climax. Donald has remembered his first and most basic error, and he is willing to challenge it by action. I have prepared him through role-playing, and I am certain I will win my two bucks.)

Session 7

GREEN. You can't guess what happened.

CORSINI. Did I win my $2?

GREEN. Oh that, yes. Here's your money. (I take the $2 and put it in my wallet.) I have been eating every day with the fellows, five others, all foremen. I asked them if I could sit at their table and they said yes, and now we always eat together. They are a nice group. They look up to me because I'm an engineer—they say I have solved a lot of problems they could not figure out. I found I have a good reputation as an engineer. I could tell they were a bit nervous about me at first, and I figured out that maybe they felt inferior to me because I make more money than they do. One of the guys—Frank—restores old cars, too, and he invited me to his house Thursday—the same night of the week I usually visit my friends, you know, the artist and his wife. Well, I accepted, and I called Jim to tell him I could not make it last week. Instead I went over to Frank's house and we spent an hour or so looking at his cars, and I gave him some advice. His wife asked me to stay for dinner and afterward we had some drinks and did a lot of talking. Then we went back to the cars and I helped fix some wires he had misconnected to the magneto on one of them. But that isn't what is good. Something else happened, more important. Can you guess?

CORSINI. You got engaged?

GREEN. Boy—are you a comedian! Well, in a way you're right. Frank's wife asked me to come to dinner again Saturday night, and when I got there they had another guest. Can you guess who it was?

CORSINI. Jackie Kennedy?

GREEN. You sure are in some mood today, Doc. No, but it was Francine, Frank's unmarried sister. We had a good time, the four of us, laughing and telling jokes. I have never been good at that but I told a few and they about fell over laughing, not so much at the jokes as how I told them—usually forgetting the punch line. But they were not malicious. Later, we all got serious, and they asked me why I had never married. All of a sudden, I decided to tell them everything: About my father and my mother and my sister and my job, and seeing you and how you had bet me $2 and took my money. They screamed over that. I suddenly felt like I belonged. Do you understand: I FELT LIKE I BELONGED!

(Had someone walked in, they would have thought that he was threatening me, standing up, shaking his fist at me, screaming at me. I looked at him with a smile on my face—a big, wide smile.)

CORSINI. I'll tell you what I think. I think you are on your way . . . nothing is going to stop you now.

GREEN. So fast? But this is only our seventh session together. I thought psychotherapy goes on for years.

CORSINI. Donald, there is an optimal time for therapy. Too little is a mistake, but so is too much. In my judgment you have decided that the basic mistake you made years ago, deciding that you were not worthwhile, that no one wanted you, was an error. You checked it out by sitting at a table, accepting an invitation to work on a car, accepting two dinner invitations, and then opening up and sharing some of yourself. All these events indicate to me that you have now rejected the second basic error—that relationships have to be superficial, that they will not last, that you have to be careful of others. Remember your memory of being afraid to go into the room where there was a stranger? You had an associated mistaken belief that you are not capable. Having the guts to ask to sit at a table with strangers tells me that that mistake has been cleared up. And the fourth one, fantasizing all the dangers, seems also to have disappeared. You just went and did what you had to do, and it worked out right, as I guessed it would.

GREEN. Some other things happened, too, even more important. Two things that I did on the job. First, one of the foremen, not those I eat with, but another man who is a prime pain, has been on my case, always screwing up and acting like a wise ass about anything I tell him to do. Well he screwed up again so I gave him one grand bawling-out at the top of my voice, in front of everybody on the factory floor. All the other foremen and some of the workers heard me. I went on and on and on. And you know what? They were all on my side, and some of them told me so later on. And the second thing—I told my supervisor that I want to quit my job.

CORSINI. Wow! Looks like the worm is turning with a vengeance.

GREEN. I realized last week why I had been having trouble getting up in the morning. It was so simple and so logical. Were you able to figure it out, Dr. Analyst? (I shook my head.) Easiest thing in the world. I didn't like my job any more. I was tired of taking a lot of bull from foremen. That was one thing. But there was something even more important. I had gotten bored with the work. I just didn't want to work at that company and at that job any more, but I didn't have the guts to admit it, even to myself. So, I was trying to get fired by coming in late. One morning while shaving I asked myself, "Hey Donald, why are you not getting up mornings?" And then, out loud, I said to myself—I was looking in the mirror at the time—"Because I want to get fired." And then I answered myself, "Why wait? Go tell your boss you are quitting. Lots of people do it all the time."

So I went to see my supervisor and told him I wanted to quit, and he didn't think that was so big a deal. He asked me what I wanted to do instead and I said I didn't know. I just knew that I wanted to be free for the first time in my life. I have enough money to take care of myself for a couple of years. I can always find a job, maybe even make more money.

CORSINI. You sure are full of surprises today, aren't you? How do you feel?

GREEN. This may surprise you, but I feel calm—like things are working out just like they should. I feel content, safe, secure, at home. By the way, at the cafeteria now, I sit with a new group every day. And Frank and I see each other a lot. I go over to his place practically every night. He is starting to confide in me. Seems his wife can't get pregnant and he is starting to tell me his problems. He wants to go on a weekend with me, his wife, and his sister, but I don't want to get involved with her. She is a nice person, but not my type. I have been talking to one of the women who works at the company with me. Matter of fact, I have a date with her tonight for dinner.

CORSINI. Donald, our time is about up. You are making such good progress that I would like to suggest that I see you only once every two weeks. OK?

GREEN. I don't know about that, Doc. We are making such good progress that I think of you as my lucky charm. I don't know whether it would be a good idea to break off so soon.

CORSINI. I am not talking about breaking off but about tapering off. If it doesn't work out, we can go back to the once-a-week schedule.

GREEN. OK. See you in two weeks, then.

This type of session, with a client suddenly making all kinds of unexpected progress in all directions, has been quite common in my experience as a therapist. To me, it is a sign that termination is called for. I don't want a client to rely on me. Sometimes I am tempted to keep an interesting client, but since I must operate in the best interests of my clients I must at least suggest tapering off, if not breaking off. The final decision is the client's, but it is my ethical obligation to tell the client my feelings and thoughts.

Session 8

CORSINI. Well hi, how goes things?

GREEN. I had a certain amount of anxiety—wanted to call you several times. But I decided to tough it out. I haven't turned in my resignation yet, on account of Cecile.

CORSINI. Cecile?

GREEN. She works in accounting, a computer expert. She's a couple of years younger than I am; was married, now divorced, no children. Real bright. We enjoy ourselves. We have dinner almost every night. Right after I see you I'll be seeing her today.

CORSINI. Sounds good.

GREEN. I have been giving a lot of thought to what I want to do. One thing is for certain. I want to change my job—even get out of that community. Start a new life. I feel restless, unsettled, wanting a change. Like a snake ready to shed its skin. I want to get into something different.

CORSINI. Well, you *are* moving along. Tell me about Cecile. Is everything going well there?

GREEN. Yes, but there is a problem with sex. Cecile and I have been doing a lot of kissing and petting. You know what I mean? I have gotten so excited that I get a big erection and then it becomes painful because I don't get any relief. You know what I mean? (I nod my head.) Well, Cecile has been married. She doesn't know I never had sex before. I wonder what to do about it. Should I go to a prostitute or see if I can get a sexual surrogate? Do you know one?

CORSINI. Donald, what do you think would be the best way to handle this problem?

GREEN. I guess telling Cecile.

CORSINI. I agree—but how about telling her after you two have sex, not before?

GREEN. That's an idea. . . . But what's your advice for me about sex?

CORSINI. Just enjoy yourself. It will all be very natural. I am sure that Cecile will be letting you know what is right for her.

GREEN. Suppose I can't perform? Then what?

CORSINI. Almost every man has had an impotence problem at some time. Often their first time. It's nothing to be ashamed of. Besides, if you couldn't perform, it would be a good thing. . . .

GREEN. Why so?

CORSINI. You would see how Cecile would react, whether she would be understanding and kind or what. Don't fake impotence for that reason, however!

GREEN (laughs). You can be sure of that. By the way, I have been talking with Cecile about quitting my job. Cecile had an idea that perhaps the two of us might go into business together. I have been working on an idea of electrifying houses to make them more convenient, using a computer which will be programmed to perform a number of functions automatically. This kind of thing has been done before, but Cecile thinks she can actually make a cheap computer for the home by buying parts from various sources. I could then wire houses for the computer or hire people to do the work. I don't mean houses that are already built but houses under construction. Imagine—you buy a house and it includes a built-in computer you can tell to do a lot of things, like turn off the phone, set the hot water heater at a certain temperature, that sort of thing. Cecile and I could set up a business together. What do you think?

> (I have a problem at this point. Suddenly, the nature of our relationship has gone from one involving depth psychology [in which I hope I am an expert] to being a business consultant [at which I am no expert]. How should I handle this?)

CORSINI. Donald, I don't want to get involved in making any recommendation about business. I am no expert. However, you are thinking of having sex with this woman, whom you have known for less than a month, and at the same time having a business relationship with her. Isn't that going too far, too fast? Why not have one first, then the other? Which one first?

GREEN. Are you kidding? You know what will be first. (We both laugh.) You ought to meet her. Would you like to, socially, that is?

CORSINI. Have you told her that you are seeing me?

GREEN. Yes. She used to see a shrink—excuse me, a therapist—herself when she was getting her divorce. I've told her all about you.

CORSINI. Donald, I have no problem with socializing with you while you are in therapy with me. But I think, in view of the relatively short time we have known each other and the short time you have known Cecile, that it would be best for her to come with you to the next session.

GREEN. OK, she'll be happy to come. I figured that might be your response. (*Everything is working out well, but something is bothering me. On the one hand, Donald appears to have rather fully overcome the stupid basic mistakes he had accumulated, and this pleases me. His behavior indicates that the mistakes that had so screwed up his life have been overcome. But is he going too fast? Does he really have a good understanding of himself? I have more or less told him that he is ready for termination, but was I too impetuous? How about this woman in his life? Can this be a complication? Perhaps it is worth going back to examine again his basic mistakes.*)

CORSINI. Donald, I'd like to go over your basic mistakes again, do you mind? (He nods indulgently.) First, I said when we did your Life Style Analysis that you did not think you were lovable or that people wanted you. What do you say about that now?

GREEN. Cecile said she thought I was one of the nicest people she had ever met. I have introduced Cecile to Frank and his wife, and they think she is very nice. Frank had hoped I would like his sister, but I didn't care much for her. You know, the people at the plant like me. Some of them drop in to see me at my office, and I have a good relationship with most of the people I work with. I realize that you were right when you said that I was OK but didn't think I was.

CORSINI. How about thinking you can only make contact with others on a superficial basis and that relationships will not last?

GREEN. That idea is gone! I have had some good discussions with the other fellows and Cecile—some of them pretty deep discussions—and I'm enjoying it! How long have these wonderful things been going on? Life is great!

CORSINI. So, on to No. 3. I said that you thought you were not capable.

GREEN. I used to think so. Now I *know* that I am not capable—but only in certain things. Cecile, who likes to dance, has been trying to teach me how, and she has about given up. I may go to a dance school—but so what? I can't be good at everything, can I?

CORSINI. I can't dance either, so we are in good company. How about basic error No. 4—frightening yourself unnecessarily with those fantasies?

GREEN. I don't have them any more. Once in a while I get scared and then I test myself. And I have succeeded in everything I have tried.

CORSINI. And I guess I don't have to ask you about face-to-face confrontations. You really are doing well. Is there anything else on your mind?

GREEN. I didn't tell you—I called Diana.

CORSINI. Diana? Oh, your sister. Tell me about it.

GREEN. Was she surprised to hear from me! Told me she had been thinking a lot about me from time to time. We had more than an hour's conversation. She is a widow now, and I had a hard time finding her—kept calling people who I thought might know her. She is living in California with her two kids, 7 and 9. She wants to see me, and I promised to visit her at Christmas. She kept telling me that she had been crazy when she was young, how she hated our parents and how she hated me—what do you think for?

CORSINI. For being a good boy?

GREEN. According to her, she hated me for always being so perfect. She thought she never could be as good as I was. Isn't that the craziest thing? I told her how I felt about her and she told me she felt like a stranger in the home and that my father and mother and me were a unit, and she was outside. Can you believe all that?

CORSINI. Easily. Well, Donald, I guess our time is up, and I will see you in two weeks.

GREEN. How about a month? I have a vacation coming, and so does Cecile, and we'll be taking it together.

CORSINI. Fine, see you in a month, then. I hope you'll enjoy your vacation.

TERMINATION OF THE THERAPY

Donald and Cecile are waiting when I enter my office. Cecile is an attractive, well-groomed, dark-haired woman about 30 years of age. I wave toward the chairs, and they sit down. I look them over with a smile and wait to see who will start.

CECILE. I am very happy to meet you, Dr. Corsini. Donald has been telling me a great deal about how you work. It's fascinating. He is quite a fan of yours.

CORSINI. Thank you . . . .

Once again I wait, and again Cecile takes the initiative.

CECILE. I knew who Donald was for almost a year before he started seeing you. It's really amazing how much he has changed! I never saw anything like it. He is like a new man—like a caterpillar becoming a butterfly.

GREEN (with a big smile). She likes the butterfly more than the caterpillar.

CORSINI. I'm curious. Would you tell me your impression of Donald before he came to see me?

CECILE. Well, you know, we work for the same company. I work in the main office and he is an engineer with a roving assignment. I always thought he was a very serious man—businesslike, no small talk. He was just interested in getting the job done—very competent and reliable. He was also self-sufficient, not at all sociable, but distant. Most people thought he was stuck up and didn't like to associate with ordinary people—a loner. But he always had a good reputation as an engineer; you want something done, he gets it done. For example, last summer, it was real hot and the air-conditioning in our office went out. I called about it on a Friday afternoon. Monday looked like a scorcher, and I dreaded coming in to work because the office would be like an oven. But when I got there the air-conditioning was on, and we found out that Mr. Green—nobody called him Donald—had come in on Saturday to work on it personally, even though it's not his responsibility. That's when I first became interested in him.

GREEN. Hey, you never told me that.

CECILE (to me). You don't know how hard it is to find a reliable man. Donald, do you remember I called you to thank you and suggested that we could have lunch together in the cafeteria, and you said you were too busy to have lunch? I felt rejected. The other girls in the office thought maybe you were gay. No one had ever seen you with a woman.

GREEN (teasing). Or with a man, for that matter. Now at least you know I'm not gay.

CORSINI. How did the two of you ever get together? Cecile, it looks as though you tried to meet him but he showed no interest.

CECILE (to Donald). Should I tell him, or will you?

GREEN. Well, dear, why don't you go first?

CECILE. It's the weirdest story. It had been about four months after I called him to ask him to have lunch and he said no. So I just gave up on him. Meantime, he had been seeing you. No one knew it, of course. Well, one day I am at my desk and he runs into the office—and I mean runs in—and everyone looks up and sees him coming up to my desk. In a loud voice, he asks me whether I will have dinner with him that night, and when I say yes, he runs out again without another word. Now I *was* confused—all this out of nowhere. Everyone wondered what had happened, whether I had been seeing him. I didn't even know whether he meant it, or what. But when I left that night, there he was at the entrance to the plant. We did have dinner, and we had a good time.

CORSINI. What do you say, Donald?

GREEN. That day, I was working on a drawing for an electrical hookup, and I suddenly didn't want to continue with it. I was just thinking of Cecile, and how stupid I had been not to accept her invitation to lunch. I began to wonder how I could make it up to her and how to approach her, and then I thought of a fable my grandmother used to tell me. One day, the devil decided to go out of business, so he wanted to sell his tools: envy, anger, jealousy, deceit, and—the best of all—discouragement. I realized then that my fantasizing about catastrophes was based on discouragement. Nothing would ever work out—that was what I had been telling myself. Then I remembered how it had worked out when I took your bet and had the courage to ask to sit at a table with the other men. At that moment I said to myself, "To hell with the devil!" and I practically ran to Cecile's office. I knew, I knew, I knew she would say yes if I asked her to meet me for dinner. And she did.

CORSINI. Quite a story—a true romance! Tell me, how did your trip together work out?

GREEN. Marvelous—a real honeymoon.

CORSINI. But you had some misgivings about it, didn't you?

GREEN (to Cecile). He's a dirty old man. He's talking about sex. (He addresses me.) Really, it worked out perfectly—no problems. Now what I want to know is, how long has sex been around, and how come I found out about it so late?

CORSINI (to Cecile). I'd like to know something Donald and I talked about. When did you find out that this was his first time—before, or after?

CECILE. Right after the . . . first time. I couldn't believe what I heard! He had been such a great lover that it didn't seem possible that I was the first woman he had ever been intimate with.

CORSINI. And how did it go for you, Donald?

GREEN. It was all very natural. I just went with it and let happen whatever was going to happen.

CORSINI. Would you say you learned anything special from that experience?

GREEN. Later, thinking it over, I decided this would be my very last fantasy. You know something? I really believe I can do just about anything I am capable of. Makes no sense, but that is how I feel. In our two weeks together Cecile and I got to know each other quite well. We are good companions, respect each other, like doing things together—and, we're planning to get married.

CORSINI. Sounds good to me. Looks as though you two can become friends, which is more important in marriage than being lovers. Do you have the same interests?

CECILE. Yes. We both like the same kinds of things, being outdoors and so on. We enjoy talking to one another. We are comfortable together.

CORSINI. Everything sounds almost too good to be true. Donald, remember when we first started I asked you how you felt about your work, family life, and friends? (Donald nods.) Let me check. Now, on the scale of 1 to 10, how satisfied are you relative to your work?

GREEN. I'd put that at about a 5 or 6. It is now just routine. I have less interest in my work than I did before. I just do it.

CORSINI. And your family life?

GREEN. Top of the scale. I've talked to my sister again, and I feel much closer to her than I ever did. And now I have Cecile. I would rate myself on family at 10.

CORSINI. And how about your social life, how satisfied are you with it?

GREEN. I would rate it about a 7. Cecile has met Jim and Mary, the couple I used to have dinner with alone. They love her, think she is the best thing that ever happened to me. We have been seeing them once a week, but now sometimes they come to my place, and Cecile and I entertain them. We see Frank and his wife, too, and I've met a couple of Cecile's friends and we've done some things with them. Also, Cecile and I go to church on Sundays together. I am really enjoying relationships with new people, and I feel much more comfortable socially.

CORSINI. Well, job satisfaction has dropped from 7 to 5, family is up from 5 to 10, and friends have gone from 2 to 7. Everything looks good, except the job situation. What are your thoughts about it?

GREEN. Actually, I was thinking of quitting my job, but Cecile suggested that I wait a bit. I talked to my supervisor and told him I wanted to change jobs, do something different. He had nothing to suggest, so I went to see the personnel officer. She told me that I was in a kind of dead-end job, and all she could suggest was to wait until the chief engineer's job is vacant or look for something else. So it looks like I'm stuck where I am.

CECILE. I had an idea, but he didn't think much of it. What would you think if he became a technical salesman for the company?

CORSINI. How do you feel about that, Donald?

GREEN. I just don't know. I have never sold anything.

CORSINI. Your work, which you had rated 7, has gone down to 5; everything else has gone up. Your job no longer challenges you. May I make a suggestion, now that you're looking forward to meeting new people? Isn't that what a salesman does?

GREEN. Yes, you could say that. I guess I got salesmen confused with television pitchmen—I despise them. Actually, I've been considering selling for the company. As a technical salesman, I would be talking to other engineers, and I know how to do that.

CORSINI. My guess is that you may find that work interesting. Remember that vocational aptitude test which showed you would like selling?

GREEN. Want to know something? Right now, I think of it as a challenge. With both of you on my side, I don't think I can fail.

CORSINI. Suppose you did fail?

GREEN. Wouldn't be the worst thing. The worst thing would be not trying. I'll give it a shot. You guys have sold me. But actually, I had pretty much decided to take a crack at it. I'll go see the sales manager about it tomorrow.

CORSINI. I can't think of anything more I would want to ask you. Do either of you have anything else on your mind?

CECILE. If we get married, do you think we should try to have children?

CORSINI. Again, this is an area outside of my expertise. Why not wait until you are married, and until Donald is satisfied with his job situation? Is your biological clock ticking?

CECILE. No, I'm just wondering about it. I'm 34, and I don't know if I can get pregnant. Like most women, I want to have a baby sometime.

CORSINI. How do you feel about being a father, Donald?

GREEN. I'm scared, to tell the truth. Seems like such a big step. I'd wait, but if Cecile wants a baby right away, I'll go along.

CORSINI. If there's nothing else you want to take up, I think we can end our session.

GREEN. Would you want to see me again?

CORSINI. Only if you have a need to see me. I think you have made remarkable progress and don't need any more therapy. But I am curious about how you experienced the therapy.

GREEN. I've been going over that in my mind. When I first met you I didn't have much feeling about you one way or another. You seemed competent and professional. I liked your commonsense attitude, you didn't use fancy terms, and I liked your diagnosis of me in the Life Style Analysis. You talked with me frankly, one to one. I got to trust you. When I tried to argue that you were attempting to make me over, you stuck to your principles and told me to go somewhere else if I didn't like the way you were operating. I thought that took a lot of guts. The big change occurred after the fourth session, when you read the list of my basic mistakes to me. What you told me was unbelievable, and yet I knew it was true. Essentially, you told me I was an OK guy but I was operating on the basis of some unconscious ideas, fallacies about myself, and that I was discouraged. I realized that I was a grown-up child, a man but still acting like I had as a kid. I saw that I had taken sides with my parents against my sister. Oh, by the way, I called my sister Diana again, and we talked some more. Good talk.

So, I asked myself: What am I? Why am I like I am? And I decided that you really knew what you were saying and that I was playing a stupid game with my life. I think the real climax came then, when I decided to accept myself. And when you bet me that I would not make a fool of myself in the cafeteria, this meant to me that you believed in me.

CORSINI. And what about Diana? You said you had had a good talk with her.

GREEN. We had another long conversation. She sees me as a success and herself as a failure. She works as a salesperson in a store, and there's no man in her life right now. I told her about Cecile, and she said she was pleased and is looking forward to seeing us both. Cecile and I are planning on visiting her in California. I really want to see her and get some things straightened out.

Doc, I think this probably *will* be our last session. But can I come back sometime if I think it's necessary?

CORSINI. Of course.

We shake hands all around and suddenly, Donald hugs me. Then Cecile hugs us both and we remain close for a moment. With no further talk, they leave the office.

A Final Note

About six months later, I received a wedding invitation from Donald and Cecile. I was unable to attend, since I had an out-of-town conference. I called Donald to explain, and he brought me up to date. He and Cecile had gone to California and had a real family reunion with his sister. Diana was coming to their wedding, and they were paying for her trip. Donald was now a technical salesman, loving the new work. As soon as they were married they would see if Cecile could get pregnant; if so, they would be moving to a larger home.

I closed the books on Donald Green as one of my better, most successful cases. But I reminded myself that any competent therapist, working in other ways, might have achieved exactly the same results I had. The credit went not only to me or to Adler or to my teachers, Dreikurs and Mosak; mostly it went to Donald Green. But without all of us, for all I knew he would still be living by himself, working on his cars, seeing his two friends, and depending on the three alarm clocks, the neighbor, and the paperboy to wake him up. ■

CRITIQUE OF DONALD GREEN'S TREATMENT BY ADLERIAN PSYCHOTHERAPY

by Harold H. Mosak

Were Corsini an artist (and I would argue that he is), he would be another Honoré Daumier or Max Beerbohm. His talent for caricature reveals itself in his ability to highlight the most prominent features of Adlerian psychotherapy and in his minimization or elimination of those aspects of treatment of lesser significance. This therapy description leaves us with a portrait which is instantly recognizable, even though the emphases create some distortions.

Adlerian psychotherapy is characterized by its basic theoretical assumptions, its commonsense outlook, and its ideal goal—*Gemeinschaftsgefühl,* or social interest, as Alfred Adler defined it. Among its assumptions are the following:

1. People should be seen as total human beings rather than being fragmentized into parts and part functions. All part functions are in the service of the whole person.

2. All behavior has purpose and is designed to move people toward their goals, rather than being the outcome of some preexisting cause.

3. While the past may be of historical importance (one reason why we collect the life-style data), it is less important from a causalistic point of view.

4. Rather than being seen as merely the outcome of causes or of a struggle with causes, people are seen as the creators of judgments and values. People are proactive rather than merely reactive. In this perspective, people can assume responsibility for their lives. Problems which create distress in the person are almost always circuitous solutions to avoid meeting the life tasks. These problems are chosen by the person unconsciously in order to guarantee the person's survival—physically, socially, and psychologically.

5. The preferred way of understanding people is through their subjective perceptions and evaluations of themselves and life. Adler indicated that the therapist must "see with the patient's eyes, hear with his ears, and feel with his heart." Carl Rogers referred to therapy as entering the client's internal frame of reference.

6. People can best be understood in a social context. For Adler, all problems were social problems. Adlerian therapists place considerable emphasis on the feeling of belonging and on interpersonal relations and transactions.

7. Living in this world, people develop a characteristic "line of movement" in their goal-seeking behavior. Even when it seems that the person is pursuing contradictory goals, a closer look will reveal that underlying these apparently contradictory goals there is a common goal.

8. People are basically social "animals" whose highest ideal is *Gemeinschaftsgefühl,* a concept incorporating such traits as caring (Mayerhoff, 1971), courage (Neuer, 1936), the courage to be imperfect (Lazarsfeld, 1966), and contribution to the common welfare (Dreikurs, 1971). All of these traits are alluded to in Corsini's chapter.

Given the caricature quality of Corsini's contribution, he has presented the flavor of how an Adlerian *might* conduct therapy with a client like Donald Green. Other Adlerian therapists might proceed somewhat differently, but all would adhere to the basic assumptions noted above. Corsini's treatment exposes the Rogerian training he received prior to embracing the Adlerian fold. He places considerable responsibility on the client and has an implicit belief in the client's ability to meet that responsibility. At one point in the Life Style Analysis, he remarks, "This is an error. He has the strength to meet and solve problems directly." Since Corsini does not inform us on what basis that assessment is made, he perhaps is referring to what Rogers taught him and me about the "growth forces" residing in the individual. While I do not negate the existence of such forces, my view is somewhat at variance. A surgeon may rely on a patient's "growth forces" but nevertheless intervene directively. Other Adlerian therapists may proceed in more directive fashion than Corsini does, or at least do so with certain patients.

Corsini also portrays Adlerian psychotherapy as a cognitive psychotherapy. In his conversations with Donald he discusses "catastrophizing" and "awfulizing" much as Albert Ellis would. Ellis himself has pointed out many of the resemblances between Adlerian and rational-emotive psychotherapy. Corsini might reasonably be characterized as a theoretical Adlerian and a technical eclectic, although in the latter he is careful never to violate Adlerian basic assumptions.

Finally, independent of the influences of his training, there is a picture of Corsini, a person with long experience, who brings his own personality, his own style, to the therapy session. While I will not comment on Corsini's personality, he can best be described as a creative, innovative, risking therapist who always has the patient's welfare at heart.

Since I have written similar chapters myself, Corsini has my sympathies. I compare this form of writing to attempting to construct a budget. There are so many items we would like to include, but budgetary considerations do not permit it. *If only* there were more pages devoted to exposition of theory. Fortunately, that is taken care of in *Current Psychotherapies* (Corsini and Wedding, 1989) and in *Individual Psychology* (Manaster and Corsini, 1982). After all the figuring, something—many things—must be omitted because of the limits of the page "budget allocation." Every omission feels like abandoning a loved, precious child.

In struggling to write such a chapter, the writer hears voices in his head lamenting, "I wish . . ." and "Wouldn't it be nice if . . ." and "If only . . . ." My wish list for Corsini's chapter would include the following items:

1. *If only* he could have elaborated more on Adlerian psychodynamics, the therapeutic process, and the various techniques used. The description of Donald's Life Style helps us to understand "what makes Donald tick," but it does not explain the Life Style procedure. Shulman and Mosak (1988) have done so, if you want to learn more about this topic.

2. There are some brief allusions to such processes as interpretation, relationship, resistance, and "transference" in psychotherapy, but we could learn more about the roles of these processes in the treatment of Donald, and in general.

3. *If only* he could have demonstrated how many Adlerians have used multiple psychotherapy with their patients, as do Dreikurs and Shulman and Mosak.

4. Many Adlerians would have placed Donald in group psychotherapy, either as an adjunct to individual therapy or as the therapy of choice. Since Corsini is a pioneer in this area, and since Donald requires both socialization and "feedback," I would assume that in actual practice Corsini would

have considered doing so. *If only* we could have observed Donald in this setting!

5. Corsini does illustrate the use of action techniques with Donald. *If only* he could have illustrated the wide range of techniques available in the psychodramatic spectrum! (Corsini, 1965; Starr, 1977).

6. Corsini presents Donald as a compliant, perhaps overly compliant patient, and the client's final statement in the initial interview lends credence to this definition of him. However, defining Donald as an overly compliant patient hardly permits a demonstration of resistance, except insofar as overcompliance itself is considered to be a manifestation of resistance. Considering that a major Adlerian assumption centers about the uniqueness of the individual (Life Style), the approach an Adlerian therapist utilizes with one patient may not be applicable to others. Corsini's approach to Donald therefore should not be regarded as the way Corsini (or another Adlerian) might approach all patients. *If only* Donald had been another kind of patient, other views and techniques might have been utilized.

7. I am more than a bit surprised that Corsini does not do more with the psychological tests given by others. While Adlerians resort to testing less than some other therapists, they do make use of them. I am puzzled because Corsini has been in the forefront of the testing movement and has constructed a number of psychological tests himself. He does rely on one test—Early Recollections—which many have described as a projective technique. Adler describes a person's Early Recollections as "the story of my life." Sought at the beginning of therapy, as it often is, it provides a quick picture of the patient's psychodynamics, without spending days conducting other psychological testing or spending months dredging up this material "on the couch." The economy of time and effort tends to keep Adlerian psychotherapy briefer than many others.

Corsini performs a service for us in introducing two ethical issues in his chapter. In the larger psychological field more attention is being devoted to such issues. However, the achievement of a unanimous viewpoint is a long way off. Many psychologists confuse legal and ethical issues. Others tend to blur the line of demarcation between what might be therapeutically contraindicated and what is unethical. Some studies of ethical opinion refer to minority opinions of unethical behavior (such as the opinion that it is unethical to shake hands with a patient) with which the majority of psychotherapists would not concur. Therefore, some might take issue with Corsini's bet with Donald, although in another article Corsini (1979) rationalizes and justifies this technique on therapeutic grounds. And there are psychotherapists who socialize with their patients, while others may view this as a violation of the ethical principle of "dual relationship." Corsini apparently treats this as a psychotherapeutic issue rather than an ethical one.

Throughout, Corsini's approach is a straightforward, commonsense one. Adlerian psychology uses no jargon or esoteric concepts; its verbalizations are understandable by anyone of modest intelligence who has comprehension of the language in which the psychotherapy is conducted. We have to envy Corsini and Donald. Everything proceeds so smoothly, and change occurs almost immediately. Donald "catches on" and accepts without much question. Change, whether deliberate or unconscious, occurs with a predictability not regularly experienced by practiced therapists. If therapy ordinarily proceeded this effortlessly and smoothly, fewer therapists (and patients) would lose sleep at night, and complaints of therapist burnout would rarely be heard. But then, we must remember that this is a caricature of the therapeutic process!

Corsini has dropped the use of the medical model. At a thoretical level, Adlerian psychotherapy is a growth model psychotherapy (Mosak & Phillips, 1980). Patients are not seen as "sick," and the goal of therapy is not "cure." Patients are seen as discouraged, and therapy is designed to change their outlook and help them grow. Therapy is a matter of education or reeducation rather than a matter of cure. Corsini attempts to educate Donald with respect to his "basic mistakes," a term currently in disfavor with some Adlerians, although we retain the concept. He measures the success of the therapy in terms of whether Donald has succeeded in relinquishing these self-defeating "basic mistakes." So far all to the good, but many therapists also focus on the resources the patient brings to the therapy and to life, and through encouragement, especially the encouragement of risk-taking behavior, they endeavor to help the patient move into a more satisfactory relationship with the life tasks—the tasks of work, relationship to others, relationship to the other sex, relationship to self, and relationship to issues of meaning and of the spirit. Using these criteria, Corsini has reason to feel the satisfaction he describes in his final paragraph.

■

REFERENCES

Adler, A. (1958). *What life should mean to you.* New York: Capricorn Books. (Originally published 1931.)

Adler, A. (1964). *Problems of neurosis.* New York: Harper & Row. (Originally published 1929.)

Adler, A. (1964). *Social interest: A challenge to mankind.* New York: Capricorn Books. (Originally published 1929.)

Corsini, R. J. (1947). Nondirective vocational guidance of prison inmates. *Journal of Clinical Psychology, 3,* 96–100. Postnote by Carl Rogers.

Corsini, R. J. (1965). *Role playing in psychotherapy.* New York: Aldine.

Corsini, R. J. (1977). My memory of Alfred Alder. In G. J. Manaster, G. Painter, D. Deutsch, & B. J. Overholt, *Alfred Adler: As we remember him.* Chicago: NASAP.

Corsini, R. J. (1979). The betting technique in counseling and psychotherapy. *Individual Psychologist, 16,* 5–11.

Corsini, R. J. (1987). Adlerian groups. In S. Long (Ed.), *Six group therapies.* New York: Plenum.

Corsini, R. J., & Wedding, D. (1989). *Current psychotherapies* (4th ed.). Itasca, IL: F. E. Peacock Publishers.

Dreikurs, R. (1971). *Social equality: The challenge of today.* Chicago: Henry Regnery.

Dreikurs, R., & Mosak, H. H. (1966). The tasks of life I. Adler's three tasks. *Individual Psychologist, 4,* 18–22.

Dreikurs, R., & Mosak, H. H. (1967). The tasks of life II. The fourth life task. *Individual Psychologist, 4,* 51–55.

Ellis, A. (1957). Rational psychotherapy and individual psychology. *Journal of Individual Psychology, 13,* 38–44.

Manaster, G. J., & Corsini, R. J. (1982). *Individual psychology.* Itasca, IL: F. E. Peacock Publishers.

Manaster, G. J., Painter, G., Deutsch, D., & Overholt, B. J. (1977). *Alfred Adler: As we remember him.* Chicago: NASAP.

Mosak, H. H. (1958). Early recollections as a projective technique. *Journal of Projective Techniques, 22,* 302–311.

Mosak, H. H. (1989). Adlerian psychotherapy. In R. J. Corsini & D. Wedding (Eds.), *Current psychotherapies* (4th ed.; pp. 65–118). Itasca, IL: F. E. Peacock Publishers.

Mosak, H. H., & Dreikurs, R. (1967). The life tasks III. The fifth life task. *Individual Psychologist, 5,* 16–22.

Mosak, H. H., & Phillips, K. S. (1980). *Demons, germs and values.* Alfred Adler Institute Monograph No. 3. Chicago: Alfred Adler Institute.

Rogers, C. R. (1951). *Client-centered therapy.* Boston: Houghton Mifflin.

Shulman, B. H., & Mosak, H. H. (1988). *A manual for life style assessment.* Muncie, IN: Accelerated Development.

Person-centered therapy, also known as client-centered therapy, and originally as nondirective therapy, is based on a relationship in which the therapist offers empathy, unconditional positive regard, and genuineness. *Empathy* is based on the therapist's interest in understanding the client's world of feelings and meanings, communicating that understanding in a natural and spontaneous manner, and ascertaining that the client feels understood. One aspect of *unconditional positive regard* is the therapist's willingness to allow clients to share their experience in the way they wish, to the depth they choose, and at their own rate. The therapist has unconditional positive regard for the uniqueness of the client's world and for the capacity of clients to resolve their problems, conflicts, and issues in the way that suits them. Thus the therapist respects the client's choice of school, course of study, occupation, marital partner, way of partnering, sexual orientation, and so on, even though these choices might differ from the therapist's preferences. *Genuineness* means the therapist is genuine, or congruent in using words that match thoughts and feelings, and does not hide behind a professional facade.

The person-centered hypothesis is that when clients receive these conditions, they respond by thinking more highly of themselves, so they become willing to accept as part of their self-concepts aspects they formerly regarded as inadmissible. They become more self-reliant in their values and standards, and their mode of experiencing becomes more free, open, and spontaneous.

This approach was formulated in 1940 by the American psychologist Carl R. Rogers (1902–1987), a pioneer in psychotherapy practice, teaching, research, and writing. Rogers impacted thousands of people around the world. With gentleness and strength, he extended his therapeutic principles to education and international conflict resolution.

Nathaniel J. Raskin

Person-Centered Therapy

SOMETHING ABOUT THE THERAPIST • *Fred Zimring*

I entered graduate school at the University of Chicago because of my general interest in personality and emotions. In addition, I was interested in personal change, since I had a strong feeling that I was not functioning as well as I wanted to.

At the time, in the 1950s, psychology was strongly oriented to animal behavior. It was thought that everything could be explained in terms of basic drives and instincts. Therefore it was with some skepticism that I first encountered Carl Rogers at the University of Chicago at an open meeting of the client-centered practicum. I had read some of Rogers's works, and his use of language seemed imprecise; the word *perception,* for example, was used in several different senses on a single page. In addition, because of the rigidly "scientific" and behavioristic nature of my first two graduate years, I thought Rogers would be impossibly "soft-headed." Everything changed for me in a few minutes of the open meeting during which a student acted as a client and Rogers acted as a therapist. In those few minutes of dialogue some small but definite changes occurred; some things came to exist for the client that hadn't existed before. This small atom of creation, occurring before my eyes, intrigued me. It seemed magical. *Where had the new material come from?*

Although this incident happened many years ago, I continue to experience this sort of creation, and it still intrigues me. When I am puzzled or bothered, and I talk to someone who knows how to listen, new thoughts, new possibilities, mysteriously occur.

This incident led me to become a student in the client-centered practicum and then a member of the Counseling Center of the University of Chicago. The Counseling Center was an active group of client-centered therapists. It made little difference if you were a student or a member of the faculty. If you demonstrated competence at doing psychotherapy, or at research, or in training or administration, you assumed that responsibility and functioned in that position. I remained on the staff of the center for five years while I was a student and then continued for the 12 years I was on the faculty of the University of Chicago.

Carl Rogers, Jack Butler, and Tom Gordon, my therapists, supervisors, and teachers, were important to my development as a therapist. Not only did I learn about myself and about psychotherapy from them, I also learned something about the unashamed pursuit of excellence. Aside from the personal changes I underwent as the result of being a client, my interest in psychotherapy as a career was reinforced by the experience of seeing personal barriers crumble and new possibilities magically occur.

After leaving Chicago and coming to Case Western Reserve University at Cleveland, Ohio as director of clinical training, I initiated a year-long practicum in client-centered therapy. I still teach this practicum, and I have been more involved with training people to do client-centered therapy than with seeing clients myself. However, I do try to see at least two clients a week, since I feel a loss when not seeing clients.

The way I do therapy has not changed much over the years. It seems to me that Rogers originated a fully-formed, cohesive method of doing individual therapy. It is based on a few simple but profound hypotheses about what human beings are like and how change can be facilitated in them by the therapist. Over the years I have tried from time to time to alter what I do with clients in many ways. Whenever I try something different from client-centered therapy, however, I find that the changes I prize most for the client do not occur.

After a career doing individual therapy, I recently have begun to work with groups and have found it interesting. In a client-centered or person-centered group there is no leader, only a facilitator. The group goes where it wants to go and discusses what it wants to discuss. What seems to happen is a change in the nature of the group. At first the group is a collection of people who consider one another from an external point of view, and then it slowly begins to work within a more subjective framework. Finally the group comes to accept the participants' internal frames of reference as being of most importance.

In addition to training therapists, the main thrust of my professional activity has been to understand why changes occur as the result of client-centered or person-centered therapy. The status of Rogers's explanations of why change occurs has seemed to me to be quite different from the status of his descriptions of how therapy should be done. His explanations for why change occurs have seemed to be initial, tentative suggestions, rather than a finished product.

I have gone on from Rogers's rather general self-theory explanations to more refined explanations drawn both from self theory and cognitive theory. I have been involved recently with description of the self phases or states first proposed by George Herbert Mead, the "Me" and the "I," and of how client-centered therapy alters these states. Explanation of what changes occur and why they occur seems to me vital.

In my opinion, many other kinds of therapy are trying to do what client-centered therapy does, but they do not do it quite so successfully. One of the main effects of many different kinds of therapy is to have clients appreciate the reality and importance of their subjective worlds. We are born into and develop in a world where objective/interpersonal realities are thought to be of primary importance and the personal/subjective world is considered less important. We learn about the reality of our subjective worlds in many different kinds of therapy. In client-centered therapy, very little of the therapist's world is intruded on the client, and the focus is on the client's internal framework. The client therefore can appreciate the reality and nature of his or her subjective world more quickly than if necessary to struggle with the therapist's frame of reference.

Another reason why client-centered therapy is more successful than other therapies is that resistance generally is less in client-centered therapy. Clients who are not pushed or led are not as likely to resist, and if they know that they can change the topic at any moment, they may feel more free to explore sensitive areas than they would in other kinds of therapy. The client is in complete control in client-centered therapy; there are no questions, no comments, no directions, and no advice from the therapist.

Training for Client-Centered Therapy

It is surprisingly hard to learn to do client-centered therapy. Student-trainees who meet once a week for two hours need three or four months before they are ready to see a client. Client-centered therapy is, in the main, empathic listening, and it may be so hard to learn to listen empathically because this skill involves the ability to hear the other person without intruding oneself. When we listen, we usually have a personal agenda which determines what we hear. Thus, when we listen to someone with a problem, our agenda includes the purpose of helping. With this purpose in the back of our minds, we frequently listen for the cause of the problem and are thinking of possible solutions. But when we do this, it is not possible to hear *exactly* what the person is saying.

Direct experience is the best way to train people in empathic listening, and role-playing is one way to obtain this experience. I have one person talk about some personal troubles (either the person's own or a friend's) for five minutes or so, while the other person, acting as the therapist, tries to understand and indicates what she or he understands about the situation. If this interaction is recorded, the person who acts as the therapist can review what the other person actually said and can check how accurate the understanding has been. It is in this active checking by the listener—the therapist trainee—that the learning occurs. This exercise can sometimes be done without an instructor present. In addition to role-playing, trainees listen to audio tapes, watch films, and read transcripts of therapy sessions. A surprising amount of material for this is available on the market. When I think a student is ready to see clients, I have an interview with the student in which I, acting as a client, talk about my concerns. If the student is facilitating and I, as client, feel I've made some progress, the student goes on to see actual clients.

Regardless of the type of psychotherapy in which a student is interested, practice in empathic listening should be a part of psychotherapy training. A therapist who doesn't know what a client is saying will find it hard to work with the client, even in the behavioral approaches. It is not easy to get this training; however, few academic programs have listening courses as part of their therapy training. Fortunately, teachers of the client-centered and person-centered approach have become more active recently. In addition to the program at La Jolla, California, where summer institutes have been held since 1965, there are a number of meetings and workshops every year through which listening skills can be learned.

The Setting for Therapy

There is nothing remarkable about the faculty office in which I do therapy. I sit about 6 feet away from the client, and I do not sit behind a desk. The office furnishings do not seem to make much difference; once clients begin to talk, they are in their own worlds. I once had a blackboard put on a wall in my office, and I was going to install a drape to cover it because I thought clients might be distracted by whatever was written on it. But the first client arrived before I had a chance to install the drape, and he noticed neither the board nor what was on it. Ten years later, when I moved, I noticed that I still had not installed the drape. In all that time, no client had commented about or seemed to be distracted by the naked blackboard.

Like most therapists, I suppose, I prefer to see people who come to me because they want help, not because they have been sent by others, such as courts or parents. It has been my experience that clients do best after having had several experiences with other forms of therapy. Many years ago we found that the most successful clients at the Counseling Center were in their third therapy experience. It is as if clients have to learn to do therapy. The severity of clients' problems has little relation to success; some of my most successful clients have had quite serious problems. Several people who were hospitalized for a number of years are now living independent lives as a result of client-centered therapy with me, for example. But I also have had clients with seemingly little wrong in terms of their personality or background when they came in, who did not change at all in therapy. Of course, the severity of the client's problem may have much to do with the length of therapy necessary to get to a satisfactory termination.

Clients come to me from many sources. The most usual source is recommendation from a former client, a friend, or relative. Years ago, when I started to do therapy, many clients came for therapy with an initial problem but had some awareness that, in addition to solving that problem, they wanted to change in a general way. Now most of my clients come because of a specific problem and leave after that problem is solved. In one case, a woman came because, some months after the death of her husband, she wasn't sleeping well and was having trouble leaving her house. She stopped therapy after two interviews because she had become aware of her anger at her husband for dying and leaving her. She was then able to sleep and could leave her house without trouble.

I am starting to see more elderly clients. Client-centered therapy, with its emphasis on the client choosing the problem and going at his or her own pace, seems ideally suited for working with the elderly.

THE THERAPY FOR DONALD GREEN

Session 2

A unique characteristic of the Rogerian approach has to do with the importance of the client's internal frame of reference. It is a basic tenet of this approach that the therapist tries to understand what the client is saying from the vantage point of the client's frame of reference and only in that framework. I do not want to understand Donald Green in any way other than his present frame of reference. If I understood him from the report of a previous interview or from psychological testing, I might not understand his world *as he sees it at the moment*. In the present case, I do not want to know anything about Donald Green that he does not tell me directly. Therefore I do not acknowledge that I know anything about the first interview. Donald begins the dialogue.

GREEN. Well, what do you want to know? Where should I start? What should I talk about?

ZIMRING. Talk about whatever is of concern to you, whatever is on your mind at the moment.

>   *(This direct statement in reply to a question, which is intended to explain how to operate in client-centered therapy, is known as "structuring," or helping the client know how to function in this particular situation.)*

GREEN. Should I talk about my childhood?

ZIMRING. I gather you are not sure how to begin. It would be most useful for you to talk about whatever is uppermost in your mind right now.

>   *(A basic tenet of the client-centered or person-centered approach is that no material is the right material to talk about. It is not more useful or therapeutic if some rather than other material is discussed. Because I genuinely believe this to be the case, the client will accept my answer. It is important for me to understand and accept the client's uncertainty if this is being experienced at the moment. At this point I think that Donald is saying, "What are the rules?" If he persists in asking questions, then I know uncertainty is central to him and my response then might be, "You feel uncertain about what to talk about.")*

GREEN. The thing that is of most concern to me is getting up in the morning. I am having difficulty getting up. I am a good worker and a responsible person. I have done a lot of things to try to get myself up in the morning. I have set alarm clocks all over the house and had the newspaper delivery boy knock on the door, and it doesn't work. I still come in late.

ZIMRING. So no matter what you do, it keeps happening.

GREEN. Yeah, it's still a problem. And I do stay late after work to make up the time. But it still looks bad. I don't know what the other employees think about Donald Green always coming in late. After 17 years with the same company, I don't know why this is happening. I don't know what to do about it.

ZIMRING. Mhm. I gather there are two things here. One is you feel helpless about it all. Puzzled and helpless.

> *(This is a typical client-centered response. In 1957, Rogers named six "necessary and sufficient conditions" for change to take place in psychotherapy. One important condition is that "the therapist experience an empathic understanding of the client's internal frame of reference." Here, I am checking my understanding of Donald's internal frame of reference, of how he sees the world at this moment. I am not checking my understanding of what he has done to alleviate the problem. Thus I do not respond to what he did to avoid coming in late, and so on.)*

GREEN. I don't know what to do about it. Why can't I wake up?

> *(Instead of taking this as a question for me to answer, I understand this remark as being about his present frame of reference, that is, his present experience of puzzlement or helplessness.)*

ZIMRING. Something you should be able to do and can't. And you don't understand why not.

GREEN. Right, right, I don't understand it. I've been there 17 years and I like my job. I've worked hard. I don't think it's that I don't want to go to work. So I don't know why I come in late.

ZIMRING. So it doesn't make sense.

> *(I make no attempt to reassure Donald that a solution is possible but rather stay with his feeling of puzzlement. You might think that a negative feeling like helplessness would get worse if we direct the client's attention to it, without any hope or reassurance. The opposite seems to be the case. If we stay with a negative feeling, the client will usually move from it, as Donald does in his next response.)*

GREEN. I don't miss every morning; this morning I managed to make it to work on time. I didn't go back to sleep after the paperboy woke me up, but maybe the only reason I managed to stay up was that I didn't feel well.

ZIMRING. You got up OK, but the reason wasn't anything you could count on.

> *(I respond to his reaction to what had happened, that he couldn't count on getting up, rather than to what had happened that morning. Responding to a client's reaction rather than to the circumstances of what happens is an important aspect of client-centered responding.)*

GREEN. Yes, maybe it won't happen that same way tomorrow.

ZIMRING. You can't count on it. . . .

> *(There could be some important material here. How was he feeling this morning? Was there any relationship between getting up in time*

and starting therapy? I could ask these and similar questions, but they are irrelevant at this point. As a matter of fact, they do not occur to me. All I am interested in is understanding what he means at the moment. If any of these questions did occur to me, they would be occurring from my framework and not from Donald's. If I were exploring my own framework, my attention would not be on him, and so I might not hear what he really means at that moment.

Listening in client-centered therapy is a most active and demanding process. The therapist makes hypotheses about what the client is saying and then checks the accuracy of these hypotheses by responding appropriately. When I am formulating questions from my own frame of reference, I am not formulating hypotheses about the client's frame of reference.)

GREEN. Yeah (pause). It was lucky how I got this job 17 years ago, right after college. My father had worked at the same company, and one of the owners recognized my name when I applied.

ZIMRING. It just sort of fell into your lap.

GREEN. Yes. I wish that man was still with the company, but he retired ten years ago. The top management of the company changes so fast that half of them would not know who I was if we passed on the street.

ZIMRING. Sort of anonymous.

GREEN. Yes. It didn't used to be that way. It used to be that the president went around the whole plant at least once a month and talked to most of the regular employees. He not only knew who you were, he knew whether or not you were married, and if you had children.

ZIMRING. It sounds as if it were more personal then.

GREEN. Yes. It used to be, when I sent a memo I knew who was going to read it. Now I don't. We have a new secretary in our section at the plant. She was on the phone, chatting away with what sounded like a friend, and I gave her something to be typed. She snapped, "You're going to have to wait your turn"; she was rude. So I said, "Do it as soon as you can," and left it on her desk. I'll be interested to see how long it takes her to get it done.

ZIMRING. It's not quite clear to me. Are you saying that you want to see whether she is just ignoring you personally, or whether she is generally doing a sloppy job?

(I do not hesitate to tell Donald that I don't understand. My major responsibility to the client is to try to understand what is being said at the moment. When I don't understand, I ask questions. If something gets in the way of my understanding, it becomes my responsibility to

remove the obstacle. If, for example, I fail to understand a client because I suddenly remember something I should have done, this internal interruption can affect my understanding of my client.

Because of this kind of possible problem, I have learned to survey my internal landscape and concerns for a few minutes before I see a client, so as little as possible intrudes itself in my mind during the session. It almost never happens that I have negative feelings about a client or about our being together, but if it should I would mention it to the client. One of Rogers's "necessary and sufficient conditions" is that the therapist be congruent in the relationship. This means that what the therapist is feeling about the client and the relationship should match what the therapist is expressing.)

GREEN. Yeah. A lot of people aren't working very hard today. Some people at the plant seem to treat it as if it was their home rather than a place to work, as if they didn't have to earn their pay.

ZIMRING. As if all they had to do was show up.

(This is an adequate but not exemplary response. I indicate that I understand Donald's opinion that a lot of people don't work hard at their jobs, but my response is about other people, not about his reaction. I focus on the client's external world and talk about it in the same way the client does. I communicate that I understand how the client sees the world, but the best kind of response would direct the client's attention to her or his own experience. However, if I had said, "It annoys you that people don't work very hard," I would have been directing Donald's attention to his annoyance. This would be an error, because he is not considering his annoyance at this moment.)

In this report of the therapy for Donald Green, I will include only the even-numbered sessions. The next session described therefore is No. 4.

Session 4

We open this session in a typical way for a client-centered interview—I wait for Donald to begin talking. I usually do not engage in much social talk—the latest news, the weather, or whatever—although if the client begins that way I do not deliberately withhold my responses. My attitude is that this is the client's hour and I am interested in where he is and what he wants to explore, and this determines what happens at the beginning of the interview.

GREEN. Hi (pause).

ZIMRING. Hi.

GREEN. We hired a woman engineer the other day. She seems OK so far. But things sure have changed; there were no women in my engineering class. Oh, there were a number of them at the college, but I didn't have much to do with them. Most of my time was spent studying, and on week-ends I worked as a waiter.

ZIMRING. Mhm.

I do not respond verbally and explicitly to everything Donald says. Frequently, understanding is conveyed by posture, facial expression, and so on. Understanding the client is important; explicit communication of that understanding is not so important.

GREEN. There was this course called Human Factors in Design. I don't know, it was a real problem for me. No matter how hard I worked, I couldn't do well in it. The instructor gave me a hard time. Whatever I did, there was no pleasing him.

> (At this point I could have said, "That must have been frustrating," or "you must have felt helpless," and Donald might have responded to either remark that my observation was correct. Even so, in the client-centered framework, either one would have been wrong. Donald had not mentioned being frustrated or feeling helpless. My response would have focused him on frustration or helplessness, material that was not in his frame of reference at that moment. Many things are true of a client, but only a few are within the client's frame of reference at a given moment.)

GREEN (continuing). I don't know that he picked on me, but I could never say or do anything right in class.

ZIMRING. There was no pleasing him.

GREEN. Yes, no matter how hard I tried. He was one of those people who, once they make up their mind about you, they won't budge. One time, we had to do a project and I submitted it in plenty of time. Then I thought of something extra to do and did it and gave it to him, still within the time limit. He wouldn't accept it because it hadn't been turned in with the original project, even though the extra project was a good one.

ZIMRING. It didn't seem fair.

> (Although Donald hasn't said he thought it was unfair, this seems to me to be what he is trying to communicate.)

GREEN. No, it wasn't (pause). You know, I've run into that a lot. Some people make up their minds, and you can't change them.
ZIMRING. Like running into a stone wall.
>   *(Using a metaphor is a good way of responding to the client. Even if the metaphor is wrong, it refers to experience, and the client has to check with his experience to find out whether it is correct.)*

GREEN. Yes, I'd have to put a gun to their heads to make them change their initial impressions. (He pauses briefly.) I usually don't make a good first impression, you know. Or rather, I don't make much of an impression. People don't seem to notice me.
ZIMRING. It's not so much that they have a bad opinion of you, it's that you don't seem to exist for them.
GREEN. That's right. The other day I was in line to order some food at a take-out place, and the woman at the counter started taking the order of the man behind me. I didn't know what to do for a second, and then I started to say something. The woman said, "I'm sorry," but she continued taking the other man's order. I just turned around and left. . . . The last time I was in Chicago I could hardly get a cab to stop for me.
ZIMRING. It's like you're invisible.
>   *(This response focuses on Donald's experience of not being visible, which has a reasonable probability of being in his frame of reference at this moment. It is an adequate response, though it ignores his inconvenience at not being seen and his feeling that he would have to do something extreme to be noticed. A better response would have acknowledged these factors.)*

Donald pauses for some time before continuing. Generally, I do not interrupt pauses. This is the client's opportunity to sense what else is of concern at the moment and to think in my presence. Beginning therapists often find that pauses make them anxious. Everyone is socially conditioned to make sure that long pauses don't occur; whenever there is a definite pause in a conversation, someone rushes in with a topic to keep it going. I allow Donald to continue when he is ready.

GREEN. Last week we were told what our salary increase for next year will be. My raise is lower than the rate of inflation was last year, so I am really taking a pay cut.
ZIMRING. You're really going to be getting less money.
GREEN. Yes, and less than some other people are getting. I don't know whether to write a letter to my supervisor or go see him. I do know

that I am not getting what I should. Last year was a good one for the company; I know they did all right and could afford to give us more. And even though I was late sometimes, I more than made up the time I missed, and my work performance has been good. My supervisor always gives me good ratings.

ZIMRING. So there's no good reason why you shouldn't get more money.
(You might infer that Donald is indignant or angry, but I do not mention these feelings because they are not in his frame of reference at this moment. He is not considering his feelings about the situation; he is concerned with his pay and is trying to communicate his opinion that he should be getting a larger raise.)

GREEN. The raise I got last year was a little larger than the average, and I performed better this year than last. I was sure my raise would be above average this year, too. I really don't know why it wasn't; it should have been.

ZIMRING. So you really expected a bigger raise and are puzzled that you didn't get one.
(In talking about "not knowing why," Donald may be beginning to consider his reactions to the situation. I choose to comment on his expectation and puzzlement, rather than on what he says about the situation itself.)

GREEN. Yes (pause). It's as if I have to do twice as much as other people to get the same credit. I know I've done more than others who got bigger raises.
(At this point, my mind is actively generating hypotheses about what Donald means. He is saying that he doesn't count to others, perhaps to those in authority. He may mean that he is more invisible than others, a theme that has appeared before. Perhaps he is considering something about unfairness, although it is not clear that this is in his present frame of reference.)

ZIMRING. Somehow what you do doesn't seem to count as much as what others do.

GREEN. That's right. It's as if other people, and what they do, exist and are of the same stuff as the rest of the world. I'm different. I am flimsier.

ZIMRING. Not as solid or real—you don't take up space in the same way.

GREEN. Yes, I don't know what it is about me. I don't have the same effect, can't make the same sort of impression as other people do.

ZIMRING. Somehow more powerless?
(I put this as a question, in a tentative tone of voice, because I am guessing that this is something he is experiencing at the moment and is trying to convey.)

GREEN. That's right! I don't know how to exist in the people world, the way others do. Other people seem to interact with each other with no trouble. I can't figure it out.

ZIMRING. It's both puzzling and darn hard.

> (This interchange is a good example of how the client moves from considering the situation he is in to considering the self. One of the most puzzling aspects of client-centered therapy is why just understanding the client's frame of reference brings about change. Here my empathic understanding encourages Donald to give more consideration to his self.)

GREEN. Yes, and I don't know what to do about it.

ZIMRING. It's a real mystery.

GREEN. Yes, it is (pause). You know, I like to keep my place quiet. . . .

> (This is a sudden change of tone. What can it mean?)

ZIMRING. You like to have it peaceful?

GREEN. Well, when it's quiet it's more restful. In the evening I like to doze. But also when it's quiet, I know that nobody is outside the house.

ZIMRING. It feels safer when it's quiet.

> (Though Donald does not choose to respond to my description of the quiet as "safer," he still may sometimes feel this way. Evidently, however, this is not central in his frame of reference at the moment. A correct response from the therapist not only describes the client's reactions but also is concerned with what the client is attending to and actively exploring at that moment. When the client does not respond to what I have said, I do not repeat it or explain what I mean. It is hard to drop or forget a hypothesis about what the other person means, but this is a skill the client-centered therapist has to acquire.)

GREEN. The funniest thing happened to me the other night. Just as I was falling asleep there was a noise outside, sort of a metallic crashing sound. Even though the door was locked and nothing could have happened to me, my whole body broke out in a sweat. Within half a minute I was wet from head to toe. It took me hours to get to sleep, and I felt sick most of the next day. Isn't that ridiculous? Nothing happened, and I still reacted like that.

ZIMRING. It was a pretty violent reaction you had, and it made no sense.

GREEN. Yes, I felt a lot like I did when I thought that woman had to get the car I had sold her repaired and was sending someone to get even with me.

ZIMRING. Both times it felt the same, as if something terrible was going to get you.

GREEN. Yes, it was awful.

Session 6

GREEN. One of the foremen at the plant has to go to the hospital for minor surgery, and I will have to supervise his unit until we know how long he is going to be off the job. I'll have to oversee manufacturing operations and make sure that the work is scheduled right. I hate this kind of work—I'm not a supervisor. I really dread it.

ZIMRING. Really hate the thought of it.

GREEN. Yes—I keep thinking about the people I'll have to supervise, going over the possibilities in my mind. The other night I woke up and couldn't get back to sleep thinking about it.

ZIMRING. On a real treadmill.

> *(There is some difference of opinion about this, but I find it useful to make metaphorical responses that have an experiential referent. Being on a treadmill involves the experience of doing something repeatedly without making any progress.)*

GREEN. Yes (slight pause). I think I am afraid of two things. On one hand, I'm afraid that when I tell them to do something I'll be ignored. I'll say something and they will look at me and just keep on doing what they were doing.

ZIMRING. As if you were invisible.

GREEN. Yes, as if I didn't exist. On the other hand, I'm afraid they will criticize whatever I say or do. Whatever I do will make somebody angry.

ZIMRING. There'll be no pleasing them.

> *(Although Donald is experiencing apprehension about supervising, it would be wrong for me to mention this, since he is not focusing on his apprehension at the moment. Instead, he is focusing on others and how he thinks they will react.)*

GREEN. Yes. I know I'm going to have trouble with some of those people. They can be so petty. Just selfish.

ZIMRING. Not caring about anything but themselves.

After a long pause, Donald volunteers a memory.

GREEN. I was thinking of my sister the other day, and how she was always mean to me. I remember once, oh, I must have been 10 years old, when Diana had a girlfriend at our house. They were trying on clothes in her room and she left her door open. Diana saw me looking and she really screamed and walloped me. It wasn't fair. I was in my own room, and if she wanted privacy all she had to do was close her door.

ZIMRING. It wasn't right to take it out on you that way.

GREEN. No—she was always doing that. I remember once when I was only 8 years old she asked me to tell the folks that she was home taking care of me when actually she was out with her friends. But I did tell them the truth when they asked me; I was too scared to lie to them. And when Diana found out I had told them, she was mad at me for weeks.

ZIMRING. She was very hard on you.

GREEN. Yes, and what made it worse was that Dad would always side with her (short pause). Well, I'm not sure he was always on her side; it was more that he was always critical of me. I remember once in high school when I was president of the Chess Club and I gave a talk on Parents' Day. My father was there. The faculty sponsor said I gave a good talk and was quite complimentary, but my father just told me about all the things I could have done better.

ZIMRING. He didn't give you much credit.

GREEN. I wasn't around him much; he was usually off by himself. But when he was there, I would always seem to mess up. I remember I was pretty good at Hi-Li, where you try to hit a rubber ball attached to a paddle by a piece of elastic. My father saw me doing it and said I should practice, that if I became good at one thing, maybe I would get good at other things.

ZIMRING (interrupting, while Donald is still talking). Sort of implied that you weren't much good at anything?

GREEN. Yes. The peculiar thing was that after that my score—the number of times I could hit the ball without missing—was always lower when he was in the house, even if he was in another room....

ZIMRING (interrupting). He didn't even have to say anything; just his presence made you worse.

> (This interruption is not the best possible response. The fault is not that it is an interruption but that I am not responding to the main thing Donald is trying to tell me. When someone is telling you something, there is a present interest or intention in the communication. That is, the person is doing more than telling you a story or telling you about something. There is a purpose, a reason—often hidden—why they are telling this story at this moment. The best client-centered response combines a mention of this present interest of the person with an understanding of the content. What Donald is intending to communicate is the peculiar effect of his father's criticism.)

GREEN. Yes.... The other day I remembered a time when we were living in a summer cottage and I was supposed to get a new bathing suit. My father was angry with me about something. After he left the room and the door was shut, I waved my hand in sort of a dismissive way at him. Unfortunately, there was a frosted glass panel in the door. When he came home that night, he told me that I was not going to get a new suit because of my gesture. I was very disappointed and scared. How he saw it through the frosted glass, I don't know.

ZIMRING. It was scary and almost seemed magical.

> (As in many responses, I mention both the feelings and the reaction Donald is talking about: "scared," and his present reaction to the incident, his puzzlement about how his father knew he made the gesture. He chooses to follow up on the latter.)

GREEN. Yes, he always seemed to know things about me.

ZIMRING. Always had you in view.

GREEN. Yes (pause). I met a man the other day whose father was working at the company while my father was working there. He said my father was at a company Christmas party he went to when he was a boy, and my father lifted him up so he could get something from the Christmas tree. You know, I can't remember my father ever holding *me* in any way.

ZIMRING. He didn't show you that kind of attention.

GREEN. I suddenly remembered something the other day that I haven't thought of for a long time. I was a small boy and I was taking a bath with my father. All of a sudden my father yelled for my mother to take me. He was disgusted and angry and I don't know why.

ZIMRING. Really a puzzle.

GREEN. Yes. I'll never forget how angry he was.

ZIMRING. It's really stayed with you.

GREEN. It wasn't fair. What could I have done that was so bad?

ZIMRING. Nothing could have been that bad.

GREEN (with emphasis). No, *nothing!*

Session 8

GREEN. I had an awful time last week. I told you I was going to have to supervise a unit at work, and it turned out the foreman was gone for four days. I found it very hard to do. I didn't want to talk to the workers on the line, but I had to.

ZIMRING. So you were really caught.

GREEN. Sometimes I actually felt like running. It was really difficult for me.

ZIMRING. Really awful.

GREEN. Yes, I knew that they were being critical, although nobody said anything to me.

ZIMRING. You knew it to be true.

> (Psychotherapists from other orientations would argue that a major problem for Donald is his expectation of disapproval and criticism, and they might see my response as reinforcing this expectation. However, all that is important for me to do is to check my understanding of what he is saying. If Donald does have incorrect or unreal expectations, as he gets to trust his own internal frame of reference he will rely less on an external frame of reference that contains expectations and perceptions of others.
>
> One of the main goals of client-centered therapy can be seen here. Rogers proposes a continuum of types of knowledge, with subjective knowledge, knowledge of one's internal frame of reference, at one end. You have most subjective knowledge when you know your own frame of reference. At the other end of the continuum is objective knowledge, which involves no internal frame of reference. Pure objective knowledge exists when you know something that has no internal frame of reference, such as knowing how a gasoline engine works. Objective knowing also exists when you know something externally, even though it may have an internal frame of reference. Thus, if you think of yourself as being of a certain age, having a particular occupation, being married, and so on, you are thinking of yourself objectively or externally. Client-centered therapy should move the client closer to the subjective end of the continuum, where the self is seen less in external terms and more in terms of personal experiences and meanings.)

GREEN. Yes (pause). I had a dream last night. . . .

ZIMRING. Oh?

GREEN. Yes. I dreamed I was talking to a professor about a paper that was due. It was hard talking to him, because he was looking down at his desk and making notes. I went away and worked on the paper, and when I finished I went back to the building where his office was. It was a big office building and the halls were dark. As I came to his office I thought I heard something down the hall. I put my assignment under his door and left in a hurry. I felt drained, like a balloon with the air escaping.

ZIMRING. You got it done and handed it in, but you were exhausted after your fright.

GREEN. Yes, I was surprised I could move.

ZIMRING. Also, was there something about hearing something down the hall?

GREEN. Yes, my heart started pounding faster.
ZIMRING. Very scary?
GREEN. Yes, but more than that. More like there was a monster down there.
ZIMRING. Terrifying and huge.
GREEN. Oh, yes.

Donald shudders slightly, closes his eyes, and moves his shoulders and arms as if he is shivering with cold.

ZIMRING. Really awful.
GREEN. Yes.

> (It does not occur to me, nor should it, that it would be "good" for him to understand what was so terrifying. It is enough for me to understand his experience. In Rogerian therapy, dreams are responded to as any other experience, without looking for symbolic material or probing for the dream's meaning. Donald's dream of going to the professor's office is treated in the same way that a report of actually going there would be. I concentrate on his experience of the dream, not on the experience implicit in the symbols of the dream.
>
> Donald's shuddering behavior raises the question of whether, or how, the therapist should respond to the client's nonverbal behavior. The intention of the client is central. If a client should say, "I feel sad," and sit there and cry, the crying would be part of the communication of sadness. It would be telling how sad the person feels and so should be responded to. However, if the client sits and cries without saying anything, and if it is not clear what the crying means to the client, the therapist would accept the crying as an open communication and wait for the client to give some indication of its meaning before responding.)

There is a long pause before Donald continues.

GREEN. I remember that I told you I like things quiet around the house, but last night it was *too* quiet.
ZIMRING. Too much of a good thing?
GREEN. Yes. When I got home I picked up a magazine to read and couldn't stop, not even to go out for supper. I just couldn't get myself to move. I didn't talk to anybody all day yesterday, either, so I went for almost 48 hours without talking to another person.
ZIMRING. It was too quiet, eh? And you got stuck.

GREEN. Yeah. After a while I got to feel peculiar, like I was getting more and more invisible. This morning I found it hard to talk to the waitress. I was surprised when she responded.
ZIMRING. You sort of expected that she would not know you were there?
GREEN. Yes, this happens to me a lot. I wish I had more people in my life. But I don't know how to talk to people. It doesn't seem hard for others, but by the time I think of something to say, the interaction is over and the person I was going to talk to is already talking to somebody else.
ZIMRING. It's a real mystery how it's done.
> (A slightly better response at this point would have been, "You'd like to interact more but don't know how to do it.")

GREEN. Right. All my life I've been by myself. I've always felt all I had to do was get my job done, but now it's not enough.
ZIMRING. Just leaves a lot lacking.
> (I understand the content of Donald's statement but not how he feels about it. While I decide to respond without guessing at his feelings, it would have been better if I had said, "At this point in your life you want more interaction with other people.")

GREEN. Yeah (pause). I can't seem to do anything right when it comes to other people.
ZIMRING. Always wrong somehow.
GREEN. I remember when my sister tried to teach me to dance. I wasn't very good at it and she made fun of me.
ZIMRING. She was hard on you.
GREEN. Yes. For months afterwards when she saw me coming she would cross her feet and pretend to stumble and fall down.
ZIMRING. Really cruel....

Donald agrees. Then he pauses and, speaking slowly, continues.

GREEN. I don't know what I am going to do. I'm always by myself.
ZIMRING. Always alone.
GREEN. Yes...and I don't know what to do about it.
ZIMRING. Feel powerless.
GREEN. Yes. I really can't do anything with people. Sometimes I don't feel like it is worth it.
ZIMRING. Sometimes it doesn't seem worth the effort?
GREEN. Right. You know, sometimes I wonder about going on.
ZIMRING. Things are just that awful sometimes.

(Clients who get to this degree of desperation test our faith in a basic client-centered premise: that, given a facilitating atmosphere, people will have the strength and resources to take care of their own lives. The therapist sometimes has an impulse to try to actively help such clients. However, a therapist who begins to worry about whether the client is suicidal or who considers reassuring the client is no longer working in the client's frame of reference. At the very moment when the client most needs to be understood, the therapist is not doing this. Over the years, it has been my experience that if we stay with clients and remain in their frame of reference while they are experiencing the bad part of life, they will come out of it on their own.)

GREEN. Yes, they are awful (pause). The other night I saw a movie that reminded me of my high school graduation. My father was angry with me; he thought I should have graduated with honors. My grades were OK but not that high, so he decided not to come to the graduation exercises. My mother said she felt bad about it but didn't want to antagonize my father, so she didn't come either. At the time it didn't bother me too much but now I really think it was wrong.

ZIMRING. Really off base.

GREEN. Yes. They should have cared more. There was no reason for them not to attend. And everyone else was surrounded by their family. It was an awful thing to do to me.

ZIMRING. They really didn't do what they should have.

GREEN. No, they didn't.

Donald has talked about his parents several times over the past few interviews. My responses, however, are only to what he has just said, not to what has come before.

Session 10

GREEN. I had a sad experience last week. My shop teacher in high school, Mr. Buck, died. He was the nicest man; he got me started rebuilding cars. I used to come back to school at night and over the weekend to work on cars. A lot of the time he would be there and we would talk together.

ZIMRING. It was a nice time.

(This response is superficial. A better response would have been, "He really helped you and you think of him fondly.")

GREEN. He was the first man who ever talked to me about himself and his life. He urged me to take advantage of my opportunities. He felt that he hadn't been very successful, ending up as a high school teacher. I remember how that startled me. Being a high school teacher seemed very successful to me.

ZIMRING. It surprised you.

GREEN. Both surprised me and was interesting. For the first time I began to see that adults are people like me and have feelings about success and failure like I do. I thought about those conversations for years.

ZIMRING. Very meaningful for you.

GREEN. Yes.... You know, I think it was the first time any adult treated me as an equal, as a person like himself.

ZIMRING. Do you mean that it was the first time anyone acknowledged that you were a person, too, or do you mean that it was the first time it occurred to you that you were a person like other people?

>(My question is concerned with what Donald is saying, but it was prompted by a theoretical assumption that is important to me: that client-centered therapy is successful because it facilitates the growth of an independent self. Thus it was no surprise to me that Donald chose this topic to discuss. I have to be careful that my theoretical assumptions do not guide much of my response to the client, because then I run a real danger of being outside the client's frame of reference.)

GREEN. I guess it was more the latter. I had always thought of children and adults as being very different, and I don't know if I had ever thought of myself as a person.

ZIMRING. It was a new thought.

GREEN. Yes (pause). Well, last week when I read in the paper that Mr. Buck had died and there was to be a memorial service at the high school, I decided to go. I was surprised at the number of people there I knew. I started talking to Ruth, a woman who had been in my class—in our senior year, I had helped her with math. We had coffee after the service. I didn't find it too hard to talk to her. She's a widow, and both of us are interested in antiques. I asked her if she wanted to go to the antique show when it comes to town and she said she would like to. I'm sort of looking forward to that, but I hope I don't make a fool of myself.

ZIMRING. It could be a nice thing, but it does make you apprehensive.

>(This response is correct in stating his ambivalence. It would have been more accurate, however, if I had mentioned the possibility of humiliation with which Donald is concerned when he says he is worried about making a fool of himself. The fact that he is apprehensive, while probably true, is not in his frame of reference, and I should not have commented on it.)

GREEN. Well, I'm not very good in social situations. Most people know what to say, but I'm just quiet most of the time. Maybe if there's something like antiques to talk about, I won't have so much trouble.

ZIMRING. Might make it easier.

GREEN. Yes, when there's a topic that I really know to talk about, like antiques, I don't feel so much that what I say will be foolish or inappropriate.

ZIMRING. It wouldn't be so dumb.

GREEN. Yes, but sometimes I feel like it's very hard.

ZIMRING. Talking to someone, you mean?

GREEN. Yes—I don't know what the other person is thinking.

ZIMRING. About what you're saying?

GREEN. Yes. Unless you're talking about a fact, how do you know the rule about what's right or wrong to say?

> (Most of the time I can understand quickly what the client says from my own experience. Here, I have to think. I can imagine myself in a social situation saying something inappropriate, something the listener might think was a foolish remark. For Donald, however, there is a mixture of abstract rules for the rightness and wrongness of conversations, which I do not quite understand, and a fear of what the listener might think, which is easy for me to understand. I choose to respond about the rules.)

ZIMRING. What are the rules?

GREEN. Yes. It's like a fantasy I had the other day as I was going to sleep of being a native who left his island for the first time and was wandering around in a strange, foreign city. It was like it was the first time I had ever seen a big city.

ZIMRING. Confusing and bewildering?

GREEN. It was like I didn't know how to talk to the people in the city. I started to ask directions of one man, and he just laughed at me and walked on. Another man just imitated my body movements and walked on without answering either. It was a bad time.

ZIMRING. I gather there were two things there. One was not to be able to communicate, the other was that they were making fun of you.

GREEN. Yes. As if, no matter how hard I tried, they thought I was an idiot.

> (At this point the connection between Donald's wanting to know the rules for what should be said in a conversation and his fear of being criticized becomes clear to me. If you know the rules everybody else uses, they can't criticize you.)

ZIMRING. You didn't know the rules and couldn't find out what they were.

GREEN. Yes, exactly (pause). In talking to some people at Mr. Buck's funeral, I learned that an old schoolmate of mine from high school had died. I've been thinking about him. Neither he nor I was part of the crowd. We didn't play football or date much. We used to have chess games, and all one summer we worked on a Model T Ford. We finally finished it and took it out for a test drive, and after a half mile, while we were going through the park, it stopped. We couldn't figure out what was wrong until it finally occurred to us that we had forgotten to put gas in the tank. It was so funny! I laughed as hard as I can ever remember.

ZIMRING. It was a great time.

GREEN. Yes, but I lost touch with him after graduation. It was like after he left town to go to college he didn't exist.

ZIMRING. Sort of out of sight, out of mind?

(I choose to respond here because Donald may be beginning a new theme about keeping contact with people. It would have been better, however, if I had waited until he indicated what his reaction was to losing contact with his friend.)

GREEN. I remember, in high school, playing chess with that friend on a Saturday night and thinking that everybody else was out on a date. It made me feel stupid. Like I was different.

ZIMRING. Not the same as everybody else.

GREEN. Yes.... I wonder what his life was like. Did he finally make some friends?

ZIMRING. Did he finally reach that goal?

GREEN. Yes, he was a nice guy, and I hope he did.

ZIMRING. He deserved it.

(When we discuss psychotherapy we tend to emphasize feelings and reactions and meanings. Values are equally important. Donald is talking about a value, an important goal: achieving friendship.)

GREEN. Yes (pause). I wonder if *I* am ever going to have any real friends.

ZIMRING. Is it ever going to work out?

GREEN. One good thing that happened last week is that I finally subscribed to cable television. It has a lot more variety, but I've got to be careful that I don't spend too much time watching TV. Too much time can be wasted that way.

ZIMRING. A real waste.

GREEN. There was a good program on gardening that my neighbor told me was going to be on, so I invited him over to watch it with me. That was pretty good.

ZIMRING. It was a nice occasion and you were pleased with it.
GREEN. Yes.

Looking back over this interview, several things strike me. Some of my responses were superficial, but this may not be as important as you might think. Frequently, the intent to understand the client is as important as, or more important than, the content of the therapist's responses. As I think about it, during this hour I was not aware of anything bothering me. If I had been, I might have said something to Donald like: "I'm not hearing you well today; would you mind telling me what you just said?" I would not hesitate to say something like this because my task is to understand, and I will do what is necessary to achieve this.

Several themes, such as Donald's increasing contact with others, emerge in this interview. I would not respond in terms of these themes unless they were the focus of his attention.

Session 12

GREEN. I spent more time with other people last week than I have in a long time. I've been working on a Model A Ford and a couple of weeks ago I sent in my application to exhibit it next month at a show. Two other guys who are also working on the Model A called me, and I got together with them. It was interesting to talk with them. One has parts I need, and the other has some equipment I can use in the final assembly of the motor. I'm further along than either of them, so I can save them some time on what they still have to do.
ZIMRING. Sounds like it was a good thing all the way around.
GREEN. Yes it was (pause). Last Sunday I felt sort of down; I really couldn't move. Then it occurred to me that it was my mother's birthday. I miss her sometimes.
ZIMRING. It was really affecting you.
    (This is not a good response; it focuses his attention on last Sunday. It would have been better to consider his more present feeling, missing his mother.)
GREEN. Uh huh. When I was young, my mother always knew where I was. It felt good working around the house when she was there.
ZIMRING. Comfortable, somehow.
GREEN. Yes, very much so. I remember sitting next to her and reading while she was sewing. You know, books always seemed more interesting when she was there.

ZIMRING. You just enjoyed things more when she was around.
> *(I do not probe for how things were better but simply stay with the fact that things were different when he was with his mother.)*

GREEN. Yes I did, unless my father was there, too. I saw a film about rabbits on television the other night. When there is some threat, like another animal, the rabbit freezes. That's what used to happen to my mother and me. We'd be sitting there, each doing our own thing, maybe she'd be reading and I'd be working on a model. Then my father would walk in and we both would freeze. We would just sit there and stare at something until he left.

ZIMRING. Both of you would stop cold when he was there.

GREEN. Yes, I always had to watch myself when he was around. And you know, although I don't like it, I still get that same feeling sometimes. Like when someone I don't know is around.

ZIMRING. You don't like it, but it still happens.
> *(This response just repeats what Donald says. It might seem that the client would consider such repetition to be obvious and superficial. But this doesn't occur. If the therapist is understanding the client, the client is in his world and not much aware of the therapist.)*

When Donald starts to talk again, he turns to another topic.

GREEN. I usually go to Jim's and Mary's on Thursday night to eat, but this week they were out of town. So I went last night instead (slight pause).

ZIMRING. Uh huh.

GREEN. After dinner, Mary usually goes to the family room and watches television while Jim and I talk. Last night it was different. She didn't leave, and we got into a long discussion, the only real talk we've ever had between the three of us. Jim started by saying that the only things people could really enjoy were those they had earned themselves. Mary said she thought that enjoyment is a personal quality which has to do with your ability to enjoy things, and it doesn't matter whether you have earned them or deserve them. Instead, she said, the question is whether you could relax and enjoy things in general. I took her side and said that if Jim was right, the wealthier the person, the happier that person should be, and that just didn't seem to be true. She and I sort of ganged up on Jim, and we had a boisterous argument. When I left to go home, Mary gave me a big hug and kiss. It was sort of an active evening.

ZIMRING. Sounds like a good time was had by all.

GREEN. Yes, but her display of affection sort of bothered me.

ZIMRING. It disturbed you in some way?

GREEN. Well, I thought it was a little much. After all, she is the wife of a friend. What if Jim had objected?

ZIMRING. You thought she stepped over the line, to some degree.

GREEN. Yes (pause). Last night wasn't a good night insofar as sleeping is concerned. I went to bed early and fell asleep fast. But then I woke up startled at every little noise. Finally, later in the night, I had an awful dream. It was one I've had before (slight pause). There was something looming in the dark. As long as I would stand and face in its direction, it would not move any closer. I knew that, even in the dream, and would try to keep facing it. But I could feel myself slowly turning away. I would shriek at myself, in my head, in the dream, not to turn, but I could feel it happening anyway. And all the time I knew that the menace was moving toward me as I turned away.

ZIMRING. So that somehow you ended up bringing the monster closer, and it was terrible not to be able to stop doing the thing that brought it closer.

GREEN. Yes, I couldn't help myself. It was the strangest thing. It was like I was standing on a turntable which just turned me, regardless of how hard I tried not to turn.

ZIMRING. Weird and uncontrollable.

(By "weird," of course, I refer to "the strangest thing." This is Donald's present experience of the dream, and so it takes precedence over his experience in the dream of not being able to control his motion. The present experience of something, even if it is a mild experience like being puzzled, is more important than the past experience being described, even if that experience was intense.)

GREEN. Yes, it was. I seldom have dreams that are that vivid, and I almost never have one where the feeling is that clear. But there was one dream I used to have when I was a kid that was vivid. I remember there was a goat in it, and the goat was in the backyard eating clothes hung out to dry on a line.

ZIMRING. Uh huh.

GREEN. Funny. I kept having that dream, but there wasn't much feeling in it.

ZIMRING. Just kept having it.

(I do not think about, or probe for, the meaning of the dream. Instead, it is up to Donald to use it as he will.)

GREEN. Yes (long pause). You know, I was thinking the other day about how I feel when people don't do what they should. For instance, I

submitted a medical insurance claim six months ago. I called them two months ago when I didn't get the check and the woman said it had gone to the review committee. It still hasn't been paid.
> *(Considering his experience of the dream has seemed to lead Donald to consider his experience in another realm—anger.)*

Session 14

GREEN. Something interesting happened the other day. I got a call from my engineering fraternity to take on a student in our program for tutoring inner-city kids in math and science.

ZIMRING. Mhm.

GREEN. So Saturday morning I went to the library and started working with a kid named Eric. He sort of surprised me and scared me a bit. He's taller and stronger than I am, even though he's only in high school. It's astounding what he didn't know, what he hadn't been taught. At first it was very hard. I would talk to him, and he wouldn't answer. He sat there with a sort of smile on his face, and I just wanted to call it off and go home. I thought I wasn't going to make a dent. But then I started to give him some math problems, using sports scores, and I found out that the problem was he didn't know much math. We had to start with third-grade math. After a while he began to enjoy what we were doing, and he really started participating. It made me feel good when he began to catch on.

ZIMRING. So it developed into a positive experience. It gave you a lot of satisfaction.

GREEN. Yes. I don't know what happened, but on the way home I stopped off for dinner at the usual place and talked to the waitress more than I ever have before. It was like somebody had oiled my talker. (He laughs.)

ZIMRING. All of a sudden it became surprisingly easy.

GREEN. Yes. Like the other day, when I oiled the hinges on my back door. Not only did it open more easily, it also stopped making all the noise it had been. Until then, I hadn't realized how hard it was to open and how much noise it was making.

ZIMRING. And I gather that talking to the waitress was like that, you sort of didn't realize how hard it had been to talk to her until somehow it became easy for awhile.

GREEN. Yes (pause). I don't know whether I told you, but we have a new production assistant. Jean's shy and finds it very hard to talk; she's still not confident. We were all having lunch in the cafeteria the other day and Mike, who is a bit of a blowhard, began to give her a hard time. He asked her about some novel he had just read and it was obvious that she didn't know anything about it. He just asked her more and more questions. I tried to change the topic to something we could all talk about, and then I asked him about something technical. That stopped the conversation. I don't like people like that. There he was, building himself up by tearing her down.

ZIMRING. Really left a bad taste in your mouth when he beat on her.

GREEN. I haven't talked much about the job recently. For a while there it was getting on my nerves. Recently, one of the foremen has been hanging around my office, talking to me, wanting my advice. The other day, I offered him a suggestion about a job in his department. We discussed it, and I think he is going to use my suggestion. Pretty good, him asking me.

ZIMRING. First you were annoyed with him but now you are pleased that he liked your idea.

GREEN. Remember that neighbor I had in to watch television a couple of weeks ago? His property is in back of mine, and last week he was burning leaves and rubbish in a big bonfire. This is strictly illegal; there are not supposed to be any open fires in our neighborhood. I was afraid the fire would spread to my property and I reached for the phone to call the police, but I couldn't do it. It was peculiar. The police would not have told him who reported the fire, but I still couldn't complete the call. It was as if my hand wouldn't obey.

ZIMRING. I gather that what was peculiar was having your body sort of take over.

GREEN. Yes, and I don't know what to do about my neighbor; I guess I'll have to talk to him.

ZIMRING. You're going to have to do something about it.

Donald agrees, and then there is a long pause before he continues.

GREEN. The other day it was my turn to present a major part of the annual report to the staff before it is mailed out to the stockholders. I've been avoiding doing this for the last few years, but I had no excuse for not doing it this time.

ZIMRING. Had to do it.

GREEN. Yes. My part of the presentation was about 20 minutes long. I felt awful before I gave it; I bet I worried about it every night for a week in advance. Couldn't get it off my mind. Whatever else I was doing, I was thinking about it in the back of my mind.

ZIMRING. It's always there.

Donald nods in agreement before going on.

GREEN. Well, I don't think I slept more than two hours Monday night. My presentation was the last one. When I got up to begin talking, I was afraid I wouldn't be able to speak, but finally I got started. One man kept looking at my left armpit; I thought maybe my coat was ripped, but I didn't know what was the matter (slight pause). When I looked later, there was nothing wrong with my coat.

ZIMRING. Hard to figure.

GREEN. Yes. I was surprised that I got through it. I actually delivered my part of the report without blocking and without making any bad mistakes. I was afraid that I was going to make a mistake and give them wrong figures without even realizing that they were wrong.

ZIMRING. Wouldn't even know that you had goofed.

GREEN. Well, I got through the report all right, much to my surprise. Didn't make any bad mistakes.

> *(Donald says something new, that he was surprised, and he also repeats something I did not mention in my last response: He did not make any serious mistakes. This tendency of the client to repeat when the therapist misses something, providing a second chance for a response, is very helpful.)*

ZIMRING. So you were surprised that you got through it without anything terrible happening.

GREEN. Yes (pause). But the strangest, most surprising part was something else. The presentation was late in the morning, just before lunch, and mine was the last presentation. From the conversations I heard as the group was breaking up, people were talking about the new menu in the cafeteria and what they would have for lunch, not about the annual report.

> *(At this point I do not have the slightest idea of why it is surprising to him that people are talking about lunch. I remain quiet until he gives me more information.)*

GREEN (continuing). When I remembered how they looked when I was presenting the report, I realized that most of them weren't listening to what I was saying. They were off in their own worlds.

ZIMRING. Not really hearing you at all.

> *(I am puzzled. He seems to be pleased, but he is talking about people not paying attention to him.)*

GREEN. Right; most of them were in their own worlds and were not thinking of me at all.

Donald smiles slightly, and I respond.

ZIMRING. Not operating in respect to you.
> *("Operating" is perhaps a strange word to use here, but it is a neutral word. I do not want to use a word with any implication of what Donald finds pleasing about the absence of the attention of the others.)*

GREEN. That's right. During my presentation, I don't think anybody was thinking of me or evaluating me. Astounding.

ZIMRING. Astounding that you could give a talk without their evaluating you.

GREEN. Yes, it's unbelievable.

The realization that people live in their own worlds and are not critically evaluating him may have been a significant insight for Donald. If so, it will have an effect even though I do not highlight or emphasize it as an insight.

Session 16

Donald sits rather slumped in his chair. He is quiet for a moment, and then he begins.

GREEN. This has been both a good week and a bad week (pause).
> *(At this point I do not say anything. To ask him, "Why, in what way?" might direct him to the content of the past week. However, his intention at the moment may be to stay with the badness: "One of the worst weeks I've had." Or his statement may be an expression of a present feeling, so his next statement could be, "I'm really down.")*

GREEN (continuing). Early in the week I took Ruth to the antique show, and it didn't turn out so good.

ZIMRING. Not so great, eh?

GREEN. No. In the first place, I got to her apartment a half hour early. I thought she said to pick her up at 7:00, but she said that our date wasn't until 7:30. Then, when we got to the show, it was not the kind of antiques in which she is interested. And I found it hard to talk to her. I was somewhat depressed afterwards.

ZIMRING. Felt down.

GREEN. Yeah. I felt like she must have thought that I made a poor choice of what to do when we went out. She tried to reassure me, but I thought at the time that she was just being polite. Now I'm not so sure.

ZIMRING. You felt down because you thought she would think that you had made a mistake in planning the evening, but now you're not so sure that she thought that.

GREEN. No, maybe she didn't, and that's good. I like her. But she's going away for a long vacation next week, and nothing's going on with anyone else.

ZIMRING. Sort of bleak.

GREEN. Sometimes I feel, "What's the use?" It doesn't seem like I'm able to lead a normal life.

> *(I am aware of the pressure to reasssure Donald. There is both the social convention that reassurance should be given when the person talking to you feels bad, and my own desire to help Donald avoid pain. I could subtly reassure him by saying, "After things didn't work out, you felt down," indirectly telling him that his negative perception of himself and negative feelings were the result of the immediate circumstances. To be helpful in the usual way by offering reassurance would be responding from outside his internal frame of reference, which should be avoided in person-centered therapy. My response therefore does not try to reassure Donald.)*

ZIMRING. Sort of seems impossible that your life will ever be normal.

GREEN. Uh huh. I don't know why I freeze so much when I'm with a woman. With men too, sometimes, but more so with women (short pause). When I got back from seeing Ruth, I couldn't stand to be by myself and went to the restaurant just to be with somebody. My neighbor was there. I talked to him for a few minutes. It was better than nothing, but. . . .

ZIMRING. But not like what you had hoped for from Ruth?

GREEN. Yes. It wasn't a bad experience. I just wish it had gone better. I really would like some social life.

ZIMRING. Something you *very much want* (with emphasis).

GREEN. Yes! I feel like somebody who is trying to talk and finally comes out with a single word, while everybody else is rapidly conversing in complete sentences. If something doesn't happen soon, I don't know what I'm going to do (pause). The other day, I was going through some things of my father's and came across the certificate they gave him when he retired. You know, he worked at the same firm I'm with now. And (slowly), it has always seemed more like his firm than mine.

ZIMRING. That you are working more in his business than in one you can identify with yourself.

> (This may be a significant insight for Donald. The perception of the business that employs him as being his father's firm may have been the source of some of Donald's negative feelings about work and partly responsible for his inability to get himself to work in the morning. Granted all that—and this is where client-centered therapy is very different from other psychotherapies—I would not lead him to explore the ramifications of the insight, that is, to consider that it may have been connected to his difficulty in getting to work on time.
>
> Does Donald lose important learnings because I do not stimulate his exploration of the insight? Probably not. The insight, if indeed it is one, is really the description of an aspect of his world which has already become different. It was his increased attending to his feelings and reactions, stimulated by the earlier therapy sessions, which brought about this observation which we are terming an insight. He will use this observation in further understanding his world, if it helps him make sense of his world.)

GREEN. One good thing happened this week. I am on the committee to organize the annual company picnic. The plan was to have the picnic from 2:00 to 7:00 in the afternoon. We tried something like that years ago in my engineering fraternity, and it didn't work. Some people come early and then leave after an hour or so. Others come late. You don't have enough people to play games or baseball at any one time. I found myself explaining why the proposed times wouldn't work, and the others agreed and shortened them.

ZIMRING. So what you said was effective.

GREEN. It felt good to get the times for the picnic right, but the best part was that I was able to say what I thought without freezing. It just happened naturally because I was concerned about the issue.

ZIMRING. Focusing on the issue rather than the people involved?

GREEN. Yes. I didn't even think about what they might be thinking about me.

ZIMRING. Somehow this didn't exist for you at that moment.

Session 18

GREEN. Went on another vacation last week. That's the third long weekend I've taken in the last two months. Went to a state park in Kentucky and went through some caves with a group that explores caves. I know one of the guys in the group from the factory here. It was a pretty good weekend. On a weekend like that you are with people most of the time, but that didn't bother me. As a matter of fact, I rather liked it.

ZIMRING. It was a nice thing. It was rather good being around people.

GREEN. Yeah, I sort of hated to come back (slight pause). I don't know why I seem to get along better with people when I'm away from home. I drove down there with Joe, the guy who works with me. At the state park we stayed in cabins and Joe and I shared one with two other men. I did go for some walks by myself, but I was with everybody else most of the time, especially in the caves—when you climb around a cave you're never by yourself. There were times when I didn't have much to say and I wished I could be alone. But I didn't freeze once the whole weekend.

ZIMRING. It puzzles you why things go so much better with people when you are away than they do when you are at home.

(As mentioned earlier, in addition to the circumstances or substance a person is trying to communicate, there is also the person's present intention in the communication. The best client-centered response combines a mention of this present interest with an understanding of the content. Part of Donald's present interest is why he is more comfortable with others when away from home. My response focuses on that question without much concern for the content, that is, the circumstances of the weekend.)

GREEN. Yes. I actually initiated conversations a couple of times, and I never do that when I am here (slight pause). When I'm away, I feel less threatened by people, more able to think and talk.

ZIMRING. It's easier.

GREEN (nods). Somehow people don't seem as critical, as disapproving.

ZIMRING. Not as judgmental.

GREEN. People seem kinder when I'm away (pause). You know, talking to you *is* having some effect. (He chuckles.) I'm not sure it's a good one, though.

ZIMRING. Not an unmixed blessing, huh?

GREEN. Right. Like, I ordered an elementary algebra textbook for Eric, the pupil I'm tutoring. The bookstore promised they would have it for me three weeks ago. It wasn't there. Then they said they would have it two weeks ago. Again, it wasn't there. That was a real inconvenience; Eric and I had to do something else. Then the bookstore assured me it absolutely would be in last week. When I called and they told me they still didn't have it, I demanded an explanation and found out that they had lost the order and had never sent it in. I really got upset then; I talked to them about keeping their promises, being businesslike, the inconvenience they had caused. Finally I got the name of the president of the bookstore chain. There was a lot of adrenaline pumping, and it felt good.

ZIMRING. So you think our talks here had something to do with learning to stand up for your rights, and it feels good to do that.

GREEN. Yes, and . . . .

ZIMRING (interrupting). But I gather that maybe it wasn't entirely a good thing.

> (This probably was not a good response. I am responding to what Donald said at the beginning of this part of the interview, to which I had already responded. Now, in the main, he is expressing his pleasure at what he has done. In client-centered therapy there is a tendency, which should be avoided, to concentrate on what is troubling the client rather than on what the client is happy about. The effect of always concentrating on troubles may be that the client believes that bad feelings are more important than joys.)

GREEN. Well, I'd hate to be doing that all the time. It got in the way of going to bed at the usual time, but I must say I slept better. And it did feel good when the president's office called from Chicago to apologize and said they are sending a copy of the book Express Mail. We'll see if it gets here.

ZIMRING. You wouldn't want to make a habit of it, but it really seemed to have some effect on the world.

GREEN. Yes. (He chuckles.) My visibility seems to be increasing.

ZIMRING. No longer quite the invisible man, eh?

GREEN. Right. You know, I realized just yesterday that I haven't worked on rebuilding cars for a week. Instead I've been working on a squirrel feeder. The squirrel can only get the food if it figures how to work the latch. I figure that will make the squirrel population on my property smarter.

ZIMRING (smiles). Sort of survival of the smartest.

GREEN. Yes . . . . I've noticed something interesting. You know all the trouble I've had waking up in the morning? Well, the other Saturday morning, when I was supposed to tutor Eric, I woke up before the alarm went off. That's the second or third time that has happened. It seems that when my mind is working on something, I can wake up easily.

ZIMRING. It happens automatically when you're working on something interesting.

GREEN (long pause). It's not only that, it's not only that I am interested. It may also be that it is easier to get up when I don't anticipate criticism. And there doesn't seem to be any of that from Eric.

TERMINATION OF THE THERAPY

At the time of this interview, Donald Green and I have not seen each other for a month. I have been on vacation for two weeks, and Donald has been visiting a branch factory on the East Coast, where there may be an opening for him.

GREEN. Well, it came through... the chief engineer at the Stamfort plant retired, and I was offered the job.

ZIMRING. Sounds as if that is a good thing.

GREEN. Yes, I thought I would not want to leave here, but they were very nice to me at Stamfort. I stayed with the man who would be my boss, and I felt good. Usually that would have been a bad situation, but I found I could talk to him and his wife. I think I'll be able to work with him without much trouble.

ZIMRING. So it feels possible to you.

(I know this response is a little less positive than his feeling. It would have been better to match his feeling more closely, but I do not emphasize the positive because I want to give him the chance to talk about any negative aspects of the situation.)

GREEN. Yes. I told them that I would do it, that I would take the job. I've been waking up at night wondering if I am doing the right thing, but most of the time I feel good about it.

ZIMRING. So, even though there are doubts sometimes, mainly it seems like the right thing to do.

GREEN. Yes. Although I've been nervous about it at times, I haven't been nearly as nervous as I would have been a few months ago.

ZIMRING. A real change.

GREEN. Uh-huh. Not only will my salary be increased, I will be doing more of what I want. I'll have a chance to design some new production techniques, something I've wanted to do for some time (pause). It will be hard to leave here, though.

ZIMRING. Although it will be hard to leave, it is something that you want to do.

GREEN. Yes. I have been hesitating to tell my friends Jim and Mary that I am going to leave. Every time I think to mention it, something else comes up.

ZIMRING. Somehow, you never get around to telling them.

GREEN. Yes. I almost never think about it until after I've left their house.

ZIMRING. It sort of slips your mind.

GREEN. Right (pause). I have a feeling that they will think I shouldn't go—that I should stay here.
ZIMRING. They'll think you're not doing the right thing.

Donald nods, then pauses. Finally he says:

GREEN. I wish there was some way I could tell them that it isn't them, that I'm not leaving because of them.
ZIMRING. Some way of telling them that.
> (*This fear of criticism and rejection has been a constant theme. Less of it has been heard recently, but it still surfaces at times.*)

GREEN. Yes, I've been avoiding having lunch with the people at the plant, too. I sort of don't want to tell them about it, either.
ZIMRING. Would sort of rather not.
GREEN. Although there's some of them I won't miss; I'm glad to be through with them. Still, there's some that have been good to me.
ZIMRING. Some that have been helpful?
> (*This is said tentatively because I am not sure that "being helpful" is what he means by "been good."*)

The next section of the interview is concerned with Donald's arrangements for moving. Not until the end of it does Donald discuss the fact that this is our last interview. In client-centered therapy, the final interview is not handled much differently from any other. Of most importance is what it means to the client that this is the final interview. Therefore I wait for him to comment on the fact that this is our last time together.

GREEN. I guess this is our last interview, since I'll be leaving next week. Do you think I am finished with therapy?
ZIMRING. How do you feel about that?
> (*I ask this because it is not clear to me what he means by this question. He could mean anything from "What do you think about my progress?" to "Will I be able to go, to navigate on my own?"*)

GREEN (laughs). Well, I guess I'm as finished as I ever will be. I feel as if I've gotten some good things done here.
ZIMRING. You sound like it has been a good experience for you, and it has been for me also.
> (*My response is in accord with Rogers's "necessary and sufficient conditions" for successful psychotherapeutic change to take place, which calls for the therapist to be congruent in the relationship, expressing*

> *his or her feelings about the client and the relationship. I had had a good experience, and it was congruent to mention it.)*

GREEN. I'll be coming back to town sometime. Would it be all right if I call and come to see you?

ZIMRING. Yes, please feel free to do so.

Frequently, clients will come back after terminating for one or two additional interviews. This decision is left in their hands. I have no problem with allowing them to choose their own pace at terminating.

Because Donald was moving, this was an involuntary termination. In a voluntary termination, the client may raise more questions about whether he or she is finished. I genuinely never have any opinion about a client's terminating, so it is easy to stay in the client's frame of reference. The whole question about being finished depends on the client's goals and how far she or he wants to go toward achieving them. Only the client can know this. Also, it is a mistake to assume that this will be the client's only chance at psychotherapy. Clients often leave therapy and then some time later, perhaps years, after it has become clear to them what more they want to achieve, they will get more therapy.

I frequently feel a sense of loss when a client leaves. I have been with clients in some touching and dramatic moments of living. It is sometimes quite painful when they terminate. I have to deal with this pain as my problem and make sure it doesn't influence, even subtly, the client's decision to finish therapy. With the exception of clients leaving town, it is surprisingly easy to keep a client in therapy. All the therapist has to do is choose client material that has to do with problems rather than with strengths and weaknesses. The therapist also can lean forward when the client talks about problems and lean backward and be less attentive when the client talks about feeling stronger. If the goal is to keep a client in therapy, it is helpful if the therapist believes that it takes a long time for therapy to be successfully completed. In the late 1940s the average client-centered case lasted about ten interviews. Ten years later, the average was perhaps twice as long. This change probably came from a change in therapists' beliefs rather than as the result of a deliberate strategy.

I did not do several things at the end of the therapy for Donald Green. I did not review the progress we had made. I was not concerned with what he still had to accomplish. I was not concerned with any strategy for making sure that the gains of the therapy would be lasting. The benefits from therapy will last because of the changes that occur during therapy. There have been a number of changes in the case of Donald Green. By the end of therapy, Donald is putting more reliance on his subjective world than on the external, objective world of logic. He is paying more attention to his feelings and to his experience. There has been an increase in the degree to which he trusts himself to make decisions which will be right for him. These changes will not be affected by what I do in the final interview.

Over the years, I have found that there are a number of subjective criteria, that is, criteria drawn from my experience, which seem to be correlated with a client's objective progress. One is how the therapy sessions felt to me. Were the hours barren and dull, without much happening, or did they flow easily? With Donald, the first hours of therapy seemed somewhat slow and difficult, but then the flow started, and both Donald and I were surprised at how quickly the end of each session arrived. Seeing Donald never felt like work to me, and I was glad that he hardly ever canceled a session.

Another subjective criterion is the ease of difficulty I have in staying in the client's internal frame of reference. Occasionally it is difficult to stay with a client without my mind wandering more than I would like. This was not the case during the interviews with Donald Green. I found myself working easily to try to understand him. Clients who are not understood frequently will repeat what they have said before changing the topic. That this seldom happened indicates to me that Donald was understood much of the time.

All in all, I was pleased with the way the therapy went. It was an enriching experience and a significant relationship for both Donald and myself. I will miss him and wish him well. Despite the closeness and intimacy we experienced, I will probably never see or hear from him again. This is sad, but it is necessary in this facet of life.

We ended therapy the way we began. It was Donald's internal frame of reference that was of primary importance, not my support and encouragement, or my external evaluation of his progress, or my estimation of the problems that still existed. ∎

CRITIQUE OF DONALD GREEN'S TREATMENT BY PERSON-CENTERED THERAPY

by Nathaniel J. Raskin

Although changes in overt behavior are the primary expectations relative to the results of therapy, they are not the only ones. Changes in individuals' phenomenology—that is to say, changes in how and about what they experience life—may be of equal or greater importance. Thus, from the point of view of an observer, a person who has had successful therapy may not have changed at all in behavior. Nevertheless, the person may experience greater internal peace, feelings of satisfaction, new attitudes toward the self, and the other covert changes in thinking and feeling. In the case of Donald Green, the person-centered therapy provided by Fred Zimring produces obvious behavioral changes, but perhaps of even greater significance is how Donald now experiences life.

Before psychotherapy, life may be dull and repetitive. After successful therapy, life may be experienced more fully and richly, with more color and variety. This certainly seems true of Donald in his encounter with Zimring, who used Carl Rogers's person-centered therapy as he understands it.

As a therapist I am pleased when there is positive behavior change but am even happier when there is change in how the person experiences the world in a more positive manner. Many events in a person's life, in addition to psychotherapy, can change behavior: a new job, meeting new people, a new relationship, and so on. Few things other than psychotherapy, however, can change how a person experiences life. And if a person is able to experience life more fully, it is highly likely that that person will be better able to cope with whatever occurs in the future.

Donald Green's behavioral changes after therapy are marked. When he begins to see Zimring he is isolated and has little to do with people. By the end of therapy, although he is hardly gregarious, he has much more people contact, and social interactions and assertiveness are easier for him. He finds it possible to initiate contact with people and is beginning to have a social relationship with a woman. Donald's major stated problem is his inability to awaken and get to work on time. Although he does not spend much time in therapy working on this problem, it disappears over the course of the therapy. On the job, he becomes more assertive, and he starts to interact more creatively with people whom he previously regarded as authority figures. As therapy goes on, he begins to engage in a greater variety of leisure and social activities.

The changes in how Donald experiences life include changes in his relation to feelings and meanings. This is a group of dimensions of experience that frequently change as a result of client-centered therapy.

One dimension of a person's relation to feelings has to do with awareness of feelings. Some people start therapy with little awareness of their emotional states. Progress for them is simply becoming more aware of their feelings. At the beginning of therapy, Donald is aware of very little feeling in his life. As therapy progresses, he reports having more feelings outside therapy as well as in it. He reports some dreams and the feelings that went along with them.

Another dimension has to do with the degree to which clients acknowledge feelings as belonging to them. It may seem strange, but people may display what look like feelings (say, give the impression of being angry) and yet not acknowledge or be aware of having these feelings. When Donald begins therapy he acknowledges past feelings to a small extent but has few feelings in the present, and he does not own these emotions. As therapy progresses, he is able to express and to accept the anger he felt when he did not receive a book when it was promised.

A third dimension of this relationship has to do with presentness of feelings. Some people, at the beginning of therapy, discuss only feelings and problems of the past. A person may talk only about mistakes made in choosing a school, or relationships with parents, or anxieties in childhood. The person will not bring up how she or he feels right now.

Some clients, and this was particularly true of Donald, strenuously avoid contact with others whom they see as dangerous. This view usually changes with successful therapy, as it did with Donald. This was apparent in his lunches with others at work, his relationship with Eric, his interactions with other men rebuilding automobiles, and his date with Ruth.

A question often asked about client-centered therapy goes somewhat as follows: How can you help a client if you do not know the cause of the problem and do not help the client solve problems? An assumption of principal importance for Carl Rogers was: *The organism has one basic tendency and striving—to actualize, maintain, and enhance the experiencing organism.* Rogers saw this as true for all life forms.

Donald had learned early in life that it is good not to cause a disturbance, not to express feelings. He may also have learned that a good person keeps things going smoothly by not having strong reactions. He mentions, early in therapy, his reactions to being judged negatively for being late getting to work. Because Zimring unconditionally accepts this reaction, Donald may have begun learning that he was not unworthy because he had this strong reaction. Over the course of therapy, as he continues to talk about his reactions, more and more of these "conditions of worth" that had been imposed by his parents disappear. He then is able to acknowledge his reactions.

Another explanation for the effects of client-centered therapy rests on Zimring's empathy. A stream of reactions continually occurs within us. We get into trouble when we do not attend to this stream and if we do not act in terms of our subjective reactions. Client-centered therapy is empathic with this stream of experiencing as it enters the awareness of the client. By responding appropriately, the therapist directs attention to it. In continually commenting on and discussing the nuances of Donald's experiences and reactions, Zimring has the effect of directing the client's attention to his own reactions.

At the beginning of therapy, Donald almost never refers to or uses his reactions as a source of data about the world. Instead he focuses on logic and circumstance. Zimring does not focus on or respond to the realities or content of the statements made by Donald, as some therapists might. Instead he focuses on Donald's experience and reactions, sticking closely to the client's subjective world—his internal frame of reference.

Some of my responses to Donald might have been different from Zimring's. For example, in response to Donald's expression of uncertainty as to what to bring up at the beginning of the second interview, I might have replied: "You are not sure how to begin," rather than Zimring's structuring response, "Talk about whatever is of concern to you, whatever is on your mind at the moment." My purpose is not to direct the client but rather to attempt to convey my awareness and appreciation of the client's attitude at the moment. But the important thing is that Zimring relates to Donald with the attitude that the client has the capacity to change, that he can direct the change, and that the nature and quality of the change are up to him.

From the outset of the therapy, Zimring is quite clear about what he has to offer Donald. He accepts it as true that if Donald receives the "necessary and sufficient" conditions implicit in client-centered therapy, he will expand his whole process of growth. To accomplish this, Zimring does not see his role as intervening, motivating, clarifying, teaching, or as *making* the process occur in any way at all. His function is to *free* his client by removing blocks to the client's experiencing processes.

In this facilitating role the client-centered therapist is implicitly demonstrating a great regard for the client. The therapist's expression of belief that the client can take charge of his or her own life helps the client to enhance self-regard and gain courage to expand awareness and to embark on new directions.

Could Zimring have predicted the specific content of Donald's new perceptions and experiences or the specific nature of his behavioral changes? I believe that he would have regarded such predictions as quite irrelevant or even as interfering with his primary task of focusing on Donald's cognitions and affections while moving from moment to moment of experiencing in therapy.

This unusual nondirective manner of relating to Donald also frees Zimring to deal with what is most meaningful to the client as he goes along in the therapy. For example, Donald might concentrate on the presenting problem of getting to work on time, or he might focus on job satisfaction or dissatisfaction, his early life, his current relationships, or whatever. Zimring is ready to go along with Donald, whichever way the client decides to go, and so he is respectful of Donald.

Zimring demonstrates a constant regard for Donald's particular pattern of change and growth. I found the therapy to be quite believable, different in some details from how other clients change, but similar in the quality of feeling or tone that accompanies self-directed growth. In following the way changes occur in person-centered therapy, you may find them unremarkable, since they emerge so easily and naturally. But if you step back, you may have the perception of an aesthetic and spectacular process—the appearance of an emerging, flowering person.

Interacting with a person in the manner of a person-centered therapist is conceptually simple. In practice it is not so easy, because the belief in the client's capacity and respect for individuals' feelings that are necessary are very profound and not easy to come by. As Zimring states, it is surprisingly hard to train students in this approach.

Zimring's extensive comments accompanying his responses to Donald also bring out the thoughtfulness that went into his work, as it does in the work of all successful client-centered therapists. He clarifies the fact that becoming a good listener requires shedding attitudes and behaviors associated with other ways of trying to help people with problems.

Of course, client-centered therapists differ in their operations. Each of us brings to the therapeutic process special qualities as well as theoretical conceptions that are personally meaningful. In Fred Zimring's career as a therapist, researcher, and educator, the notion of subjective experience is a dominant one. He emphasizes this in his work with Donald Green and his explanations of what happens within the client. In so doing, he helps to show why experience is such a central concept in the person-centered theory of personality reorganization.

■

REFERENCES

Kirschenbaum, H., & Henderson, V. L. (Eds.). (1989). *The Carl Rogers reader.* Boston: Houghton Mifflin.

Mead, G. H. (1934). *Mind, self and society: From the standpoint of a social behaviorist.* Chicago: University of Chicago Press.

Rogers, C. R. (1951). *Client-centered therapy: Its current practice, implications and theory.* Boston: Houghton Mifflin.

Rogers, C. R. (1957). The necessary and sufficient conditions of personality change. *Journal of Consulting Psychology, 21,* 95–103.

Rogers, C. R. (1961). *On becoming a person.* Boston: Houghton Mifflin.

Rogers, C. R. (1980). *A way of being.* Boston: Houghton Mifflin.

Rogers, C. R., & Dymond, R. (Eds.). (1954). *Psychotherapy and personality change.* Chicago: University of Chicago Press.

Rational-emotive therapy (RET) is a pioneering form of cognitive-behavioral therapy (CBT) which holds that people do not really *get* disturbed by the things that happen to them; they largely upset themselves *about* these things. When their goals and desires are thwarted at point A (Activating Events in their lives), so that they feel anxious, depressed, or enraged and act self-defeatingly at point C (emotional and behavioral Consequences of these unfortunate Activating Events), they largely *upset themselves* at point B (by their beliefs).

People first have a set of rational Beliefs (rBs) which consist of *preferences* or *wishes*—such as, "I don't *like* these thwarting Activating Events *but* they're not *too* bad and I can *stand* them and still lead a reasonably happy life." If they *only* have such preferences, when they are frustrated they produce *appropriate* negative feelings, such as sorrow, regret, and displeasure. But often they *also* have a set of irrational Beliefs (iBs) which consist of absolutist, grandiose *demands* or *commands*—such as, "I *must* not experience these thwarting Activating Events! It's *awful* when I do! I can't *bear* it! I'm a *bad person* for letting them occur, and the world is a *rotten* place for presenting them to me!" Consequently they have *in*appropriate feelings such as panic and despair.

RET contends that people can rid themselves of their *in*appropriate and self-defeating feelings and behaviors if they: (1) acknowledge their irrational Beliefs; (2) scientifically Dispute them (at point D) until they give them up; (3) strongly work at *feeling* differently; and (4) *act* against them in a determined, persistent manner. They then arrive at a new Effective Philosophy (at point E) which enables them to retain their appropriate feelings and behaviors and minimize their self-sabotaging actions.

Albert Ellis

Rational-Emotive Therapy

SOMETHING ABOUT THE THERAPIST • *Leonor Lega*

I am now a therapist and a supervisor at the Institute for Rational-Emotive Therapy in New York City, where I am also the director of training and therapy for Spanish-speaking people. In addition, I am a college professor, and for the past three years I have been the chairperson of the Psychology Department at St. Peter's College in Jersey City, New Jersey. About half of my clients in New York are Spanish-speaking, and the other half are English-speaking. I also speak French, Italian, and Portuguese, but I do not have experience as a therapist in these three languages.

I was born in Philadelphia while my father was training in gastroenterology at the University of Pennsylvania, but I grew up in Colombia, South America. My family returned to that country when I was one month old. I attended high school at Liceo Benalcazar and college at Universidad del Valle, both in Cali.

I left Colombia to attend graduate school at Temple University in Philadelphia, where I completed my masters and my Ph.D. in psychology. I did my postdoctoral training as a fellow at the RET Institute in New York under the supervision of Albert Ellis, Janet Wolfe, and Ray DiGiuseppe. I also received training in counseling psychology in South America. As part of my training throughout my professional development, I have been in therapy both in Colombia and in the United States, and both in Spanish and in English.

Several people have played a very important role in my development as a therapist. My parents, Jorge and Leonor Lega, and my grandmother, Leonor de Campo, provided me with a home environment in which service to the community was a very important value. My father founded two medical schools in Cali, Colombia; my mother was part of a group which founded the Museum of Modern Art; and my grandmother was the president of the Red Cross for over 40 years.

In my early education, Ana de Dominguez and Betsabe Zapata at Liceo Benalcazar and Ruben Lechter at Universidad del Valle supported my interest in a career oriented to helping other people. Later on, Surang Kowatrakul at Temple University helped me discover the importance of an individual's own frame of reference through the study of people from a cross-cultural perspective. At the Institute for Rational-Emotive Therapy since 1981, my professional and personal development has been heavily influenced by Albert Ellis and Janet Wolfe, who have been generous as mentors and friends.

Many of the clients I see have problems with depression and anxiety. Much of my work is in the areas of assertiveness training, women's and couples' therapy, and cross-cultural issues such as acculturation.

I have worked with Spanish-speaking clients in a variety of settings: as a counseling psychologist in Cali; as a licensed psychologist at the Institute for Rational-Emotive Therapy in New York; and as a researcher for the Title IV Bilingual Program for the Philadelphia School District. I have been a consultant for the U.S. Immigration and Naturalization Service Cuban Entrants Program; for the Board of Education of Hudson County, New Jersey, Human Relations Program for Bilinguals; and for several National Institute of Mental Health grants at settings which include the Cuban National Planning Council and the Hispanic Research Center at Fordham University in New York.

In addition, my work experience includes supervision and training of health professionals who work with Spanish-speaking clients in the United States and abroad, such as postdoctoral fellows at the Institutes for Rational-Emotive Therapy in New York and Mexico City. I have also supervised and trained heads of medical divisions in Latin America for a major multinational corporation.

I have lectured at the University of Amsterdam and the University of Leiden in the Netherlands and at Universidad del Valle and Universidad del Atlantico in Colombia, among others. I have conducted a large number of workshops in the United States, Latin America, and Europe.

If I were to give advice to would-be therapists, I would suggest that they try to get a wide knowledge in psychology and related areas as part of their basic education. Students interested in learning the RET system should first register in a Primary Certificate Program and then continue with either the Intermediate and Associate Fellowship Programs or the Postdoctoral Fellowship Program. For those who do not meet the minimum qualification for primary certificate candidacy (a master's degree in psychology or counseling, an M.S.W., an M.D., or an R.N.), the Paraprofessional Certificate Program would be an option. To qualify for this program, a person must work as a counselor in a chartered or certified agency and receive ongoing professional supervision.

The Setting for Therapy

I do my clinical work at the Institute for Rational-Emotive Therapy in New York. Here I see clients individually, co-lead a women's group and a postdoctoral fellows' supervision group with Dr. Wolfe, and give public and professional workshops. The institute handles 350 clients a week in individual or group sessions. Since its opening in 1965, some 80,000 people have participated in professional and public workshops. Its fellowship program has included trainees from North and South America, Europe, and Asia. It also publishes and distributes many pamphlets, books, audio and video cassettes, and other psychoeducational materials on rational-emotive therapy.

The institute has five floors with several offices, a large auditorium, and two additional meeting rooms. On the first floor there is a receptionist and a waiting area with books and magazines. At present there are 25 psychologists on the staff, including interns and fellows. Offices are furnished with chairs and small tables, a clock, and additional items such as a box of tissues. Usually the client and the therapist sit facing each other. Only during relaxation and biofeedback are clients likely to lie down on a couch. RET is an active, directive form of therapy, and eye contact is important.

Client referrals come from a variety of sources which range from an ad in the Yellow Pages of the telephone directory to suggestions made by other clients, therapists, or family and friends. Prior to the first interview, clients are asked to fill out an intake package, including a biographical information form and several tests and inventories. Some of these are readministered every month to monitor clients' progress. When clients come in for the first time, the receptionist announces their arrival to the therapist and asks them to go upstairs. I usually meet them by the elevator on my floor at least once to show them the way to my office or the interview room.

Therapists normally see clients once a week for a period of 45 minutes, though on occasion the session may be just 30 minutes long, or a client may be seen every other week. For clients in group therapy, there are initial individual interviews to determine if this is the appropriate therapeutic intervention for each person. Group rules are given to all the first time they join the group. The institute publishes a catalog describing upcoming events and available materials twice a year to facilitate the use of books, tapes, workshops, and so on, as therapy tools.

Interns and postdoctoral fellows are supervised every week by licensed psychologists. Most senior staff members give workshops in other cities in the United States and foreign countries, in addition to their work in New York.

THE THERAPY FOR DONALD GREEN

Session 2

Since the first interview with Donald Green (Chapter 1) had the purpose of collecting information about the client but did not follow any particular therapy format, I will assume it was conducted by someone who was not doing rational-emotive therapy. Of course, we gather diagnostic data in RET, but we also try to identify and dispute—or help change—irrational beliefs as early as the first interview. As the second interview begins, Donald and I introduce ourselves.

LEGA. Hello, I am Dr. Leonor Lega. Please come in.
GREEN. Hello, I'm Donald Green.
LEGA. With your consent, I have the transcript of your first interview as well as your psychological report with the results of tests and other evaluations.
GREEN. Yeah, that's fine with me.
LEGA. Is there any particular aspect of that first interview—or anything else which may not be included in the report—anything you would like to talk about now?
GREEN. Well, I don't know. There are several things.
LEGA. Let's choose the one that concerns you the most at present. We will get to the others as well, but let's pick a starting problem.
GREEN. I guess . . . my job, then.

Donald seems uncomfortable and is not giving very long answers. He also has difficulty making eye contact.

LEGA. Very well. Tell me a bit more about this problem.
GREEN. It's about my coming to work late so often. I already have a black mark on my job record because of it, and people are talking. In fact, my supervisor suggested I should ask for help with this.
LEGA. And how do you feel about all this?
GREEN. I feel bad about it.
LEGA. Let's describe that feeling more precisely. Is it worried? Or anxious? Or . . . ?
GREEN. I guess anxious, and at times fed up with the whole thing. But I don't tell anyone I am feeling mad at them, because I know they are trying to help me.
LEGA. And if you got mad at someone who is trying to help you . . . ?
GREEN. I guess that would not be a nice thing to do.
LEGA. And how would you feel about it?
GREEN. I guess I'd feel guilty.
LEGA. That is right. So, in short, you feel anxious about your lateness and the consequences it may have, and angry at the people who talk about it, and, at times, guilty about the lateness and your anger. Is that so?
GREEN. Yes, and frustrated, too. You see, I even go to work on weekends without asking for overtime. So why can't this count for something? I also have three alarm clocks, and my neighbor calls me in the morning, and the paperboy knocks on my door. It's not like I'm not trying to do something about it.
LEGA. And that is *AWFUL!* (I use a deep voice to overemphasize the last word.)
GREEN (smiling a bit). Well, yeah.
LEGA (also smiling). And how is it awful?
GREEN. Well, I could lose my job.
LEGA. That would be unfortunate, and certainly a reason to be concerned. But how is it *awful* and *terrible*? (Again, I emphasize these two words.)
GREEN. OK, I guess it's not horrible.
LEGA. That's right. You see, in RET we believe that the way we view the world largely determines how we feel about it and how we behave or react toward it. Many people think that *situations*, what we call the A's or Activating Events, make us feel or behave in a particular way. We call our reactions the C's, or consequences. But, if that were so, every-

one would react in the exact same way under the same circumstances. Wouldn't you say that is true?

> (In RET we use what Albert Ellis calls the ABC's. A is the Activating Event, the situation or circumstance about which the problem occurs. C is the Consequence, which can be a behavior or an emotion, or both. B is the Belief, or the view the person takes of the activating event which largely creates C, and that is the central point of much of rational-emotive therapy.)

GREEN. Yes, that may be so.

LEGA. Let's take your situation, for example. A would be getting late to work. C, which in this case is an emotion, would be anxiety, worry. Is that the case?

GREEN. Yes. Also anger.

LEGA. Well, would you say that everyone who gets to work late feels exactly the same way you do?

GREEN. No. I know people who really don't care.

LEGA. Correct. So, do you see my point? A's, or situations, do not cause C's, or emotions, though they contribute to them. When we say, "She made me angry," or "It makes me nervous," we are wrongly making that assumption. What connects a situation with a consequence is what we call B's, or *beliefs*, or the way we view the situation at the particular time. Going back to your example, your B, or belief, was "It is *awful* and *terrible* to be late." And that thought is what made you feel anxious, not the lateness in itself.

GREEN. I see what you mean.

LEGA. Now, we were also saying that if we think about it more carefully, lateness is not *awful* and *terrible* but rather *unfortunate*. Is that correct?

GREEN. Yes, I guess it wouldn't be the end of the world.

LEGA. No, it wouldn't. But, at the moment you are upset, you are *telling yourself*, "It would be *catastrophic* and a *big disaster* to lose my job!"

GREEN. Yes, I think that is true.

LEGA. And how do you feel then?

GREEN. Very anxious.

LEGA. That is right. Let's do an experiment. Close your eyes, please.

> (The technique I plan to use is called rational-emotive imagery.)

LEGA. Vividly imagine that you are arriving to work very late and your supervisor is angry at you.

GREEN (after a pause). OK, I can imagine that.

LEGA. Fine. How do you feel in your gut?

GREEN. Exceptionally anxious.

LEGA. Very good. Now, keep that same image and change your feelings from *anxiety* and panic to just disappointment and *concern*. Tell me when you only feel disappointed and concerned—and *not* anxious.
GREEN (after a long pause). OK, now.
LEGA. Very well. Please open your eyes and tell me, how did you change your feelings?
GREEN. I told myself, "It's too bad that I'm late again, but I have been a good employee, and that will count for something if they are considering firing me from my job."
LEGA. So the situation is not really as desperate as you may view it sometimes. That is good. One way to do this is to try to get a more realistic picture of the situation.

> (This technique is called empirical disputing when utilized by cognitive therapists. However, in RET the preference is for philosophic disputing, in which the aim is to help clients change their basic philosophy rather than their perceptions of the world. In doing philosophical disputing, it is assumed that clients have underlying commands and demands—especially, that they must do well and be approved—and that a main goal of therapy is for them to clearly see and surrender their absolutist musts.)

LEGA. But let's assume that you *do* get fired. How could you still remain *concerned* rather than become desperate with *anxiety*?
GREEN. I guess I could tell myself that it is not the end of the world, that I could probably find another job.
LEGA. Good! But you had better also see that to create concern and disappointment, you are telling yourself "I *preferably* should not come late and be fired," while to create panic and low frustration tolerance you are telling yourself something like "Under all conditions I *absolutely must not* come late and be fired!" So always look for your command, your *must*, and change it back to a *preference*. When you only *prefer* to be on time and keep your job, you will see that it is not awful, terrible, and catastrophic if you don't, and that you *can* stand it even if you are fired.
GREEN. I get your point. But I still would not feel good about it.
LEGA. No, you will feel *appropriately* sorry and frustrated. Many people misinterpret RET and wrongly believe it makes one *un*emotional. Not at all! We are not saying that irrational, nonfunctional beliefs lead to negative emotions, while rational, functional thinking leads only to positive feelings. You may be thinking rationally and *still* experience negative emotions. In fact, it would not even be that healthy to only

feel positively at all times. Nobody expects you to be happy if you lose someone dear to you, or if you lose a good job. What we go after in RET is the added, unnecessary burden that irrational thinking puts on top of an already unfortunate situation.

Irrational thinking is nonfunctional because instead of working *toward* your goal, which in this case is to keep the job you have, it works *against* that goal. If you are consumed with worry and anxiety, your work performance will probably suffer, and you will *increase the probability* of being fired. But you can de-awfulize your view of the situation and work against your low frustration tolerance by accepting that it *is* possible to live with the discomfort of having to be at work on time. You can acknowledge that the long-term consequences of being constantly late are much worse than the short-term, pain-in-the-neck effort of not being late for work. Then you will be working toward your goal, thinking more rationally, and feeling less upset.

GREEN. So I am really wasting my energy by working extra hours rather than doing something about my lateness.

LEGA. Exactly. I would bet that you spend a lot of time in the morning going from alarm clock to alarm clock, to the phone, to the door, worrying.... "I'm going to be late, and I *must* not be! How awful!"

I mimic an anxious person and smile, and Donald begins to smile, too. I go on:

LEGA. "I'm going to lose my job—how terrible!"

GREEN (laughing). I see your point. That is exactly what I do.

LEGA. Yes. Now, use your dysfunctional feelings of anxiety as a red flag. Tell yourself that if you are anxious it is because you are giving yourself irrational messages, and if you would stop and think, you would find these messages. At present it is hard to stop and think, because you have been practicing the wrong thinking habits, and anxiety seems almost automatic. It is going to take a lot of practice to replace those irrational ideas with rational, functional ways of thinking.

GREEN. What you are saying sounds logical, but I think changing my thoughts and feelings is going to be so hard....

LEGA. That is right. And you do not *have* to change. This is only one alternative. You may decide not to do anything about your thinking, or your lateness, or your job. But it seems to me that if this is what you have been doing, or not doing (smiles), all your life, and it has given you poor results, it may be worth it to try it the RET way. What do you think?

GREEN. You are right.
LEGA. I wish there were another way for you to get over your anxiety, but the only ones I can think of would require work on your part.
GREEN. Yeah. I'm afraid there is no easy way out.
LEGA. No. And all I can do is to coach you. I cannot *make you* more rational; I can only *assist you* in *helping yourself* be more rational. The real therapy, someone said once, is not the one that takes place in the 45-minute session you have with me every week, but the week in between sessions where you have to go out there in the world and function.
GREEN. Yes, I see. And I really want to help myself.
LEGA. Very good. Before we finish today's session, I would like to give you some homework.
    (Homework is another technique used in RET.)
GREEN. Homework?
LEGA. Yes. To change, you will have to practice and practice, remember? (I smile.)
GREEN *(returning the smile)*. Oh, yeah.
LEGA. I want you to do an exercise using this RET Self-Help Form. You should work at using this form at least *twice* during the coming week.

I give Donald a copy of the RET Self-Help Form (see Figure 4.1). We go over it to make sure he has no questions.

LEGA. Now here is a reward/penalty system that goes with the Self-Report Form.
    (RET is cognitive-behavioral therapy, so we use reinforcers to complement the homework.)
LEGA. Tell me something you find rewarding. Any hobbies?
GREEN. Yes, I like to fix up old cars.
LEGA. Very well. Now tell me something you dislike.
GREEN. Getting to work on time.

At this, we both laugh.

LEGA. I know, but we cannot use that one. How about washing dishes? or cleaning the toilet bowl?
GREEN. Yes, cleaning the toilet is bad.
LEGA. Next week after you finish doing your homework, reward yourself: Go to the garage and work at fixing your cars. But if you fail to do the homework, not only do you forego work in the garage, you also clean

the toilet bowl instead. Follow these instructions for the minimum of two times you have agreed to do your homework.
GREEN. OK.
LEGA. Very well. See you next week.

Session 3

LEGA. Hello, Donald. Please sit down.
GREEN. Hello, Dr. Lega.
LEGA. How are you today?
GREEN. Fine, thank you.
LEGA. How was your homework? Any difficulties or questions?

Checking homework is part of a regular RET session. I normally give it 5 or 10 minutes at the beginning and assign new homework at the end of the session. This format is not rigid, but it is important to cover homework in each session. This is a good tool for determining therapy results, goals, and main areas of difficulty.

GREEN. The form was helpful. I worked on it twice, as we agreed, and I am becoming aware of the things I tell myself. I used to think my feelings came about automatically, but I am beginning to see that they really don't. They follow my thoughts.
LEGA. That is correct. And you will find that the more you practice seeing your irrational beliefs and disputing them, the faster you will be able to pull yourself out of a rut.
GREEN. Disputing—that's where I'm still having problems. I can often identify my irrational beliefs, but disputing them does not seem to work too well.
LEGA. How much of it are you *really believing?*
GREEN. Well.... (He nods.)
LEGA. You see, just saying rational sentences won't do. You may talk to yourself sensibly, but if you do not forcefully and persistently attack your irrationalities, you are just "parroting," not really believing good ideas. Remember, we are looking for a change in your belief system, which means a change in your philosophy of life. And since RET is based on the scientific method, by training yourself to arrive at conclusions that are logical and realistic, and that are not made in a dogmatic, absolute way, you will develop a rational way of interpreting the world.

RET SELF-HELP FORM

Institute for Rational-Emotive Therapy
45 East 65th Street, New York, N.Y. 10021
(212) 535-0822

(A) **ACTIVATING EVENTS**, thoughts, or feelings that happened just before I felt emotionally disturbed or acted self-defeatingly: _____

(C) **CONSEQUENCE or CONDITION**—disturbed feeling or self-defeating behavior—that I produced and would like to change: _____

(B) BELIEFS—Irrational BELIEFS (IBs) leading to my CONSEQUENCE (emotional disturbance or self-defeating behavior). Circle all that apply to these ACTIVATING EVENTS (A).	(D) DISPUTES for each circled IRRATIONAL BELIEF. Examples: *"Why* MUST I do very well?" *"Where is it written* that I am a BAD PERSON?" *"Where is the evidence* that I MUST be approved or accepted?"	(E) EFFECTIVE RATIONAL BELIEFS (RBs) to replace my IRRATIONAL BELIEFS (IBs). Examples: *"I'd* PREFER *to do very well but I don't* HAVE TO." *"I am a* PERSON WHO *acted badly, not a BAD PERSON." "There is no evidence that I HAVE TO be approved, though I would* LIKE *to be."*
1. I MUST do well or very well!		
2. I am a BAD OR WORTHLESS PERSON when I act weakly or stupidly.		
3. I MUST be approved or accepted by people I find important!		
4. I NEED to be loved by someone who matters to me a lot!		
5. I am a BAD, UNLOVABLE PERSON if I get rejected.		
6. People MUST treat me fairly and give me what I NEED!		

(OVER)

FIGURE 4.1 RET Self-Help Form

7. People MUST live up to my expectations or it is TERRIBLE!		
8. People who act immorally are undeserving, ROTTEN PEOPLE!		
9. I CAN'T STAND really bad things or very difficult people!		
10. My life MUST have few major hassles or troubles.		
11. It's AWFUL or HORRIBLE when major things don't go my way!		
12. I CAN'T STAND IT when life is really unfair!		
13. I NEED a good deal of immediate gratification and HAVE to feel miserable when I don't get it!		
<u>Additional Irrational Beliefs:</u>		

(F) **FEELINGS and BEHAVIORS** I experienced after arriving at my EFFECTIVE RATIONAL BELIEFS: _____

I WILL WORK HARD TO REPEAT MY EFFECTIVE RATIONAL BELIEFS FORCEFULLY TO MYSELF ON MANY OCCASIONS SO THAT I CAN MAKE MYSELF LESS DISTURBED NOW AND ACT LESS SELF-DEFEATINGLY IN THE FUTURE.

Joyce Sichel, Ph.D. and Albert Ellis, Ph.D.
Copyright © 1984 by the Institute for Rational-Emotive Therapy.

FIGURE 4.1 (continued)

Now, let's go on to specifics. Let's review your presenting problem and help you stop needlessly upsetting yourself about it.

Going back to the material we used for disputing in the last session, I help Donald summarize it and produce for himself rational self-statements that change his lateness, his self-downing, and his anger. Checking his irrationalities this way is somewhat like using a thermometer to find out if someone still has a fever, so we can tell whether or not a prescribed medicine is working.

LEGA. I have an additional suggestion to make. We tell our clients to write down their rational beliefs or self-statements on small cards and carry them with them. We ask them to get these cards out and read them when they are having emotional difficulties. This helps them develop new muscle, an "emotional" muscle. It takes practice. What are some helpful statements you can write down?

GREEN. I guess: "It is not *awful* and *terrible* if I have to be at work on time," and "I *can* stand discomfort now, so I can avoid long-term disadvantages."

LEGA. Good. Keep using this method this week and see what happens, OK?

GREEN. OK.

LEGA. So, what shall we work on today?

(In order to illustrate how the RET approach deals with various problem issues, I am addressing a different problem at each session. In reality, dealing with a single problem can take several sessions.)

GREEN. I guess... that I'm a loner. I have only two friends that I see for dinner once a week. I live alone; I'm 42 years old; I'm single. My parents are dead. I have a sister but I have not seen her for ten years. And I haven't seen any other member of my family, like uncles or aunts.

LEGA. Do you date? Do you have any social life with people at work?

GREEN. I have never dated in my life, except for the senior prom in high school. I go to the two company parties every year, but I go alone.... I normally eat by myself in the cafeteria.... No, I guess I don't do much socializing.

LEGA. And you would like to change that?

GREEN (looking down and lowering his voice). Yes. I guess that, deep inside, I feel like a social failure.

LEGA. Very well, Donald. I see several issues here. Let me try to sort them out, and please correct me if I am wrong, OK?

Donald nods in agreement.

LEGA. One issue has to do with your feelings of discomfort in social situations like the company picnic and Christmas party, lunch in the cafeteria, and going out on dates. Perhaps you have feelings of anxiety because you do not know what to do or say on such occasions. Therefore, you feel awkward. In RET we call this discomfort anxiety.

I am watching Donald for nonverbal cues, and I see him nod as I speak.

LEGA. Another issue may have to do with feeling uncomfortable about your *own* discomfort, or putting yourself down and feeling secondary anxiety because you are experiencing anxiety in the first place.
GREEN. Oh yes! I know that my anxiety about social situations is wrong, so I put myself down for having it.
LEGA. A third issue has to do with feelings of anxiety and depression about your own failure. You put yourself down because you have failed at something, namely at relating to other people. In RET, we call this ego anxiety.
GREEN (looking as if he is about to cry). You've hit it right on the head, Dr. Lega.
LEGA. And which feeling occurs most often?
GREEN. Perhaps not knowing what to do in social situations.
LEGA. Then let's work with that one first. Can you think of a specific example?
GREEN. Yes, at the last Christmas party Cecile, a woman who works in accounting, was just standing around and I was thinking about approaching her, but I could not do it. I like her very much, but I was tongue-tied.
LEGA. Why?
GREEN. Because I was too anxious.
LEGA. That is how you *felt*. But it was because you were *telling* yourself something. What was running through your head as you stood there, wanting to talk to this woman and getting all anxious about it?
GREEN. I guess that it would be very bad if I said the wrong thing, or if she would reject me.... It would prove that I am an unlovable person!

LEGA. Well, let's assume she really did reject you. Say she runs away screaming the moment you say "hello."

We smile at one another.

LEGA. What would happen then? What would you tell yourself?
GREEN. It would be awful!
LEGA. And how would it be awful?
GREEN. Because she would think I am stupid, and everybody would see how clumsy I am, and.... I would feel pretty terrible about myself.
LEGA. All you have said indicates that it would be pretty *uncomfortable*, but how would it be *awful* and *terrible*?
GREEN. Well....
LEGA. Well?
GREEN. I get your point. I am doing it again, right? I'm viewing a situation as terrible and exaggerating it inside my head.
LEGA. Very good! That is exactly what is going on. It would be *very* uncomfortable but it would not be a horror. So what, instead, could you tell yourself about *it*?
GREEN. That it is *only* discomfort and that I can live with it, as I did with getting to work late.
LEGA. That is excellent, Donald. But you also said that being rejected would prove that you are an unlovable person. And that you would feel terrible about *yourself*. How would your whole *personhood* be bad or unlovable just because one or a few women reject you?
GREEN. Well... uh... I suppose it wouldn't be.
LEGA. Right! That's the right answer. But *why* wouldn't *you* be unlovable if you exhibited some awkward social behavior?
GREEN. Because... uh... because I have other traits and behaviors that are not so bad.
LEGA. Right! But you had better believe that much more strongly. In RET, we show people that no matter how awkward or bad some of the traits and behaviors are, *they*, as *persons*, are *more than* their individual behaviors. They have thousands of traits, some good and some bad, so they, as whole persons, are too complex and too changing to be given a single, global rating. Do you see that?
GREEN. Yes, a little. But I guess I'd better keep working to see that better.
LEGA. Yes, and *stronger*. You can *forcefully, strongly* show yourself, many times, that you are *you*, and never are just a few of your traits. So you can rate your social awkwardness, give *it* a low rating, but refrain from

rating *yourself*, your whole personhood. You can feel badly about being clumsy and being rejected. But never put *yourself* down, don't call *you* a bad *person*.

GREEN. Because I'll only harm myself if I do?

LEGA. Yes, I'm glad you see that. Giving a global rating to yourself, your *youness* will make you anxious and increase your social clumsiness and withdrawal. But rating only your *awkwardness* as bad could help you work on it and improve it.

Now let's go into the next aspect of your social problem. When you stand there and refuse to talk to a woman, you tell yourself "It is awful," and then you say: "It is even worse that I am feeling this anxious!" So you first upset yourself about a potential rejection by saying, "It would be excruciatingly painful and would prove I am unlovable and no good!" We call that your primary anxiety. On top of that, you get yourself even more upset by becoming anxious about your anxiety, telling yourself, "It's terrible to be anxious! That makes me a stupid, inadequate *person*." In RET, we call this your secondary anxiety.

GREEN. Yes, that is what happens. And it feels so bad that I have to leave the situation and not talk to the people I really would like to talk to.

LEGA. You see how your thinking is irrational and gets you in trouble? Not only do you feel bad, but it takes you further away from what you want, which is to talk to women and make some friends.

GREEN. So what can I do about it?

LEGA. You can convince yourself: "My awkwardness is *only* uncomfortable and I *can* stand it. I am not going to die from it. Otherwise I would have been dead for a long time already. I will stay here, put up with my discomfort and concentrate on the party, music, food, and other people's conversations, rather than on my own anxiety." And you can strongly convince yourself, "Feeling rejected and being anxious are undesirable or bad traits. But *I* am never a bad or rotten *person* for having these unfortunate traits. I can always accept *myself*, and then work to change these behaviors." If you did that, how would you feel?

GREEN. Not as bad as I do now.

LEGA. Yes, Donald. And remember, *you* create your own anxiety by giving yourself the wrong, irrational messages. You are the only one who can change them. And it takes work and practice.

GREEN. So shall I do my homework around this issue of social anxiety?

LEGA. Yes, but this time it would be preferable if you not only include disputing at home, using an imaginary situation, but if you also use a real setting. I want you to practice rational self-statements on your own, of course. But I also want you to go to a table during lunch at work, a table with one or two other people, and say something to them. It would be preferable if you sat down with them, but a one- to two-minute conversation would do for now. Do that three times this week. You will see that working at both your thinking and your behavior will bring results much sooner.

GREEN. But what do I talk about?

LEGA. Try something about work—something you have in common. It is better to stay away from personal matters at the beginning. Ask about their work, or talk about cars or the weather. It doesn't matter if your conversation is superficial. What matters is that you are doing it *despite* your discomfort.

GREEN. OK. Sounds good. Thank you.

LEGA. See you next week.

Session 4

LEGA. Well, Donald, did you do your homework?

GREEN. I did; I talked to a guy at work and discovered that he is also interested in old cars. You were right. I would never have known that if I hadn't sat down with him at lunch.

LEGA. That's right, Donald. Do you see how we can increase the probability of achieving our goals by thinking and acting rationally rather than irrationally? We feel better, too. Of course, there are no guarantees. Everything is a probability statement, but why not work *for* rather than *against* your desires and goals?

GREEN. Dr. Lega, I have to tell you, I'm doing better in that respect, but I still have a lot of difficulty talking to women.

LEGA. Then let's work at it. What else happened?

GREEN. Remember the woman at the Christmas party I wanted to talk to? Well, I was talking with some other guys at lunch and she came up to our table with another woman, a friend of hers. They sat down with us, and from that moment on, I could not open my mouth.

LEGA. And what were you telling yourself about opening it?

GREEN. Part was discomfort, and I was happily surprised to see that it decreased as I used the disputing. But part of it was thinking that I had to say something interesting, something amusing, something outstanding.

LEGA. And why *must* you say or do the *perfect* thing?

GREEN. Because I think that if I would be more sociable I could have more friends and I would not feel as lonely and depressed as I do sometimes....

LEGA. That's why it's *desirable* to talk well. But where is it written that you *must* act desirably?

GREEN. I guess only in my head.

LEGA. Yes, *only* there. And what happens if you don't speak as well as you supposedly *must*?

GREEN. I feel that I have been a failure in life, empty... no real friends, no wife and children.... I am even worse off than my father, who at least managed to get married and have children....

LEGA. And how does the lack of friends or a mate make *you* a "failure"?

GREEN. Because everybody else can do it and I can't.

LEGA. That does not really follow, Donald. I could say that, in the worst case, if you had *nobody*, which by the way is not true because you do have some friends, it would only show that you are private and alone. You would be bad at friendship, but how would that show that you are a "failure in life"?

GREEN (after a long pause). I guess it doesn't.

LEGA. No, it doesn't. You are taking *one* aspect of your life, your social aspect, and you are generalizing it to your essence, to your value as a human being. You are wrongly concluding that you, in your totality, are worthless. Now, is that conclusion correct?

GREEN. No, I guess not.

LEGA. Why wouldn't it be correct?

GREEN. Because there are other aspects of me that are good. I am a hard-working guy, and I am loyal to my company even if I am often late for work.

LEGA. Exactly. And if you were *totally bad,* a bad person, it would mean that *everything you have done and will ever do* would be bad as well. It is philosophically incorrect to say that someone who is *essentially* bad can produce anything good. It would be illogical and wrong.

GREEN. Yes, that is how I feel sometimes.

LEGA. That is how you *think*, Donald. The *feeling* resulting from it would be depression. Does that sound familiar?

GREEN. Yes, it does. So should I just concentrate on my good points to build up my self-esteem?

LEGA. That is a common mistake we make, Donald, and it gets us into trouble too. You see, if we build up our "self-esteem" by wrongly concluding that we are "good people" because we do good things, we are making the same overall generalization we did before. We are concluding that *one behavior*, or even *one role*, defines us *totally* and *completely* as human beings, defines *our essence*. And we set ourselves up because even if we do things right this time, there is no guarantee that we would not do them wrong next time. And there we go, we would become a bad person again!

GREEN. I see. So, is that why I feel that I should say the perfect thing?

LEGA. Exactly. You are equating your self-worth with the results of your behavior. So the slightest mistake becomes a major issue, since it shows what a "rotten person" you are. Isn't that thinking irrational? Do you see how it can get you depressed and keep you from pursuing what you want?

GREEN. Yes. I do. So, there is no good in self-esteem?

LEGA. Instead of self-esteem, let's work toward *self-acceptance*, which means seeing yourself as a human being with good aspects, or traits, as well as bad ones, but not as a good or a bad *person*. Dr. Albert Ellis uses a good illustration for this point: humans hold traits like a fruit basket holds fruits. Even if some fruits are good and others are bad, as human performances or traits can be, this does not change the essence of the basket, which need not be rated. Moreover, since the basket may contain good oranges, bad pears, and mediocre apples, can we legitimately give it a single *global* rating?

GREEN. But what about something like a crime? Shouldn't criminals be condemned and punished?

LEGA. Yes, their *behavior* is wrong, bad, and it better have penalties. We do not want to help people become sociopaths, with no concern for others. We can condemn their behavior but not their *personhood*. Their behavior, as bad as it may be, still does not make them bad *humans*.

GREEN. That is very interesting. It makes a lot of sense. I always felt that when my father punished me for things like breaking the toilet watertank or losing my cap, he was doing that because I was a bad boy.

LEGA. And I wouldn't be surprised if he told you so, too. We *learn* irrational thinking. Parents are a very good source, sometimes. As Dr. Ellis would say: "Blood is sicker than water." (We both laugh.)

GREEN. I've been meaning to ask you how important you think early experiences are....

LEGA. They are important only to the extent that we keep them alive. If we hang on to something that has been gone for a long time, it is because we are giving it some meaning at present.

GREEN. Well, I was thinking about a time when I was playing doctor with the girl next door and my mother caught us. We were about 8 years old. Do you think that has something to do with my difficulties with women?

LEGA. You may have learned then that it was something you were not supposed to do, and perhaps you concluded that you were a bad boy for behaving badly. A way of avoiding this was to avoid the situation altogether. However, what was, and still is, at the bottom of it is the irrational thinking that makes behavior equal to self-worth. You see? You then rated *yourself* for your "error," and you are still rating *you* today. So it was and still is the *rating*, and not your mother's catching you that caused—and still causes—your anxiety.

GREEN. Yes, you are right.

LEGA. And if we add your low frustration tolerance to this picture, where your thinking *demands* that things come easy, you have a perfect excuse not to have to bother with the effort to meet women. You can always justify it by blaming someone else, like Mom or Dad, saying to yourself: "I was traumatized at an early age, so I cannot do anything about it. It is perfectly OK for me not to make any efforts. They would be useless anyway."

GREEN. You know, things are getting so clear.... I can see how I give myself all those excuses....

LEGA. Psychologists call them rationalizations, or false excuses which we give ourselves to try to reduce anxiety in the immediate situation but which get us into trouble in the long run. Some people confuse this with thinking rationally. The difference between the two is mainly in how functional their consequences are. Rational thinking leads to effective short- and long-term behaviors and emotions, while rationalizations do not.

GREEN. I guess that's what happens when I tell myself that it is going to be impossible for me to make friends or to meet a woman because I come from such a strange family. My parents rarely talked to one another, my sister had her own life and I have not seen her or heard of her for ten years...(long pause).

LEGA. And you conclude that it is impossible for you to do something about it, so why bother? That is your low frustration tolerance. What else do you conclude?

GREEN. That (sigh)...there is something wrong with *me*.

LEGA. And there is perhaps a lack of social skills. But how does that lack make you less of a human being?

GREEN. It doesn't. I know. I can see that if I work at it I am not doomed to be a loner all my life.

LEGA. So, next time you catch yourself thinking irrationally and feeling depressed and anxious as a result of it, how can you dispute your irrational beliefs?

GREEN. I can tell myself that I am a human being and that I am bound to make mistakes, but they do not make me a bad person. I may feel uncomfortable about making them, but that is only discomfort. It would be better for me to put up with it and try to talk to people, so I would get some practice and eventually increase the probability of meeting someone and making more friends. . . . I feel better already, Dr. Lega.

LEGA. Very good, Donald. You may end up feeling sad, as well, but not depressed. Let's see about your homework for next week, which is called a cost-benefit ratio. We use this technique in RET to help people see the advantages of using rational thinking and getting a more realistic perspective of life, of others, and of themselves. You may use it for your social skills or for your lateness. It goes as follows: On a piece of paper, write down all the advantages and disadvantages of thinking rationally and all the advantages and disadvantages of thinking irrationally that you can imagine. Then, compare both ways of thinking. Most likely, the list of advantages will be longer and carry more weight for rational thinking than for irrational thinking. The reverse will probably be true when you compare their disadvantages.

Session 5

GREEN. Dr. Lega, I picked up an RET catalog on my way out last time, and I think I would like to find out more about assertiveness training—maybe enroll in a workshop.

LEGA. That's a very good idea, Donald. You will be working at both changing your thinking behind your assertiveness difficulties and building up better communication skills.

> (RET practitioners often encourage their clients to take specialized workshops on topics relevant to their therapy issues. They also use bibliotherapy, or the reading of selected books and pamphlets to help increase their clients' range of coping strategies.)

LEGA. How was the homework?

As usual, I go over the homework for a few minutes. Donald is showing improvement through changes in his thoughts, feelings, and behavior. He comments that he is feeling less depressed.

GREEN. I guess I mean I am *making* myself less depressed . . . (smiles). I'm getting together with Frank, that guy from work who fixes up cars the way I do; on Saturday, we are going to see an exhibit of old cars at the

Coliseum. However, I'm beginning to notice that although I am less depressed, I'm feeling more angry. Perhaps my anger was there before, and I am only noticing it now, when I am not so anxious and depressed.

LEGA. That is possible, Donald. I remember you said at the beginning of therapy that at times you were fed up with the whole issue of lateness. You felt mad at other people, but you would not tell them about it.

GREEN. That's a pretty good memory, Dr. Lega!

LEGA. So what are head-shrinks for, Donald? (We both smile.) Now, can you give me an example of just what is going on?

> *(Although at times we have abstract, philosophical discussions with clients, the use of specific examples facilitates the identification and disputing of irrational beliefs. This is important to keep in mind, particularly with clients like Donald. Because of their low frustration tolerance, these clients may want to use more theoretical discussions as a way to "goof off.")*

GREEN. The other morning, when my third alarm clock went off, it was particularly difficult for me to get out of bed. When I finally did, I felt very angry.

LEGA. Because...?

GREEN (looking tense). Because...why is it so difficult for *me*? Other people have it easier. Why do I always have to conform to rigid rules? Soon there's going to be a new supervisor, since the one I like is planning to retire. This new guy will probably give me trouble because I am late. How unfair! After all, I come to work on weekends. Why is this lateness business so important to everyone?

LEGA. Well, Donald, you are bringing up two sources of anger, as far as I can see. One is anger at the world in general, and the other is anger at this new supervisor in particular. When you think that it *shouldn't* be so difficult for you, and that the world *should* be fair and give everyone an equal share of grief, it is part of your low frustration tolerance. You make yourself upset because you believe LIFE IS TOO HARD!

> *(I emphasize this last part by changing my tone of voice. I have picked up the low frustration tolerance aspect first, because Donald has already been working on it and it is more familiar to him.)*

GREEN. But it *is* true. Life is *unfair*!

LEGA. Yes, it sometimes is. But why *shouldn't* it be? Where is it written that the world *must* be fair?

GREEN (looking pensive). Well...I guess it is not written anywhere... but I still think it would be better!

LEGA. I agree that it would be *nicer*, and *preferable*, but you are *demanding* fairness. You are making it a *must* rather than a *preference*, and by doing so, you are only making yourself upset. The world is still going to be frustrating, with or without your shoulds.

GREEN. So, I had better just accept it, right? Well, it is easy for you to say. You do not feel the way I do.

LEGA. That is probably right, Donald. And that is because I probably *think* differently than you do. That does not mean that I never felt like you do now. I did, I still do on occasion, but I have worked hard at changing my demandingness and, little by little, anger and anxiety come less and less often. And when they do, I talk myself out of them faster than before. By practicing, you can do the same. You may feel sorrow and annoyance, but only occasionally will you make yourself angry and panicked.

(In RET, therapists may work as role models for clients.)

GREEN. Really (looking perplexed)?

LEGA. Really. It works, but it does take practice. So, what can you tell yourself. . . ?

I work with Donald on the difference between a *demand* and a *preference*. We discuss how this difference helps with accepting situations that cannot be changed, or with modifying those that can be changed by more functional thinking, feelings, and behaviors.

LEGA. Now let's go back to that morning when you felt so angry. We have covered the aspect that applies to life in general, but you also felt angry at your new supervisor in particular. By the way, this person has not been hired yet, and for all we know this particular incident may never happen. But let's pursue it as an example of how to deal with anger. You were feeling angry at him. Is that true?

GREEN. Yes, and I can see now how I was demanding fairness from him as well as from life in general.

LEGA. That is right. I see, though, one more element, one more irrational thought. Let's continue to pursue it. Let's assume that your new supervisor will act in an unfair way toward you. Let's assume that he tells you that the extra work you do on weekends does not count, that only promptness does, and he says this in a nasty tone of voice. If you want, let's even assume he tells you that you are fired. And let's put aside other feelings and concentrate on your anger toward him, OK?

Donald nods in agreement.

LEGA. What runs through your head while you feel so angry?
GREEN. That he is so unfair, and he shouldn't be that way....
LEGA. And if he behaves that way, what does it mean?
GREEN. That he is a rotten person!
LEGA. Very good. And where is the irrationality in this conclusion?
GREEN (after a pause). Am I overgeneralizing again?
LEGA. I'm afraid so. In a way, aren't you concluding about him, based on his behavior, what you used to conclude about yourself, based on your behavior?
GREEN. I see. You are right. I guess I am thinking that because he is acting bad toward me he is no good. And I am getting myself angry at this. Perhaps even so angry that I would become paralyzed. And I would want to get back at him, but because I have difficulty speaking up, I might get to work late just to show him this in an indirect way.
LEGA. And you set yourself up to lose on two accounts: one, your anger does not make him behave any better than he does, and two, you increase the probability of losing your job.

Donald nods.

LEGA (continuing). How can you dispute this irrational belief, so you can change your anger at him to annoyance at his acts?
GREEN. I could tell myself that he is not a bad person for behaving badly, that he is a human being and so will make mistakes.
LEGA. Yes, and even if he would *always* be unfair toward you, which we really do not know yet, it would only prove that he acts badly as a supervisor, a role he often plays badly. But this does not make him a bad human being.

For the sake of brevity, the rest of this session is omitted here.

Session 6

In the past several weeks, Donald has continued to make progress. He is feeling less anxious, less depressed, and less angry, and he is late for work only on occasion. He still has a very limited network of friends, however. As we begin the sixth session, I note his progress.

LEGA. You have made great progress in a lot of the issues you brought up when you first came to therapy.
GREEN. Yes, Dr. Lega, this therapy—and you—have been very helpful.
LEGA. Well, Donald, you have helped yourself. I am only your coach, remember?

We both smile, and then I continue.

LEGA. So, what shall we work on today? Any problems or issues?
GREEN. You tell me.
LEGA. I was thinking that the area of interpersonal relations could use some help. I would like to make a suggestion: How would you feel about joining a group for therapy?
GREEN. A group? I never thought about it. Why do you think it would help?
LEGA. Because you would get to work with other people, and you could practice the RET skills you've learned on them and get their input, too.
GREEN. Does it mean I would have to stop therapy with you?
LEGA. Not necessarily. We would continue to meet regularly and if at some point it gets to be too much, we could meet every other week instead of every week. Or you could leave the group and continue with individual therapy only, if in a few months you prefer to do so. What do you say?
GREEN. OK, I'm willing to give it a try.
LEGA. Good. By the way, what's happening with Cecile, the woman you like in accounting?
GREEN. Not much. We say hello to each other now, but I still cannot bring myself to say anything else.
LEGA. What keeps you from doing this?
GREEN. I guess I would feel ashamed if I made a fool of myself. I know—you're going to tell me that I'd better dispute my self-doubting and my low frustration tolerance. Believe me, Dr. Lega, I have been doing this. But I think I have this big problem with shame. I know it is linked with self-acceptance.
LEGA. You know, Donald, I think I have an almost perfect exercise for you—a shame-attacking exercise.
> (*Shame-attacking exercises are a technique that is often used by RET therapists.*)
GREEN. Sounds interesting!

LEGA. This is what you do. First, let's think of something you would normally label as shameful; nothing that would get you into trouble, of course. Like calling out the stops on the subway or bus: "Forty-second street! Thirty-fourth is next." Or saying to someone you pass in the street, "I'm sorry, could you tell me what year this is? I've just come out of a mental hospital, and I guess I was there longer than I expected." The purpose is to get through this exercise feeling uncomfortable but not ashamed. Use it to dispute your tendency to down yourself. That is where shame and guilt come from, remember?
GREEN. Oh... well, I'm not so sure I could do that.
LEGA. For the same reasons, I guess you continue to make yourself ashamed about everything else. Guess what they would be....
GREEN (reluctantly). OK, OK. I'll give it a try.
LEGA. Very good. I will check this with you next week.

This session continues with other material which, in the interest of brevity, will be omitted here.

Session 7

The combination of individual and group therapy seems to be working well for Donald. He finally has a two-minute conversation with Cecile, the woman at work. He is going to group therapy, and the group gave him the homework assignment of going to a bar and staying there for 15 minutes. He has completed this assignment after several unsuccessful trials, with everyone in the group urging him on.

LEGA. Well, Donald, you seem to be moving right along in your therapy. Now, how about some goal-setting? I believe the crisis intervention phase of your therapy is over; your job no longer seems to be threatened by your lateness. We can go on to a new phase of therapy for growth. How about spending some time on increasing the number and frequency of pleasurable activities in your life?
GREEN. That sounds very good to me.
LEGA. All right, then, let's do an exercise. I want you to close your eyes and imagine yourself in the future, five years from now. Imagine your life is the *best* it can be. Try to fill in as many details as possible.

I wait a few minutes and then continue.

LEGA. Now I want you to remain in the future, still five years from now, but this time your life is the *worst* it can possibly be. I want details here, too.

After waiting a few more minutes, I go on.

LEGA. Finally, I want you to place yourself in the future, just a year from now, and imagine how your life will be realistically speaking.

Again I wait a few minutes, and then I say:

LEGA. OK, Donald, open your eyes and tell me what you have imagined.
GREEN. When I imagined my life at its best, I pictured myself having many friends, a wife and children, no problems at work, and making lots of money. When I switched to the worst my life could possibly be, I saw myself alone, without a job...perhaps even being crazy....

Donald's voice trails off, and I urge him to continue.

GREEN. In reality, a year from now, I would probably be working at the same place. Hopefully, I would have some new friends and maybe even a special friend....(He smiles.)
LEGA. Very good. Now let's use this form for goal-setting for the next three months.

I give Donald the Three-Month Goal Form (see Figure 4.2). This is an effective resource for goal-setting, because it allows the client to work with the therapist in determining which thoughts, feelings, and behaviors are to be increased or decreased in a set period of time.

LEGA. Try to fill out the form using some of the elements from the exercise we've just completed. We covered some thoughts you may want to increase and decrease and some of your feelings as well. How about bodily sensations you may want to decrease?
GREEN. The lump in my stomach.
LEGA. Very good. And which one would you like to increase?
GREEN. An overall sensation of relaxation, I guess.
LEGA. For that particular one, you could use a relaxation tape we have.
GREEN. Fine, thanks.

```
                        THREE-MONTH GOAL FORM


    Things I want to accomplish by_____
                                         (date)


    BEHAVIORS YOU WISH TO INCREASE:_____
    _____
    _____


    BEHAVIORS YOU WISH TO DECREASE:_____
    _____.
    _____
    _____


    FEELINGS YOU WISH TO INCREASE:_____
    _____


    FEELINGS YOU WISH TO DECREASE:_____
    _____


    SENSATIONS YOU WISH TO INCREASE:_____
    _____
    _____


    SENSATIONS YOU WISH TO DECREASE:_____
    _____
    _____


    THOUGHTS YOU WISH TO INCREASE:_____
    _____
    _____


    THOUGHTS YOU WISH TO DECREASE:_____
    _____
    _____


    Institute for Rational-Emotive Therapy/45 East 65th St./New York, N.Y. 10021
```

FIGURE 4.2 Client's three-month goal form

LEGA. And which behavior do you wish to decrease?
GREEN. Some of the running around in circles I still do sometimes in the morning before going to work.
LEGA. Fine. And which behavior would you like to increase?
GREEN. Perhaps—talking to women.
LEGA. That's very good, Donald. I'll see you next week.

Sessions 8–20

Donald and I work at getting him to give up his anxiety and anger and enjoy himself more, and we are making progress. He is making some friends and he finally has managed to carry on a conversation with a woman he met at a coffee shop while he was doing another homework assignment from his group. After the 20th session we begin to consider the possibility of terminating therapy.

TERMINATION OF THE THERAPY

In rational-emotive therapy, termination of the therapy can take many forms. In the most commonly used form, after an agreement for termination has been reached between therapist and client, the client gives a two-week notice.

GREEN. So, do you think I would be able to function well if I stop coming to see you?
LEGA. Well, what do you think?
GREEN. I am not so sure. I am ambivalent about the whole thing.
LEGA. OK, let's look at what is going on behind that ambivalence.
GREEN. On the one hand, I have made a lot of progress in my work, in my social relations, and in managing my life with less anxiety, depression, and anger than before. On the other hand, I was looking at my goal sheet the other day, and I see that I still have not had any intimate relationship with a woman.
LEGA. Well, Donald, I agree. A lot of progress has been made, and yes, finding a woman is still up in the air. But before getting into that topic, let me ask you something. You said in your first interview that you were having crazy fantasies about the Internal Revenue Service, but don't we all? (I smile.) And there was another fantasy about a car you had fixed up for a woman. Are such fantasies still occurring?

GREEN. Only once or twice in the past few months, and they did not last very long. I think I have learned to talk myself out of them pretty effectively.

LEGA. That sounds interesting. How do you do it?

GREEN. First, when I catch myself obsessing I use it as a red flag. So I snap a rubber band I have been wearing around my wrist and I say to myself: "Stop! This is only inside my head and I am putting it there because of my tendency to overexaggerate things." Then I try to concentrate on something else, something pleasant, like one of the cars I saw at the last show.

LEGA. Very good, Donald. It is also your fear of performing badly, right? Now, let's go back to the area of intimacy and the difficulties of establishing a relationship with a woman. Any specifics?

GREEN. I met a woman at one of the car shows a few weeks ago. I got her phone number and finally managed to call her and ask her out. She said she couldn't make it this time, but to call her again. So I hung up and started feeling down and anxious.

LEGA. What was running through your head at the time?

GREEN. I knew you were going to ask me that! Well, I was telling myself, "I really blew it!" and "She does not like me at all. She is just trying to be nice."

LEGA. There we go again, Donald. Does this thinking remind you of other occasions where the same ideas have popped into your head?

GREEN (pause). Yes, I guess so.

LEGA. So what can you tell yourself in order to change those ideas?

GREEN. That she may have been really busy this time, and that even if she does not want to see me it does not mean that I am a bad guy or that I will never be able to find anybody to date.

LEGA. I could not have said it better. So, when will you *believe* it?

We both laugh.

GREEN. You know, a lot of the things I tell myself seem to end up being the same nonsense. Is that true?

LEGA. In a way, yes. According to RET, we can classify irrational beliefs into three main categories: One which includes all our self-downing statements and leads to depression; a second one which includes the statements downing other people and results in anger; and a third one which is low frustration tolerance, where we whine and scream about life being *too* hard and that it *has* to be more fair.

GREEN. And I can dispute them to replace my irrational beliefs with more functional, rational ones, so I feel and function better....

LEGA. That's right. You can remove self-downing by criticizing only your acts and not your *self*. You then change depression to sadness and regret. You can stop damning others by only rating their *behaviors* and thereby change your anger to feelings of displeasure. And you can increase your tolerance to frustration by changing things you can change and *accepting* what you cannot change. You then reduce self-pity and wind up with feelings of discomfort and determination to work for greater comfort.

GREEN. The RET model seems so easy....

LEGA. No, it is *simple* but often not *easy*. It frequently is difficult to *use* it on a *regular* basis. It takes a lot of work to overcome years of traditional thinking habits. Practice is crucial. In fact, let me make an interesting point: How long have you been in therapy with me, Donald?

GREEN. About six months, I think. Once every week or so.

LEGA. So, it is around 20 sessions, is that correct?

GREEN. Yes.

LEGA. And how old are you?

GREEN. Forty-two.

LEGA. So you have been practicing rational thinking for 20 hours with me and perhaps another 100 hours on your own. But you have been practicing irrational thinking for at least 30-odd years!

GREEN. I see your point.

LEGA. The question is, which one—rational or irrational thinking—are you going to practice for the *next* 30-odd years?

We smile at one another.

GREEN (after a pause). I think I get it. It is up to me, right?

LEGA. That's right, Donald. You now have the tools to make yourself more rational and functional, so you can feel and act better. But you are the one who has to continue to do so. As we have noted before, I cannot do it for you.

GREEN. You are right, Dr. Lega.

A week later, Donald decides to give the two-week termination notice. We meet one more time.

GREEN. ...and I thought about all the things we have discussed, and I think I am ready to give the world a try on my own.

LEGA. You also know that you can always contact me here. In fact, I would like you to call me in a couple of months and let me know how you are doing.

GREEN. I'll do that (pause). Dr. Lega...thanks.

Two months later, Donald Green calls for an appointment. He is doing well at work and is dating a couple of women. He continues to attend some of the RET workshops. Several months after that, he calls to report that he is continuing to do well.

About two years later, Donald comes in again for several sessions, bringing a woman he has been dating. They may be moving in together and want to explore the direction of their relationship and the commonality of their goals. I have three joint sessions with them, and they decide to live together. A year later, I receive a letter from Donald thanking me again for my help and saying that they are doing well and are planning to be married. ■

CRITIQUE OF DONALD GREEN'S TREATMENT BY RATIONAL-EMOTIVE THERAPY

by Albert Ellis

Leonor Lega's therapy presentation indicates some of the most important aspects of rational-emotive therapy (RET) in a brief, condensed format. The main relevant things she does with Donald Green in the second session include the following:

1. She starts with a presenting behavioral problem (Donald's lateness to work) but also quickly ferrets out his emotional disturbances about this self-defeating behavior (that is, she reveals and works with his severe feelings of anxiety and anger).

2. She looks for and finds some of his secondary disturbances—his guilt about his lateness and about his anger. In RET, we routinely investigate and work at removing people's guilt about having their primary problems.

3. She very quickly gets to some of the things Donald is telling himself to create his anxiety—that it is *awful* and *terrible* if he loses his job because of his lateness.

4. She briefly disputes and challenges his awfulizing.

5. She starts to teach Donald the ABC's of RET—shows him that A's (Activating Events, such as lateness to work) do not cause him to have disturbed C's (emotional Consequences, such as anxiety). Instead, Donald's B's (his irrational Beliefs *about* these Activating Events) do upset him.

6. Lega shows Donald that if he only would stay with rational Beliefs (such as "It is unfortunate if I lose my job") rather than irrational Beliefs ("It is horrible and catastrophic if I lose it"), he would make himself feel not *in*appropriately anxious but *appropriately* sorry and frustrated. His appropriate feelings would then help him do something about getting to work on time and not losing his job.

7. She starts to give Donald emotive and behavioral exercises (such as rational emotive imagery) to help him feel sorry and concerned but *not* extremely anxious about the possible loss of his job.

8. She uses empirical or realistic disputation to show Donald that he probably *won't* lose his job. And she also uses philosophical (and more elegant) disputing to show him that even if the worst possibility occurs and he does lose his position, he can still find happiness and also look for another job.

9. She teaches Donald the key RET theory—that human *preferences* lead to appropriate negative feelings when one's desires are not fulfilled, but absolutist *musts, shoulds,* and other *demands* lead to emotional and behavioral disturbances.

10. Lega shows Donald that insight alone into his irrational Beliefs will not change him. He had *also* better work and practice—yes, work and practice!—at *using* this insight and *acting* on it.

11. She gives him cognitive homework—the RET Self-Help Form—to do between sessions and arranges for rewards and penalties to encourage him to do this homework. RET invariably includes a number of cognitive, emotive, and behavioral methods, including rewards and penalties.

In the third session, Lega continues active-directive RET with Donald, utilizing these techniques:

1. She checks to see how he has done his homework.

2. She shows him that *forcefulness* is part of RET and that he had therefore better *vigorously* challenge his irrational Beliefs and *strongly* convince himself of rational coping statements.

3. She helps Donald devise some specific rational Beliefs and tells him to write them down and go over them several times during the following week.

4. She starts working with another of Donald's major problems—his severe social anxiety. She shows him that he has ego anxiety about failing in social relations but also has discomfort anxiety or low frustration tolerance about how hard it is to overcome his social awkwardness.

5. She also points out his secondary social anxiety—his putting himself down for *being* anxious.

6. Lega particularly helps Donald see one of the basic RET philosophies—that even if his social (or other) *behavior* is inept or bad he is never a *bad person* but *can always accept himself as a human.*

7. Again, she deals with Donald's discomfort anxiety or low frustration tolerance as well as his self-downing, because *both* these important aspects of disturbance are sought out and dealt with in RET.

8. In addition to a cognitive disputing assignment, Lega gives Donald an activity homework task—taking the risk of talking to some people at lunch.

9. She also gives him some skill training in how to hold a conversation and recommends some of the skill-training workshops that are given regularly at the Institute for Rational-Emotive Therapy in New York.

In succeeding sessions with Donald, Lega keeps checking his homework, gives him new RET exercises and homework, continues to reveal his main irrational Beliefs, and shows him how to dispute these Beliefs and how to come up with alternative rational Beliefs. She especially works on his feelings of inadequacy and worthlessness (as in the fourth session). She keeps emphasizing that he is never a bad person, even when he performs badly and defeats his own ends.

Where most therapists would largely work with Donald's self-blaming and feelings of worthlessness, Lega also points out and works with his low frustration tolerance. This is what we usually do in rational-emotive therapy—assume that clients not only have ego problems and irrationally put themselves down but also have discomfort anxiety or low frustration tolerance problems. They demand that life be easier and fairer than it actually is, and therefore they overly rebel against it to their own detriment. Lega keeps showing Donald the enormous difference between his *preferences*—which in RET are almost always seen as being legitimate—and his grandiose *demands* and *commands*—which frequently get him into emotional and behavioral difficulties.

As the sessions proceed, Lega also works with Donald on setting some goals for himself for the future and on actualizing himself better. RET has two main aspects. First, it deals with people's emotional and behavioral problems and helps them overcome these difficulties. Second, it shows them how they can actualize themselves and really fulfill and enjoy themselves to a greater extent than they have tended to do in the past and present. Lega gets to this second aspect and indicates to Donald how he can give some thought and action to present and future self-actualization.

The material presented in this case is necessarily brief and omits some of the important aspects of RET that would be covered in a more detailed presentation. These include:

1. The issue of self-rating and self-worth would be gone into more thoroughly. Donald would be shown that he can choose either an "elegant" or an "inelegant" solution to this problem. In the elegant solution, Donald would be shown how to refuse to rate his self, his being, or his personhood *at all* and instead to rate *only* his deeds, performances, and traits. In the inelegant solution, he would unconditionally rate himself or accept himself as "good" just because he exists, just because he is alive and human, just because he chooses to do so (Ellis, 1962, 1972, 1973, 1976, 1988; Ellis & Becker, 1982; Ellis & Harper, 1975). Thus he would convince himself: "I am alive and want to remain alive and happy. I accept myself as a 'good' or 'deserving' person just because I choose to do so and will never defame myself or damn myself, even when I behave poorly and even when significant others do not approve of me."

2. Donald would be shown that his panic attacks and obsessions with great dangers probably stem from his great need for certainty. When panicked, he is probably irrationally telling himself, partly as a result of some early experience which he had defined as "catastrophic," that he absolutely *has to* be free from any physical or other real dangers. And if he keeps saying to himself, "I *must* not be in danger! I *must* not suffer any great pain!" he will keep obsessing himself, in waking life and in his dreams, with this "terror" or "horror."

3. Usually, Donald's dire need to be loved, especially by a woman, would show itself in his need to have his therapist completely like and favor him. This would affect his relationship with Lega and would be dealt with in RET sessions. He would finally come to believe that it is highly *preferable*, but not absolutely *necessary*, that even his therapist like or love him. This aspect of his dire need for love would have been dealt with in more detail in a longer presentation.

4. Donald could be shown that he has a real potential for friendship, and also presumably for love relationships, as indicated in his long relationship with Jim, his artist friend, and Mary, Jim's wife. His loneliness and his desire for the therapist's approval also indicate that he really *wants* more intimate contacts.

5. Although RET does not emphasize dreams and their interpretations, Donald could be shown that his dreams tend to be related to the same basic needy philosophies that he has during his waking life—especially his dire need for approval and his demanding certainty that he not be in any kind of great danger.

6. If I were Donald's therapist, I would try to show him that his father and mother both had serious relationship problems and seemed to be quite socially anxious. Therefore, his own shyness and social anxiety may have a hereditary element. If so, I would point out to him how difficult, but still not impossible, it would be for him to overcome this innate, as well as acquired, handicap.

7. Donald's sex inhibitions could be more thoroughly explored. Even if he has a long history of being very shy with women, he could have resorted to prostitutes and to easily available sex partners. Why didn't he? Did he have other sex or emotional problems in this connection? If so, what was he telling himself that was creating and maintaining these problems?

8. RET particularly emphasizes people's anxiety about their anxiety. Although Lega does this in her sessions with Donald, she could have pointed out that he is putting himself down for his crazy fantasies, vowing that he *must* not have them, and thereby augmenting them. His phobia about the barking of dogs probably stems from his fear of *having* this fear and from frantically telling himself, "I *must* not be so nutty! I'm really too crazy and may well end up in the loony bin!"

9. Donald's low frustration tolerance could be further explored, particularly his anger (in one of his dreams and in his waking life) at not getting more out of life. He prevents himself from fully enjoying himself because of his great fear of failure, but then he tells himself, "I *must* lead a happier existence!" and makes his condition much worse.

10. Although Donald seemingly can live nicely by himself and insists on doing so, he seems to have an enormous dire *need* (not merely a *desire*) for love and intimacy. And this very need makes him so afraid of intimacy that he thoroughly avoids it. He could have been shown how he really craves love and approval, irrationally *insists* on having it, and thereby blocks getting it.

No series of therapy sessions is ever complete, because, in review, it is always possible to find missed opportunities that might have been taken. But Leonor Lega's presentation of her sessions with Donald Green nicely illustrates some of the main principles and practices of RET. Sessions of this nature hardly ensure therapeutic success. Nothing, in fact, does! But if RET is practiced along the lines she has indicated, there is a good chance that clients will be helped with some of their most serious emotional and behavioral problems.

■

REFERENCES

Ellis, A. (1962). *Reason and emotion in psychotherapy*. Secaucus, NJ: Citadel Press.

Ellis, A. (1972). *Psychotherapy and the value of a human being*. New York: Institute for Rational-Emotive Therapy. Reprinted in A. Ellis & R. Grieger (Eds.), *Handbook of rational-emotive therapy*. New York: Springer.

Ellis, A. (1973). *Humanistic psychotherapy: The rational-emotive approach*. New York: McGraw-Hill.

Ellis, A. (1976). *RET abolishes most of the human ego*. New York: Institute for Rational-Emotive Therapy.

Ellis, A. (1988). *How to stubbornly refuse to make yourself miserable about anything—yes, anything!* Secaucus, NJ: Lyle Stuart.

Ellis, A., & Becker, I. (1982). *A guide to personal happiness*. North Hollywood, CA: Wilshire Books.

Ellis, A., & Harper, R. A. (1975). *A new guide to rational living*. North Hollywood, CA: Wilshire Books.

Behavior therapy is based on the principles and procedures of experimental psychology, particularly social learning theory. According to this theory, behavior—both normal and most abnormal behavior—is maintained and modified by environmental events. The influence of these external events on individuals is largely determined by cognitive processes, which in turn are affected by the social and environmental consequences of behavior. Behavior therapy theory emphasizes the constant reciprocity between personal actions and environmental consequences in the analysis and development of methods for self-directed behavior change.

In behavior therapy, treatment involves a detailed, continuing assessment of each client's problems, focusing primarily on current determinants of behavior. The assumption is that people are best described by what they think, feel, and do in specific situations. Once therapists form an understanding of the determinants of a client's problem, they typically select several different techniques to be included in a multimodal treatment program designed to modify all aspects of the problem. Treatment methods are precisely specified and based on the results of controlled research, wherever possible.

Aside from technical expertise, behavior therapists should possess the clinical and interpersonal skills essential to any effective treatment method. These therapists function as problem-solvers who provide emotional support and engage clients in mutually agreed-upon efforts to change their behavior.

G. T. Wilson

Behavior Therapy

SOMETHING ABOUT THE THERAPIST • *Barbara McCrady*

I always knew I'd be a professional. In fourth grade, my career was to be law; by high school it was medicine; in college, it was neuroanatomy research. I completed an undergraduate degree in biological science, and in my last year of college and for a year after that, I worked in a neuroanatomy research lab. The work was difficult, stimulating, and was the kind of basic research that would clearly contribute knowledge that would benefit people. But as a child who came of age in the 1960s, the sense that my work would affect the world someday, in the distant future, was not satisfying enough. That was how I came to psychology.

As an undergraduate at Purdue University, I took only two psychology courses—introductory and abnormal. The professor who taught abnormal psychology, Robert Toal, was a community-oriented psychologist who devoted many lectures to concepts of community activism and change. His lectures fired my imagination, and when I became dissatisfied with basic research, I came back to them. I also was devoted to a television series called "Bronson's Way," which featured a man who rode his motorcycle from town to town, involving himself in people's problems in each place he visited. One week he worked with an emotionally disturbed child, and in the way of all television shows, he touched this child profoundly in the course of the hour. My restiveness with biology, the inspiration of Professor Toal, the success of a fictitious television character, and my high school memories of teaching swimming to mentally retarded children culminated in my rather impetuous decision to enter clinical psychology. Although I knew absolutely nothing about this field when I entered it, this was a decision I have never regretted.

When I applied to graduate programs, I planned to become a community psychologist, organizing and helping to empower community groups for change. My husband and I wanted to go to California (another dream of children of the 1960s), so I applied to and was accepted at the University of California at Los Angeles. However, he was able to obtain a draft-deferred job in Rhode Island, which was a consideration during the Vietnam War, and we decided to move to the East Coast.

The University of Rhode Island (URI) had just begun a doctoral program in clinical psychology, after having had a master's-level program for many years. After we moved East, I went to talk to the department chair at URI. Being naive probably was helpful, because I thought I could just begin graduate school that fall. Instead, the department chair, Stan Berger, told me that they had admitted their first-year class, but he encouraged me to take undergraduate psychology courses and then apply for the following fall. After the first semester, a graduate student in the experimental psychology program had to leave, resulting in an open assistantship. Some of the faculty who knew me through coursework suggested that I be admitted to fill the assistantship. With that, I became a graduate student in clinical psychology, still not really knowing what I had begun!

The orientation of the University of Rhode Island clinical psychology program in 1970 was primarily humanistic/interpersonal. The core themes of the program, human potential and sensitivity, resonated with my own values. Personal growth experiences were integral to the program, and students were given feedback about their interpersonal styles. I experienced much of this as dislocating, as it was so different from my previous academic experiences in biology, chemistry, and physics. While I was attracted to the humanistic approach, the courses in behavior therapy and operant methods appealed to me as a scientist. However, since the department emphasized the importance of experiential methods, I felt that the more cognitive and analytic approach of the behavioral courses was less "genuine" and therefore less valuable.

I saw a number of clients through the psychological clinic at URI, working particularly with couples with marital or sexual problems. I liked couples therapy and learned behavioral and systems couples techniques through supervision with Jim and Jan Prochaska. Jan also became my first role model for a woman professional who was married and had a child. Jim was fairly behavioral in his orientation, and I learned behavioral approaches from him, but I did not view these as central to my thinking as a therapist.

My two practicum placements during graduate school did much to broaden my thinking about clinical psychology. My first placement, at a child and family services agency, exposed me to people with limited personal and economic resources. I did individual and couples therapy and taught sex education to inner-city black teenagers. My second placement was at a private psychiatric hospital, where I did traditional psychological testing and outpatient therapy and functioned as a treatment-team leader for a limited number of inpatients. I learned about severe psychopathology and the complexities of working within a treatment-team milieu. I also began to work with two people who were important to me for years to come—Tom Paolino, a psychiatrist, and Dick Longabaugh, a psychologist.

Even though I saw a good number of clients in therapy, read about and discussed therapy frequently, and had close supervision, my ideas about therapy remained fairly unformed during graduate school. I had some sense that the relationship between the client and therapist is critical to the therapy process, that respect for the intrinsic potential of a human being is essential, and that being open and genuine would create a climate that would allow the client to change and grow. My formulation of therapy was unsatisfying, however, because it lacked the kind of scientific rigor that I had grown to respect as a biologist and a biological researcher.

When I applied to internships I wanted community experience. I accepted a clinical internship at Worcester State Hospital, where community experiences and individual, couples, and family therapy training were combined with responsibility for an open psychiatric unit at the state hospital. The associate director of the internship, Larry Peterson, was a talented and devoted behavior therapist who had the absolute conviction that behavior therapy is the most successful and reasoned approach to treatment. His conviction infuriated me; we debated regularly, and I resisted his certainty. At the same time, he was a superb supervisor, and the clients I saw under his supervision did well, a bit to my surprise. I also found that when I would ask for references to approaches or techniques Larry recommended, he was able to refer me to research publications as well as clinically descriptive material. As my clients did well and I began to read more widely in behavior therapy, I began to rethink my opinions of behavior therapy. Our most notable success was with a lesbian woman in her 40s who had had years of unsuccessful therapy for problems with depression and anger. Larry encouraged me to focus on relaxation and assertiveness skills with her, and she responded wonderfully. She worked out several difficult issues with her lover and her job and became much less depressed. She terminated therapy successfully, leaving me with the sense that what we had done in therapy had made sense, to her and to me.

I did not become a "convert," however, until I began to work with a young woman client under the supervision of Susan Vogel. Susan provided the kind of intense supervision in interpersonal therapy that I was seeking. The client, Lisa, responded, to a point, but finally she said rather plaintively, "Now I *know* what I'm doing in my relationships, but I don't know *how* to change." That single sentence represented the moment for me that I became a behavior therapist, for at that point I realized that behavior therapy could be used to help clients achieve their goals and actualize their potential as human beings. Before, I had perceived behavior therapy as mechanistic, without a value base, and as manipulative. Lisa's comment helped me realize that I could use the methods of behavioral assessment to help clients clarify their own goals, and I could use behavioral treatment techniques to provide them with the competencies necessary to achieve these goals. When it became clear to me that I could effect an integration between my humanistic values and my scientific hardheadedness, my transition to being a behavior therapist was an easy one.

After I completed my internship, I took a position working with Tom Paolino and Dick Longabaugh at Butler Hospital in Providence, Rhode Island. Tom had been awarded a grant from the state to study an innovative method of treating alcoholic couples through joint hospitalizations. I was hired to develop and implement a research study to evaluate the effectiveness of the joint-hospitalization approach. I had virtually no background in alcoholism but had fairly extensive experience with couples, and I had good research experience from my days as a biologist. I took the position for pragmatic reasons—I needed a job while I completed my dissertation—but the position became formative for my career. I worked in the research position for a year, completed my dissertation, and was offered a position at Butler and as a faculty member in the Brown University Program in Medicine. I was hesitant, due to my continuing desire to work in the community, but I decided that I could spend a few years as a medical school academic psychologist.

During the eight years I was on the faculty at Brown, I began two major programs—a psychological consultation and assessment program for the hospital, and a treatment program for problem drinkers. I became heavily involved in alcoholism treatment research while continuing my interest in couples' aspects of treatment, obtaining research grants, and publishing my work. I also saw a wide range of clients in both inpatient and outpatient treatment, including schizophrenics, manic-depressive patients, anorexics, alcoholics, women with issues of independence and identity, distressed couples, and people who were just unhappy.

When I first joined the faculty, David Barlow had just come to Brown and Butler Hospital. He began a clinical psychology internship training program with a strong behavioral orientation. I supervised interns, and, through seminars, reading, supervision, research, and experience, I solidified my skills and identity as a behavior therapist.

Three clients stand out most clearly in the large caseload I had over these eight years. I think each of them taught me a special lesson as a therapist and helped me to develop and expand my skills as a behavior therapist. Lou was a 50-year-old alcoholic man who also had a serious driving phobia. He went through our alcoholism treatment program and did well. He continued in outpatient treatment with me, and we worked hard on his driving phobia and on his continued abstinence from alcohol. After about six months he was doing well enough to stop treatment, but he asked if he could "check in" periodically. We began to meet on a gradually decreasing schedule, first monthly, then every three months, then finally every six months for a 15-minute appointment. About two years after Lou had left the day hospital, his son, who was also an alcoholic, fell asleep in a chair with a lighted cigarette in his hand. Lou's house burned, and his son was burned to death. Lou stayed sober through this horrible experience, saying simply "drinking won't change what happened." I remember Lou because of his courage and the lessons he taught me about the importance of long-term contact with some clients and how important people's thinking is in determining their behavior.

The second client who stands out in my Butler memories is Jaynie. A young professional woman, she had significant problems in her relationships at work and with men, as well as her chronic anxiety. For the first two or three months I saw her, she refused to have the door to my office closed. Only several months later did I learn that she was strongly attracted to me sexually and that she was confused about her sexual identity. She taught me much about handling extremely uncomfortable feelings as a therapist and the need to tailor the pace as well as the content of the therapy, and she taught me that clients may have problems that they do not reveal to a therapist for a long time.

The third client was a 62-year-old woman who was admitted to the in-patient hospital with severe depression. She felt utterly hopeless, was acutely suicidal, and wept in a way that was painful for all of us to hear. She did not respond to antidepressant medication or to intensive, cognitively oriented treatment for her depression. Finally we decided that electroconvulsive therapy (ECT) was the most appropriate treatment for her and transferred her to the care of a psychiatrist who specialized in ECT. For me, this was a terribly difficult decision, because I felt fairly negative about ECT, and my client was terrified. However, after three or four treatments, her depression lifted dramatically. The woman who felt hopeless became animated and began to care about herself and her life again. She sought me out to thank me profusely for recommending the ECT to her. My shock at her response sent me back to the library, where I looked more thoroughly at the quite respectable literature on the effectiveness of ECT, particularly for the pattern of depression she had experienced. From her I relearned the lesson that I need to be informed about the effectiveness and indications for a treatment, even if I do not particularly like the treatment. I also developed a healthy respect for the role of physiologically based treatments, under some circumstances.

In 1983, I left Rhode Island to join the faculty at Rutgers University. My position at Rutgers combines several of my passions as a psychologist. I am a member of the faculty of the psychology department, teach graduate courses, and supervise graduate students in their research and clinical work. I also am the clinical director of the Center of Alcohol Studies (CAS), the oldest alcohol research center in the world. At CAS, I conduct research on issues related to alcoholism treatment and have developed a series of innovative alcoholism treatment programs in the local community. I spend part of my time in the development and administration of these programs, which also serve as sites for clinical training for our students and for our research on alcoholism treatment.

Now, 13 years out of graduate school, I am firmly a behavior therapist. For me, behavior therapy combines my respect for science with my respect for people. As is evident from Terry Wilson's (1989) writing, the data on the effectiveness of behavioral approaches are impressive, supporting its equal or superior effectiveness in the treatment of the majority of psychological problems. It is also important to me that the approach of behavior therapy places responsibility on the therapist for developing a plan for treatment and for continually evaluating the effectiveness of that plan. The constant evaluation and modification of treatment allow for a flexible and self-critical approach to therapy which I believe challenges the therapist and does not blame the client, unlike trait-theory-oriented treatments. Also important is my sense that behavior therapy is highly respectful of people's capacities and dreams. We respect the client's ability to say "I would like to become X," and we become a consultant who can provide the client with tools to try to become "X," rather than an omniscient or all-knowing therapist who manipulates or maneuvers the client to change. I also think that behavior therapy is eminently teachable and that the treatment can be well enough specified that it lends itself particularly well to research. Finally, behavior therapy fits with my worldview—that human behavior is a product of the interaction between the person and the environment, rather than a function solely of forces within or outside the individual.

Training to Become a Behavior Therapist

It is probably clear from the discussion of my own path to becoming a behavior therapist that I would recommend serious consideration of behavior therapy to any student who wants to become a therapist. In the next 20 years I think behavior therapy will become ascendant because of the strong research base for the approach and the serious efforts to curtail the costs of health care. Behavior therapy is well suited to briefer interventions, and, because goals of treatment are well-specified and progress is well-documented, insurance companies are likely to be more amenable to reimbursing the costs of treatment.

There are several important components in the process of becoming a behavior therapist. A firm academic grounding in psychological theory and research, plus personal experience with clinical research, will provide training for the kind of rigorous and critical thinking skills I believe the behavior therapist should acquire. The student should also learn to turn to the scientific literature as a source of answers for questions, rather than relying solely on personal experience and clinical supervision. However, close supervision which pushes the student to formulate cases, monitor progress, and evaluate outcomes is crucial. In addition to this rigorous kind of training, therapists need to be exposed to a range of life experiences, both to become familiar with problems outside their own experience and to become humble about the limited range of knowledge and experience any individual can have. Additionally, in becoming therapists students need to develop a level of self-awareness and to come to understand how they cope with personal problems, react emotionally to situations, and think about problems and people. Some students develop this self-awareness and understanding through life experience, some through clinical supervision, and some through their own therapy.

The Setting for Therapy

At this point in my career, I occasionally see private clients in my office at the Center of Alcohol Studies. The building is a rather typical two-story, red-brick structure on the campus. My office looks like a combination of traditional professor's office, with piles of papers, journals, and computer printouts, and a private practitioner's office, with comfortable chairs and a low table. The overall impression is probably one of comfortable chaos.

I see most clients under certain special circumstances. One is in a consultation and outpatient substance-abuse treatment program at one of the community hospitals in New Brunswick, New Jersey, run by a clinical team consisting of a physician, psychologists, a nurse who is also a certified alcoholism counselor, and graduate students in clinical psychology. Here I see hospitalized medical patients who have or are suspected to have problems as a result of their alcohol or drug use. Evaluations and treatment are conducted at bedside, while these patients are undergoing medical treatment. They are an unusually challenging group to work with, because most of the patients have not labeled themselves as having an alcohol or drug-use problem, and none of them is seeking psychological help. Thus my challenge as a clinician is to help them begin to label themselves as having problems and to help them consider the notion of changing some aspects of their behavior, either through treatment or on their own. Since I have previously worked only with clients who were seeking treatment, this aspect of my work is unusual. As part of the outpatient program at this hospital, I also run a couples clinic which serves as a base for my continued research on couples' approaches to alcoholism treatment.

In addition to my consultation work, another psychologist and I run an employee-assistance program for the New Jersey Dental Association. Through this program, I see dentists with alcohol, drug, or psychological problems. My primary roles are evaluation, referral, and monitoring of treatment and progress, rather than direct treatment. These clients present some of the most complicated problems I have seen, including serious drug abuse, legal problems, and concurrent emotional, family, and financial problems.

We recently opened a unit for college students with alcohol and drug problems. Students live in the inpatient unit of the student health center at Rutgers and continue to attend classes and maintain other aspects of their student identity while participating in an intensive treatment program. This new assignment has allowed me to return to a familiar role, as therapist for patients in residential treatment.

THE THERAPY FOR DONALD GREEN

Session 2

There are a number of differences between the way I normally conduct an initial interview and the first interview with Donald Green presented in

Chapter 1. I would have spent more time obtaining detailed information on the client's presenting complaints. I would have informed him how I work as a therapist and shared some of my expectations about his role as a client. In an initial session, I would not have asked about his dreams. At the end of the interview, I would have given him a brief homework assignment to bring to the next session. Because of these differences from my usual way of beginning therapy, the second session will include some of the information that I normally would have included in the first session.

Donald Green enters my office for the second session, putting out his hand rather tentatively.

GREEN. How are you today, Doc?

MCCRADY. I'm OK, how about you?

GREEN. Oh, OK.

MCCRADY. Last week, in our first session, we discussed a number of things that were bothering you. I was wondering if you had any reactions to that session, or if there were any other concerns you had that we didn't talk about.

GREEN. Well, I guess I felt kind of embarrassed after I left. I figured that you probably thought I was kind of a jerk, with no friends, no wife, and all those strange things that I worry about. I thought about not coming back, but my boss is really concerned that the new supervisor who will take his place when he retires will not put up with my being late so much, and you seemed nice and understanding.

MCCRADY. It sounds as though you have done a lot of thinking about how I might have reacted to you. I'll tell you—my strongest reactions were that you seemed pretty unhappy, and it took a lot of courage to tell me so much about yourself when you had just met me.
> (I think Donald probably does a lot of "mind reading," where he decides on what another person thinks and then acts on that belief, and this probably has contributed to his discomfort around people. I want to begin right away to challenge his assumptions by correcting any mind reading he has done with me. I plan to introduce more specific interventions later on that will help him with this problem if my initial guess is correct.)

MCCRADY. Did you think of any other problems that might be important to bring up at this point?

GREEN. No, not really.

MCCRADY. OK then, I'd like to spend some time this session in getting a clearer picture of your problems with being late for work. I also want to make sure that we discuss your overall goals for treatment, so we can agree on what we're trying to accomplish during our sessions.

GREEN. Sounds fine to me.

MCCRADY. Then let's begin with the lateness at work. When did you say this started?

GREEN. Oh, about three years ago, I think.

MCCRADY. Can you tell me something about your life at that time—were there any changes in your work or personal life around then?

GREEN. No, not really. Nothing I can think of. It just seemed to come out of the blue.

MCCRADY. OK, then, let's look more at the present. Can you tell me more about your usual morning routine? I'm interested specifically in knowing when you get up, what you do between the time you get up and the time you leave for work, and something about your commute, since you live fairly far out in the country.

GREEN. I don't really do anything unusual in the morning—just what everyone does. I get up, shower, shave, eat breakfast—you know, things like that. I don't think you'll find anything in that to really *explain* my problems.

MCCRADY. I guess right now I'm not trying to completely explain your problem, Donald. But in order to help you make any changes, we need to start with a careful description of what's happening right now. The approach I take in therapy may be a little like your work—first we have to carefully describe and understand how something is working right now, figure out what is wrong with it, and then we can begin to develop a plan to make changes. My job with you is kind of like that of a consultant—I'll help you learn how to discover what patterns in your life are contributing to the things you are unhappy about, and then I can help you learn ways to change some of those patterns. Does that make sense to you?

> (Donald has given me a natural opening to describe a bit about my behavioral approach to treatment. I like to emphasize two parts of treatment—assessment and change—as distinct components of the therapy. I define myself as a consultant because I believe that captures the behavioral therapist's role well—not an omnipotent stranger in a "one-up" position, but rather a colleague in a sense, who has special expertise to be shared with the client. I do not use the term "psychotherapy" but rather use terms such as "therapy," "behavior therapy," or "learning-based treatment.")

Donald thinks a moment before he replies.

GREEN. You know, what you're saying is a lot different from what I thought therapy was supposed to be. I thought I would just have to talk a lot, and eventually I'd feel different. I thought that in therapy you have to talk about your parents and your childhood. I think I like your approach better, if I understand it. It seems to make sense to me.

McCRADY. I'm glad I could clarify things for you. Keep asking me questions as we go along, and I'll do my best to keep explaining to you what and why I'm suggesting the things I do. Now, let's go back to your morning routine. Start with the time you get up.

GREEN. Well, as I told you last week, I am a really heavy sleeper, and I have this elaborate routine to make sure I do get up. I go to bed at 11:00 every night, read for about a half hour, and turn out the light. My first alarm goes off at 6:30, and the paperboy comes at 6:45.

McCRADY. Does the wake-up routine work for you, or do you end up going back to sleep after all the alarms, neighbors, and paperboys get you up?

GREEN. Sometimes it works, but sometimes I go back to sleep after everyone's gone. But if I get up on time, I still may be late for work. I'm just in a fog in the morning and can't seem to get going.

McCRADY. So sometimes you get up on time, but that doesn't really help you in getting to work on time?

GREEN. That's right. I just don't understand it.

McCRADY. Could you tell me more about how you feel when you first get up?

GREEN. I'm sleepy and seem to move very slowly. I've always been that way—that's not any different than it ever was.

McCRADY. Do you ever feel like you don't know where you are when you're first getting up or have no idea what day it is?

GREEN. Well, maybe when I first wake up, but I just lie there for a minute, and then I remember what I have to do that day.

McCRADY. Do you ever have trouble with your balance when you first get up?

GREEN. No, that never happens to me.
>   (*The questions about disorientation and ataxia [balance] are relevant to a diagnosis of hypersomnia disorder. Donald does not have symptoms consistent with hypersomnia. If he did, I would have referred him to a sleep lab for a formal evaluation, because about 85% of hyper-*

somnia cases seen in sleep disorder centers have a physical cause or contributing factor. A routine physical examination by an internist or general practitioner would be insufficient to diagnose such a disorder. Since he does not appear to have a primary sleep disorder, I can continue with more specific behavioral interviewing.)

McCrady. OK. What do you do after you get up?

Green. Well, I, ah, I go to the bathroom first. That usually takes me a while. I subscribe to a couple of auto mechanics magazines, and I read those while I'm in the bathroom. Sometimes the articles are really interesting. Anyway, then I shower and shave, and then I go to the kitchen to eat breakfast.

McCrady. What do you usually have?

Green. Usually just a cup of coffee and a couple of sweet rolls. I usually read the front section of the paper then. Then I brush my teeth and check to make sure everything's OK around the house. Then I leave.

McCrady. What kind of things do you check?

Green. Oh, you know, I make sure that all the windows are closed, that the oven and stove are off, that the pilot lights are burning, that all the lights are off—things like that.

McCrady. How long does all this take after breakfast?

Green. Not too long, but it varies. Sometimes after I leave I'm not sure if I turned off all the lights or something, so I go back to be certain.

McCrady. OK, that gives me a general idea of your usual routine. Does it vary on any mornings?

Green. No, not really.

McCrady. Good. I'd also like to know a bit about your commute, and your schedule first thing once you get to work.

Green. It takes me about a half hour to get to work. Usually the traffic's not too bad, but once in a while if there's an accident or something it'll take me longer. I used to leave the house an hour before I had to be at work, so that even if there was a tie-up I wouldn't be late. Now, I'm just happy if I'm not too late. Did you ask me something else too?

McCrady. Yes, I was interested in your schedule and routine when you first get to work.

Green. When I come in, I go past my supervisor's office, but I don't usually see him. His secretary, Miss Donahue, is really nice to me and always says "Good morning." I say hello to her, too, but we never talk much after that. I think she'd keep on talking if I ever stopped by her desk. When I'm late, though, she's usually not there, because she's already delivering the morning memos. Then I go to my office and review reports from the day before. If there were any problems, in pollution ratings or whatever, I have to go talk to the plant foreman who is responsible for each one. They get kind of angry when I say anything—that's definitely the worst part of my job.

> *(For a behavior therapist, defining the antecedents, consequences, and thoughts and feelings surrounding a problem is essential to developing a plan for change. I am using behavioral interviewing to look for specific details rather than the kind of global information Donald first gave when I asked about his routine.)*

MCCRADY. I think I'm beginning to get an image of what your morning is like. Often, some of the variations in a person's routine are also important to figuring out how to bring about change in a problem. So what I'd like to have you do for the next week is to begin to keep careful track of your morning routine. Let's put together a time log on which you can keep track of your daily activities. For now, I think you should include the time you get up, what devices you use to get up, and the time you spend on each part of your routine at home. Include your commuting time and then maybe a log of the first hours at work—where you are, who you see, and what you do. Also, you should mark down anything different that happens. I'd like you to fill it out each day. Keep the form with you as you go through your routine, and mark down each thing as you finish it. On your morning break at work, write down any additional things that happened. Does this make sense to you?

> *(By careful questioning, I've begun to get an idea of some of the factors that may be contributing to Donald's lateness. I suspect that he spends excessive time reading and engages in obsessional checking routines about the house. I also suspect that his eating and exercise habits may be contributing to his "logy" feeling in the morning. It sounds as though his lateness may be partially an avoidance of uncomfortable interpersonal situations at work—with the secretary and with the people Donald is supposed to work with. I suspect that he is minimizing the time devoted to certain activities and is unaware of any possible link between his lateness and the social situation at work. Therefore, to get a clearer picture of his routine, I need to develop a way to collect day-to-day information about his functioning. The Self-Recording Form for comfort-discomfort in various activities will provide a format for doing this.)*

I give Donald the Self-Recording Form for Daily Routine (see Figure 5.1), along with specific instructions for daily recording of his degree of comfort-discomfort. Donald looks over the form before commenting.

GREEN. This makes a *lot* of sense. Do you think it will really help?

McCRADY. I'm sure it will give us a better picture of the lateness problem. From there, we can begin to decide how to help you change it. Is it fair for me to assume that you want to go back to being on time for work?

GREEN. Absolutely. I like my job and want to keep it.

McCRADY. OK, I just want to be sure that we are working toward the same goal here. We talked about many of your other concerns last week, too, and before we run out of time today I'd like to review some of these other problems. We won't be able to go into each of them in the same detail as we did with the lateness, but I'd like to see if we can agree on the problem areas you'd like to work on during treatment. During the week, I'm going to pull together some questionnaires to use that will help me understand these problems better, and then we can develop plans for dealing with each of them. By the beginning of our fourth session I hope we can set fairly specific goals for each of these other problem areas. Then we'll agree on an initial number of sessions for treatment.

> *(As a behavior therapist, I want the client to participate fully in defining problems and setting goals for treatment. Treatment involves an explicit contract, either verbal or written, which includes specification of the goals of the treatment and expectations for the client and the therapist. With Donald, because he presents several rather major problems that encompass much of his life, I think a problem-specific focus is particularly important. If we do not define and agree on priorities in his treatment, it would be easy to jump from one area to another, without really effecting any significant changes in any area.)*

GREEN. OK, Doc.

McCRADY. It seems to me there were four other major problems you talked about in our first session. You spoke about feeling isolated, lonely, and uncomfortable around other people, and you seemed to have a rather negative view of yourself. You also said you were concerned about those catastrophes you imagine, and I think you mentioned a fear of barking dogs. Are these basically the other major things you're feeling unhappy about?

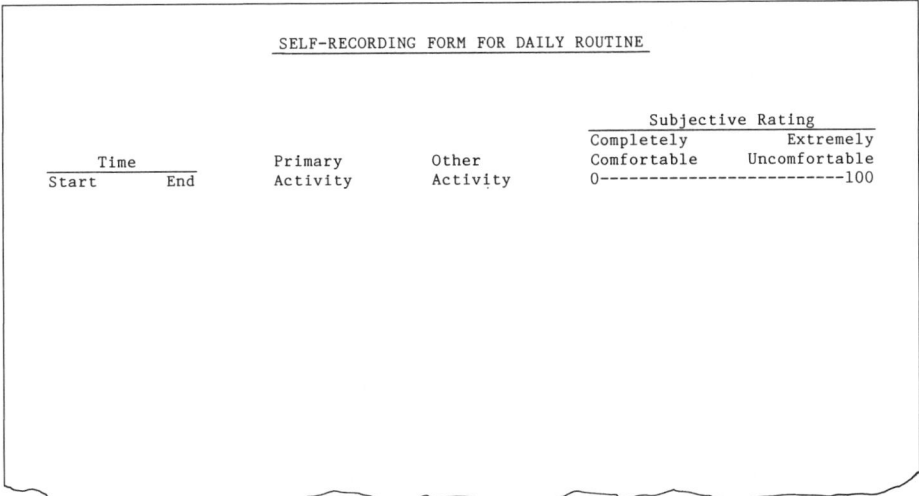

FIGURE 5.1 Self-recording form for daily routine

GREEN. Yes, but the barking of dogs isn't really a major problem. The other things you mention are real problems to me. Do you think I can actually change? I've been this way my whole life.

MCCRADY. I think you have a good chance of making some changes. Even with me, you seem to be able to talk easily and tell me about yourself. A good part of being able to get to know other people is being able to share something of yourself, and I think you already have some of what you need to do that. We must learn more about what makes it hard for you to share, and then I can try to help you learn how to do it. I can't promise that you'll become the life of the party, but you don't have to live out your life in a room by yourself, either.

> (I want to give Donald some feedback and a sense of hope about therapy, based on the information I have so far. As a behavior therapist, I try to reinforce positive behavior of the client, rather than maintaining the more neutral therapeutic posture characteristic of psychodynamically oriented therapists.)

MCCRADY. As you think about these problems, and the problem with lateness that brought you to see me, do you have any idea about what is most important for you to work on first? I'm not asking you to decide what's most important to you as a person, or to say what bothers you the most—just to say where you want to start.

GREEN. I *have* to start getting to work on time. If I can do that, I'll feel much better. I hate feeling like I'm so weak that I can't control something so simple. Maybe then we can talk about some of these other things, but I'm still not sure that there's any point to it. I think my personality is pretty well set. I'm worse than my father—I'm afraid I'll always be alone.

MCCRADY. OK, so our first goal will be to get your work schedule back on track. We'll begin to work on that and also to assess these other problems more carefully. I understand how hopeless you feel, because you've been this way a long time. But let's see how we do together and whether some of these problems begin to appear more manageable. We have to stop for today, but be sure you fill out your forms each day this week. We'll look at them together at our next session.

GREEN. Thanks, Doc.

Donald and I shake hands, and he bumps into the corner of a low table as he turns around to leave.

Session 3

Donald arrives early for our third session and comes into my office with a serious look on his face.

GREEN. I did those forms all week, Doc, and things aren't any better.

MCCRADY. That's OK, Donald. The forms are just to help us see the patterns that are keeping you in this habit of being late. Just writing things down won't change things very much.

GREEN. I guess I know that you didn't promise anything, but I kind of hoped things would change anyway. But let me show you what I did.

Donald hands me his filled-in report forms (for Thursday and Friday mornings, see Figure 5.2). For the next 20 minutes, we go over each day of his work week. Our appointments are on Wednesdays, so we review the week from Thursday to Wednesday. Thursday morning, Donald had gotten up on time, was ready to shower by the time the paperboy arrived, and left for work early. He arrived on time and was greeted warmly by Miss Donahue, who commented that she hadn't seen him in two weeks and tried to engage him in conversation. He went to his office and did solitary work for the first hour of the day. Thursday night there was a thunderstorm, and on

SELF-RECORDING FORM FOR DAILY ROUTINE

Time		Primary	Other	Subjective Rating	
Start	End	Activity	Activity	Completely Comfortable 0	Extremely Uncomfortable 100
THURS.					
6:30		GOT UP		15	
6:30	8:00	SHOWER, DRESS, EAT, CHECK HOUSE		15	
8:00		LEFT HOUSE		20	
8:30		ARRIVED AT WORK	SAW MISS D.		70
8:30	9:30	WORKED IN OFFICE		35	
FRI.					
6:30	6:45	GOT UP		15	
6:45	8:00	SHOWER, DRESS, EAT		15	
8:00	8:10	CHECK HOUSE (STORM)		20	
8:10		LEFT HOUSE		20	
8:15		RETURNED HOME			80
8:15	8:20	RECHECKED HOUSE		20	
8:20		LEFT AGAIN			
8:50		ARRIVED AT WORK	SAW MISS D		75
8:55	9:45	WORKED IN OFFICE		45	
9:45		TALKED TO FOREMAN			80

FIGURE 5.2 Example of Donald Green's self-recording form for daily routine

Friday morning Donald got up only when the paperboy came to the door. After breakfast he checked every electrical appliance in the house to be sure that nothing had been damaged by the storm. Five minutes after he left the house, he returned because he had forgotten to check the pilot lights on the stove (they were all on). He arrived at work about 20 minutes late but still was greeted by Miss Donahue, who told him how nice it was to see him two days in a row.

Monday morning was a disaster. Donald had received a new magazine in the mail and stayed up until midnight Sunday reading it. He was tired in the morning and went back to bed after the paperboy delivered the paper. When he finally did get up, 45 minutes late, he scanned two articles before he even showered. He decided to skip breakfast and left the house without checking anything. Ten minutes from the house, he realized that he had left his bedroom window open and returned. He then decided he should check the whole house, in case he had forgotten anything else, and ended up arriving at work more than an hour late. By then, Miss Donahue was not in sight, and he had missed most of the Monday morning engineers' meeting. Tuesday and Wednesday mornings, he got up when the paperboy arrived, spent only a few minutes reading and checking the house but longer showering and having breakfast, and arrived at work about 40 minutes late.

The objective information on the forms yielded several hypotheses about the nature of Donald's lateness. However, the comfort ratings on the forms for each activity provided even more information. Donald rated his interactions with Miss Donahue at 70 and 75, at the uncomfortable end of the scale, despite their brevity. He rated arrivals when he did not interact with Miss Donahue at 30, closer to comfort than discomfort. His discomfort at the engineers' meeting rated 90. In addition, his discomfort rating when he left in the morning without checking the house was 80, but it dropped to 20 after he returned and completed his checking ritual. If he checked before leaving, his discomfort ratings were also 20.

McCrady. Well, Donald, as we look these sheets over, a couple of things strike me. It looks as though you got pretty uncomfortable on those mornings when you ran into Miss Donahue and at that engineers' meeting. Can you tell me more about what makes those situations uncomfortable for you?

Green. I don't think Miss Donahue has much to do with my problem. I think that I just have trouble getting going in the morning.

McCrady. That may be so, but it does strike me that you are much more comfortable on days when you get to work and don't see her. Let's just try to explore this a little more. It is possible that she has nothing to do with your lateness, but that's what we're trying to do—to see if there are factors which contribute to your being late but which aren't immediately obvious. Besides, you have already said that you're pretty uncomfortable around people but would like to change that, so by talking about Miss Donahue and the meeting I can get a better understanding of what makes those situations so uncomfortable.

Green. I still don't think she's my problem, but I'll tell you that I feel very awkward around her. I never know what to say, and I know that she's never been married, so I think she wants to go out with me. She's nice, but I can't imagine going out on a date or kissing her or anything. I don't know if she really wants to go out with me. I don't know why she would—she's very stylish—always has her nails and hair done real nice. I'm not much to look at.

McCrady. So you do a lot of thinking about what she thinks of you, why she's talking to you, and you feel pretty tongue-tied? Is that a fair summary of what you're saying?

Green. Exactly.

McCrady. How about at the engineers' meeting—what kind of thoughts and feelings do you have there?

Green. I just hate those meetings. Each engineer is supposed to give a five-minute update on what he's doing. I get all sweaty and nervous before it's my turn and don't even hear half of what they say. Then I worry that someone will ask me a question and I won't know what they're talking about. By the time it's my turn, I'm a wreck. They all know it, which doesn't help much. Sometimes the chief engineer just skips me, and then I'm even more embarrassed. I know he does it just because I get so nervous.

McCrady. It sounds as though you do similar worrying in the meeting and with Miss Donahue. You worry so much about what other people think of you that it interferes with your own ability to think. It also sounds as though you get physically uncomfortable—is that right?

Green. Yeah, you're right, I shouldn't get so nervous all the time.

McCrady. I'm not trying to evaluate you, I'm just trying to describe what I think happens to you. It seems clear to me that you face some pretty uncomfortable situations every day at work, and some days are more uncomfortable than others. I could see how these situations would lead you to want to dawdle in the morning, but, as you said, we don't know yet if they are an important part of your being late.

GREEN. I notice that I spend a lot of time checking the house every day. As a homeowner, I think I should do these things—what would happen if there was a gas leak or something? I could lose everything, and innocent people would get hurt if the house exploded.

McCRADY. And I can see that the checking seems to take up a lot of time, especially on those days that you return to the house. Do you ever find anything out of place while you're checking?

GREEN. No, never. I'm pretty careful. Are you telling me not to check things any more?

McCRADY. No, Donald, I'm not trying to give you any instructions right now, just trying to see what's been happening. I notice that you rate yourself as pretty uncomfortable when you first get up in the morning. Is that discomfort the same as the discomfort about checking or those situations at work?

GREEN. No, not at all. In those other situations I feel real nervous inside. When I first get up, I just feel kind of lousy and tired, like I just can't get moving. I keep thinking that my bed feels so good, and there's nothing really to look forward to, nothing to get up for.

McCRADY. Can you describe your thoughts in the morning a little more?

GREEN. Well, I don't want to keep complaining all the time to you, but I don't think my life's very, well, you know, right. I'm over 40, no friends, no wife...I mean, look at me. I'm not much to look at. Sometimes it's just very hard to get up and face another day. There's nothing to look forward to, and it seems as though nothing will ever change. I guess I get pretty down on myself. I shouldn't complain so much—I have a good job and even have my own house.

McCRADY. It sounds as though you get to thinking about all the things you're dissatisfied with. That also makes it hard to want to get up.

GREEN. That's right.

McCRADY. It seems to me that we can sort out at least four different things that are contributing to your problems with getting to work on time. First, you've said that you're a heavy sleeper and always have been. You've handled that by relying on more and more external things to wake you up. Second, your unhappiness with many things in your life sometimes seems to slow you down in the morning. Third, you do lose a lot of time checking and rechecking things in the house, and sometimes that makes you late. And my hunch is that some of the things that make you uncomfortable at work also slow you down in the morning, like having to face people you don't feel comfortable with.

Does that sound like a fair summary of what we've talked about and what's on the sheets?

GREEN. Well, it sure does sound complicated. Do I have to change everything in my life before I can get to work on time again? That would be pretty hopeless.

McCRADY. No, I think we can tackle some of these things slowly and still help you with your schedule. I think the place to start with this is to just pick one thing that's responsible for making you late and try to make some changes in that. Then we can see what happens. . . . OK?

Donald nods in agreement.

McCRADY. Now let's shift gears for a few minutes. I want to give you some questionnaires to fill out to help me get a better picture of some of the other problems we discussed last week. I have several here that I'd like you to spend some time on this week. This first one is called the Thought Inventory. It was developed to help us understand the kinds of worries you have when you fantasize catastrophes. I just want you to fill out the second half, from question 23 on. The first half is more for people who are consistently afraid of one thing, which they try to avoid.

I give Donald the Thought Inventory, which describes many of the thoughts associated with rituals, as well as many irrational fears people have. To get a sense of the types of things he worries about, I ask him only to complete the section on irrational fears. The inventory asks a respondent to indicate what "unpleasant consequences" he or she is worrying about, such as "Contracting a serious disease," "Having a bad accident happen to me," and "An intruder breaking into my home, car, etc." (Steketee & Foa, 1985, p. 128).

GREEN (pointing to the form). So I should just answer this part?

McCRADY. Right. These other three questionnaires ask you about your feelings around other people and how you feel about expressing your feelings and opinions. I think filling them out will be pretty straightforward.

Next I give Donald the Social Avoidance and Distress Scale and the Fear of Negative Evaluation Scale, both developed by Watson and Friend (1949). These two questionnaires should give me a good picture of his thoughts about interpersonal situations. In addition, I give him the Assertiveness Inventory, which asks him to describe how likely he is to behave assertively in a variety of situations (Gambrill & Richey, 1975).

McCRADY. Finally, I'd like you to complete this questionnaire to help me understand better how you've been feeling in general. The instructions are here at the top.

I give Donald the last questionnaire, the Beck Depression Inventory, a simple self-report questionnaire that evaluates symptoms of depression. Although I do not think that Donald is clinically depressed, I believe it is important to evaluate his depression more fully (Beck, Rush, Shaw, & Emery, 1979).

GREEN. So you want me to fill all these out this week?
McCRADY. That's right. I also want you to keep using the Self-Recording Form to keep track of your morning routine. Don't feel that you have to change anything yet, because we want to be sure that we haven't missed anything major that's affecting you. Next week, we'll go over these questionnaires and your forms, and then we'll get a clear plan for treatment.
GREEN. OK, I'll see you then.

Sessions 2 and 3 have been crucial to my development of a behavioral formulation of Donald's presenting problems. The detailed interviewing has given me a clear picture of the variety of antecedents to his lateness problem, and I have provided him with the assessment tools I will use to evaluate this and his other problems. This data collection method is at the heart of the behavioral approach. I want Donald to feel fully involved in this, so he will become a cooperative partner in the change process. In the next session, I plan to provide him with detailed feedback about the problems and my proposed treatment plan. Normally I am able to do this by the end of the third session, because I would have begun the self-recording after Session 1 and the questionnaires after Session 2. However, even without these questionnaires, I have a fairly good idea of what has contributed to some of Donald's major problems and how I think they relate to one another. Between this session and the next, I want to develop a case formulation. In connection with this I will also prepare a problem list, a DSM-III-R diagnosis, and a plan for treatment for Donald.

Case Formulation

At this point, I have a fairly good picture of the problems Donald is experiencing and some hypotheses about the relationships among these problems. Donald's problems seem to include (1) behavioral deficits in terms of skills needed to interact with other people; (2) behavioral excesses in terms of his house-checking behavior; (3) cognitive problems, which include negative self-evaluative statements, anticipations of aversive consequences in a range of situations, and ruminative, distorted thoughts; (4) physiological problems with anxiety; and (5) problems with weight, eating habits (which I only infer at this point from his description of his breakfasts), and lack of exercise. It seems to me that Donald's lateness at work is related to several factors, including his heavy sleeping, social anxiety, general physical condition, and checking rituals. His social anxiety and lack of social skills contribute to his social isolation, which enhances his negative image of himself. I also think that his weight and general physical appearance are both a result of and a contributing factor to his social isolation.

A theme that seems to pervade much of his functioning is a fear of negative evaluation and a fear of criticism or punishment by others. This is most evident in his work situation; he is uncomfortable in social situations that require confrontation, or even extended conversations on his part. It also fits with his relatively isolated life-style, his few friends, and his solitary hobby of repairing cars. The "catastrophes" he imagines also seem consistent with this theme; the two he has described relate to the concept of doing something wrong and expecting to be caught or punished. His dreams are also consistent with this theme, with the major elements including fear of failure, looking foolish, or being punished. I do not think that this hypothesized experience of fear of negative evaluation occurs in all situations, but it does seem to occur across a range of situations. This formulation, which focuses on both specific problems and hypothesized themes that occur across a variety of situations, is similar to the approach that Turkat and Maisto (1985) take to the behavioral treatment of clients diagnosed as having personality disorders.

Although I do not focus much on the historical roots of clients' presenting problems, it seems clear that Donald's parents were poor models for positive social skills. His father was socially isolated, and his mother never appeared to express her feelings or desires directly. His memory of his par-

```
GREEN, DONALD

    1. Lateness at work
    2. Social anxiety
    3. Social skills deficits
    4. Social isolation
    5. Ruminative thoughts
    6. Negative self-image
    7. Fear of barking dogs
```

FIGURE 5.3
Problem list for Donald Green

ents suggests that they did little to enhance his feeling of being valuable or lovable. He describes his father as avoiding him and his mother as caring for him but providing no physical affection. His memories suggest that his father allowed little room for imperfection, and he reports being criticized or punished by his father for his mistakes.

Problem List. After completing my case formulation, I always develop a problem list for clients and establish a DSM-III-R diagnosis. The problem list provides a vehicle for weekly case notes and helps me keep my focus clear during treatment. Donald's initial problem list is shown in Figure 5.3.

DSM-III-R Diagnosis. Establishing a diagnosis is less consistent with a behavioral approach to assessment because it focuses primarily on symptoms and makes the assumption that clients have "disorders." Behavioral approaches focus instead on presenting problems, without attempting to decide whether they fit a pattern that suits a particular diagnostic label. However, diagnosis is important for communicating with other health-care professionals and for determining whether a client does have a diagnosable problem for which there is a known treatment of choice. Moreover, it is required for insurance purposes. My diagnostic formulation is based on the *Diagnostic and Statistical Manual of Mental Disorders* published by the American Psychiatric Association (see Figure 5.4). For Donald, the diagnosis is as follows:

Axis I: V71.09 No diagnosis or condition of Axis I.
Axis II: 301.82 Avoidant Personality Disorder, characterized by being easily hurt, having none or only one close friend, avoiding social or occupational activities that involve significant interpersonal contact, and being reticent in social situations for fear of saying something inappropriate.

Axis III: None.
Axis IV: Psychosocial Stressors: Work pressure.
Severity: 2-Mild
Axis V: Current Global Assessment of Functioning (GAF): 65
Highest GAF past year: 65

The other diagnoses I considered for Donald include hypersomnia, occupational problem (not attributable to mental disorder), and schizoid or schizotypal personality disorder. His sleep problems are not sufficiently severe to warrant a hypersomnia diagnosis, and it appears that his work problems are related to his problems with social avoidance and to a minor compulsive checking ritual. The other two personality disorder diagnoses I considered are more appropriate for clients who lack a desire for social interaction and who are aloof and withdrawn. Donald, in contrast, appears to want more interaction but is too uncomfortable to seek it out. It is important to note, however, that Morey's (1988) research suggests a large degree of overlap between the avoidant and schizoid personality disorder diagnoses, and many clients, such as Donald, present features of both.

The *Diagnostic and Statistical Manual of Mental Disorders*, third edition, revised (DSM-III-R) uses a multiaxial approach to diagnosis which assumes that a client must be assessed and understood along multiple dimensions of functioning. There are five "axes" for diagnosis:

Axis I: **Clinical Syndromes.** These represent acute emotional or behavioral problems for which people seek treatment.

Axis II: **Developmental Disorders and Personality Disorders.** These are problems that usually begin in childhood or the adolescent years and continue fairly unchanged into a person's adult life.

Axis III: **Physical Disorders and Conditions.** This axis allows the clinician to note any physical problems that might be relevant to the client's emotional or behavioral problems.

Axis IV: **Severity of Psychosocial Stressors.** This axis allows the clinician to indicate the amount of stress that the client has been experiencing in the last year. Ratings are from 1 (no stress) to 6 (catastrophic stress).

Axis V: **Global Assessment of Functioning.** For this axis, the clinician makes an overall rating (from 1 to 90) of the client's overall psychological, social, and occupational functioning.

FIGURE 5.4 DSM-III-R Axes for diagnosis of mental disorders

Plan for Treatment. My complete plan for Donald's treatment includes the following points:

1. Lateness at work
   a. A mild exercise program to increase the immediate positive value of getting up in the morning.
   b. Imagery techniques to increase the ability to get up without so many external agents.
   c. A response-prevention program to decrease the time involved with checking rituals.
   d. A social skills training program to enhance ability to talk with Miss Donahue without undue anxiety.
2. Social anxiety
   a. Relaxation training.
   b. Cognitive-restructuring techniques to increase positive self-statements about social interactions and to decrease fear of negative evaluations by others.
3. Social skills deficits
   a. Further role-playing to evaluate his social skills deficits.
   b. Social skills training, including the elements emphasized by Hollin and Trower (1988) as optimal components of social skills training, such as instruction, modeling, rehearsal, feedback, and homework.
   c. A specific emphasis on assertion skills, especially as related to work situations.
4. Social isolation
   a. Gradual exposure program to decrease social isolation.
   b. Some clarification of interests and identification of optimal settings for meeting people with similar interests.
5. Ruminative thoughts
   a. Monitoring for the appearance of any new "catastrophic thinking."
   b. Cognitive restructuring with exposure if any new ruminative patterns develop.
6. Negative self-image
   a. Treatment primarily through plans for dealing with social anxiety, social isolation, and social skills deficits, as well as exercise program.
7. Fear of barking dogs
   a. No treatment planned, unless Donald decides later that he wants help with this problem.

Session 4

At the beginning of this session, I collect Donald's questionnaires and Self-Recording Forms. After reviewing them and scoring them quickly, I ask a number of follow-up questions to obtain more detailed information about some of his responses. On the Beck Depression Inventory he scores a 7, which suggests that he is only mildly depressed. He endorsed items such as, "I am so sad or unhappy that it is very painful," "I feel that I won't ever get over my troubles," "I am disappointed in myself," "I am critical of myself for my weaknesses or mistakes," and "I have thoughts of harming myself but I would not carry them out." These answers are consistent with his self-presentation as being unhappy about his life situation.

The three measures related to social skills make the nature of some of his social-interpersonal difficulties clearer. On the Gambrill and Richey Assertiveness Inventory he reported that he rarely does things that require assertiveness. For example, he said he never asks others for favors, rarely expresses his feelings or opinions, and usually gives in to other people's requests or demands, even if he thinks they are unreasonable. This inventory also asks clients to rate how uncomfortable various situations would make them, and Donald indicated that he would experience a "fair amount" or "much" discomfort in almost all the situations. The only behaviors that did not make him very uncomfortable were such things as apologizing if he feels he is wrong or admitting his ignorance about something. His answers on the Social Avoidance and Distress Scale (SAD) and the Fear of Negative Evaluation Scale (FNE) indicate that he feels uncomfortable in many social situations and worries intensely about others' evaluations of him. His score of 24 on the SAD suggests an extreme degree of social avoidance (the mean on the SAD is 9.00, with a standard deviation of 8.07). He scores 25 on the FNE, also well above the mean of 15.47 (standard deviation of 8.62).

These questionnaires and the interviewing have given me a fair picture of Donald's problems in social situations. However, I also want to be able to observe how he interacts in different situations that involve other people. I decide to try some role-playing with him but to postpone that part of the assessment until we begin to work directly with his social discomfort.

On the Thought Inventory, he indicated that he worries most about being criticized or ridiculed by other people, being responsible for making a serious mistake, or ruining his reputation. He is relatively unconcerned about other types of catastrophes, such as illness, death, or accidents.

After discussing the results of the questionnaires with Donald and clarifying some of his answers, I ask him for his reaction to them.

McCRADY. You did a nice job with these questionnaires and the recording sheets. Did you have any thoughts as you went through them?
GREEN. They really got me thinking more and more about myself. These two (pointing to the FNE and the SAD) in particular seem to be made just for me. They describe exactly how I feel when I'm around other people.
McCRADY. I'm glad they seem so relevant to you. Now let's take a little time to agree on some goals for the treatment. Let's try to make the goals as specific as we can for each of the problems you'd like some help with. I'd also like to tell you a little about some of the things I think we will do during treatment.
GREEN. OK, Doc.

After some discussion, Donald and I agree on an Initial Treatment Contract (see Figure 5.5) which embodies several elements that are important to a behavioral approach. First, it is time-limited. I do not expect to complete treatment with Donald in ten sessions, but breaking down the treatment into smaller segments emphasizes the need to evaluate progress in some regular fashion. Second, the contract sets specific, small goals, the ones I think can be achieved in a relatively brief time. This should enhance Donald's feelings of self-efficacy about change. Also, the goals are specific, so we will know if we have achieved them or not. And the goals are directed toward the major problems Donald presented.

Up to this point, Donald and I have spent most of the session discussing the questionnaires, the treatment contract, and the treatment goals. I leave some time at the end to begin to implement the plan for dealing with the problem of lateness at work.

McCRADY. Now we can begin to put into effect the plan for dealing with your lateness. I think the place to start is with helping you develop some new techniques for getting up on time and having something to do right away that makes it more worthwhile for you to get up—something you can really look forward to in the morning.
GREEN. What do you have in mind?
McCRADY. Two things. First, I'd like to see if we can help you become more reliant upon yourself to get up. We can use some imagery techniques to help you learn to get up without all the help from neighbors and paperboys. And, I'd like to see you develop some kind of mild exercise program for when you get up.
GREEN. That doesn't sound like me—I'm not a weightlifter or long distance runner—look at me.

INITIAL TREATMENT CONTRACT

1. We will meet for ten sessions, then evaluate our progress.

2. The goals of treatment for Donald are:

    a. To begin arriving at work at the scheduled time.

    b. To be able to carry on brief conversations with people at work without becoming excessively anxious.

    c. To begin to learn how to give directions to people at work.

    d. To improve how he feels by exercising.

3. Donald agrees that his responsibilities in treatment are to come to scheduled appointments on time, to call at least 24 hours ahead if he has to change or cancel an appointment, to pay bills on time, and to do homework assignments to the best of his ability.

4. Dr. McCrady's responsibilities are to be at scheduled appointments on time, to provide the most effective treatment that she is aware of for Donald's problems, to be available for emergencies, and to arrange appropriate coverage when she is not available.

Signed:_____   _____
         Donald Green   Barbara McCrady, Ph.D.

         _____
              Date

FIGURE 5.5 Initial treatment contract for Donald Green with Barbara McCrady

McCrady. I don't mean that. What I was remembering was how in our first session you mentioned how much you liked walking tours on vacations. You really lit up when you talked about them. What about a two- or three-mile walk each morning?

Green. I don't know—I have enough trouble getting up. Won't that just make it worse? I'll have *more* to worry about instead of less.

McCrady. Maybe, but tell me how you feel about walking.

Green. You're right—I like walking. When I'm on vacation, I do get up early and take walks. It's quiet then, and no one's around, and you can notice everything.

McCrady. All right, then, can we agree on beginning by working out a walking program and trying the imagery techniques?

Green. I guess.

McCrady. I also suspect that we'll have to develop some kind of program to help you get your checking of the house under control, but let's hold off on that for now.

Green. OK, maybe I can just cut that down. I have never really thought about how much time I waste doing that.

McCrady. Well, don't try to take on too much at once. Let's start with the plan for the walking program. Is there a walk you'd enjoy that originates near your house?

Green. Yes, there's a park about a half-mile away. I could walk there and walk around the park for a while.

McCrady. Let's set a small goal for starters—how about just walking to the park and back?

Green. That'd be no problem—it would only take me about 20 minutes.

McCrady. Can you make changes in your wake-up routine to get up 20 minutes earlier?

Green. I'm not sure, but I'll try.

McCrady. Well, see how this works out. Next week we'll begin to work on some imagery to help you with getting up in the morning without so many external aids. Keep track on your Self-Recording Form of the walking you do, along with everything else you've been recording.

Green. OK. You know, I'm beginning to feel pretty hopeful about this therapy. It seems like things really could get better.

Sessions 5–12

Now that I've given some specific examples of how I work as a behavior therapist, I will shift to a more narrative format to describe most of the remainder of the treatment. My approach remains fairly consistent throughout—working at a very detailed level to specify actual behavior, thoughts, and feelings; reinforcing progress; and trying to effect changes in small steps. Each session begins with a review of homework and any important events of the week and ends with the assignment of new homework.

In the next several sessions, we focus on Donald's lateness problems at work. He takes to the exercise program immediately and complies faithfully. Over the next six weeks he gradually increases his walks to three miles each morning.

I then introduce some imagery or covert rehearsal techniques to help Donald get up without so many external aids. I have him sit back in his chair, close his eyes, and imagine his alarm clock. First he imagines himself setting the alarm for the time he wants to get up in the morning. Then he imagines the clock again, with the morning time displayed, and then I have him imagine the clock ringing. The imagery continues with his turning off the clock, getting up immediately, and feeling pleased with himself for getting up so easily.

Donald becomes quite anxious when I initially have him close his eyes. He cannot keep them closed and begins to breathe rapidly and to perspire. I have to discontinue the covert rehearsal to discuss his discomfort. He indicates that he feels foolish with his eyes closed and is certain I am looking at him and thinking about how stupid he looks and how stupid his problems are. I try to reassure him by telling him that my main concern is to help him get through this problem. Then I tell him that I am not sure this approach will work, so I also have some anxiety about it. This revelation surprises him; he says he thought that I was always completely self-confident. It helps him become more comfortable with the covert rehearsal procedure, and then he can go through it, though he still is somewhat anxious.

We rehearse this technique six to eight times during the session and I assign it as homework, to be practiced at least three times a day, with the last rehearsal when he goes to bed. We make no immediate change in his use of external aids.

Although in the first week of the rehearsal Donald notices no changes in his awakening pattern, by the second week he begins to awaken when the alarm goes off. In Session 7, he decides to tell his neighbor and the paperboy not to call him or wait for him any more, because he feels confident that he can get up without them. However, he continues to set the three alarm clocks and place them at strategic points around the house. Then, in the first week Donald tries to get up without the neighbor and paperboy, he oversleeps the first two work days and skips his morning walk. He is surprised at how much he misses the walk. After that, he is able to get up when the alarm goes off.

Other reasons for Donald's lateness still have to be addressed, however. After Session 5 he tries to eliminate his checking rituals on his own and is successful for three days, but he is extremely anxious when he does not return to check things and cannot sustain this pattern. I address the checking ritual directly in Session 7, and we spend some time identifying its behavioral and cognitive components. His checking is rather predictable—he would check that all the windows are closed and locked, the faucets are all turned off, the pilot lights on the stove and oven are lit, all the lights are off, the heat is turned down, and the doors are locked. Once he gets in the car, he would begin worrying that he had forgotten to check something. Sometimes he could remember what he had checked and could continue on to work; other times he could not reassure himself and would return to the house.

The treatment of obsessive-compulsive rituals, including checking, is discussed by Steketee and Foa in David Barlow's (1985) handbook on the treatment of psychological disorders. They emphasize that the most effective treatments include exposure to the feared object or situation, combined with response prevention, in which the client is not allowed to engage in the ritualistic behavior. The response-prevention procedure usually results in high client anxiety at the beginning, with the anxiety gradually reducing over time. The procedure is based on the learning principle of extinction. Because of the high client anxiety associated with the procedure, response prevention usually needs to be done under the direct supervision of a therapist.

It is difficult to determine how to implement response prevention for Donald unless I make many trips to his home, which is impractical and probably would elicit a great deal of anxiety from him. I ask Donald about checking in general, and, as I expect, he checks in other situations as well. Therefore I arrange a situation at my office that will allow us to implement a response-prevention program. Since I am seeing Donald in the evening, the kitchen in my building is not being used. Before he comes in, I make sure that both coffee makers and all the lights are on, the faucet is dripping, and one burner of the stove is still hot. We make it Donald's responsibility to turn off the coffee makers and lights, shut the faucet, and check the stove and oven. After he does that, he is to come to my office for our appointment.

For the first part of the session, Donald discusses his thoughts about the kitchen and his desire to again check on what he has already checked. We discuss ways he can talk to himself about the desire to check, such as, "It's

OK to be anxious, I don't have to do anything about it," or "It will be just fine even if I don't check." I have him rate his anxiety at five-minute intervals on a 0-100 scale, similar to the subjective comfort-discomfort rating on the Self-Reporting Form. When we graph the anxiety ratings, we see that in each session his anxiety peaks and then decreases. We also construct a list of situations in which he has checked and arrange them in hierarchical order, from least anxiety-provoking to most anxiety-provoking. Between sessions, I have Donald use response prevention on his own, beginning with less difficult checking situations, such as turning off the lights in his office and locking his car, and gradually moving to more difficult situations. We schedule two response-prevention sessions each day. He uses the back of his daily recording sheet to write down his anxiety rating at five-minute intervals.

After three sessions of response prevention in the office, Donald is ready to try something at home. I begin by having him check everything in the house once and then agreeing that he can recheck anything except the lights, the least difficult item for him to check at home. After a few days his anxiety about checking the lights begins to decrease, and we gradually add other items he is to avoid checking. By Session 12, I assign him to implement the response-prevention program for all checking when he leaves in the morning. We agree that he will call me if he feels that he must return to the house. He has two days the first week where his anxiety is very high, and he calls both mornings. We deal with the anxiety on the phone as we had in the office, and after that he is able to resist the impulse to return to check.

The combination of imagery techniques, exercise program, and response prevention to deal with the checking is effective in decreasing Donald's lateness. This is evident in a graph we have been constructing during our sessions which shows his discomfort rating on arriving at work, his discomfort on leaving home, and his record of being late getting to work (see Figure 5.6). We get the data from the Self-Reporting Forms he has been filling out. However, his discomfort level is still high when he arrives at work, and I am concerned that he will begin to be late again as an avoidance response to the uncomfortable situations at work.

Sessions 13 and 14

At the beginning of Session 13, we review Donald's progress with the lateness problem. We look at the graphs of discomfort ratings we have been constructing each week and discuss his feelings about his progress.

174 BEHAVIOR THERAPY

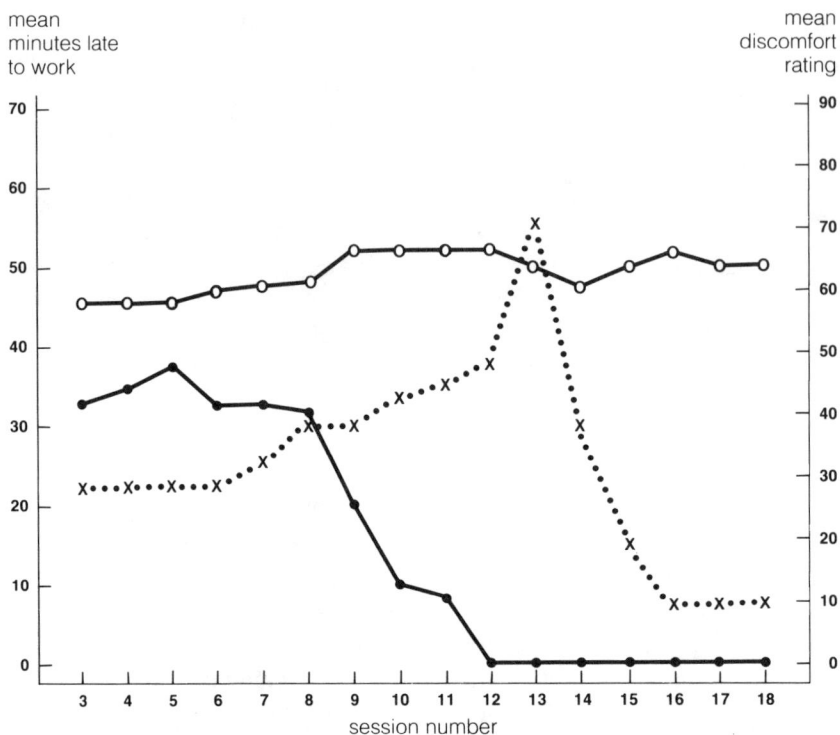

FIGURE 5.6 Graph of lateness and discomfort ratings for Donald Green

McCrady. It looks as though you've made good progress toward being on time for work. How are you feeling about it?

Green. I guess I feel OK. My supervisor seems happy that I'm on time, and I like it that I can get up and out of the house when I want to.

McCrady. So do you feel as if this problem's pretty well resolved?

Green. I guess so, although I don't feel very confident about it yet.

McCrady. That's understandable—you were late for three years and have only been getting to work on time for a couple of weeks. We'll keep working on the imagery, your exercise, and watching the checking for a while. But there's something else that might be keeping you uncomfortable. I've noticed that your discomfort ratings when you get to work are still pretty high.

Green. Yeah, I noticed that too.

McCrady. It seems to me that your feelings when you're around people may be making it difficult for you at work. Remember that another of

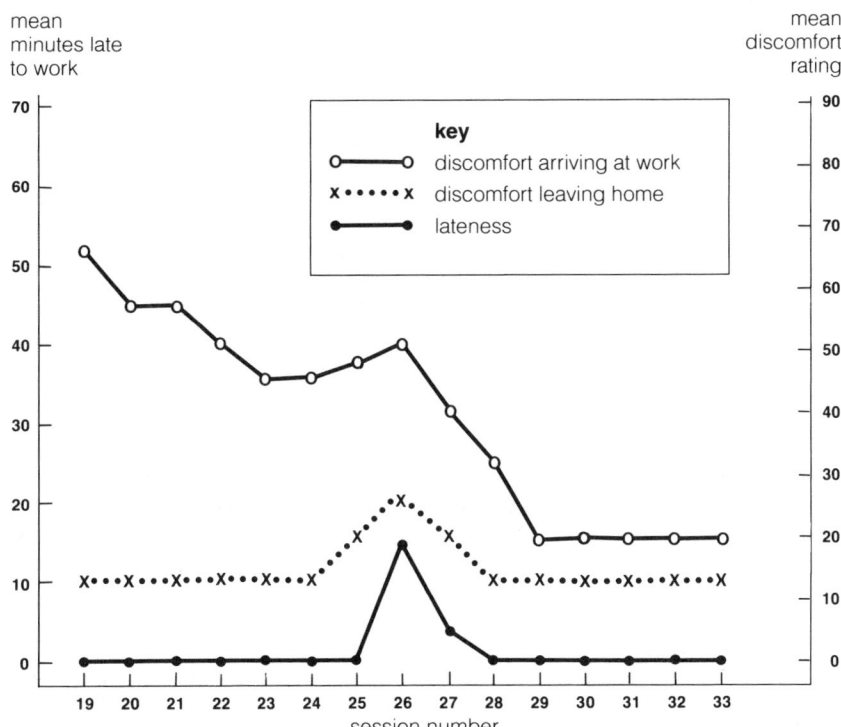

the goals we set was to help you learn some ways to interact with other people more comfortably than you do now.
GREEN. I was wondering when you were going to get around to that.
MCCRADY. Is it something you've been thinking about for a while now?
GREEN. Uh-huh.
MCCRADY. Why didn't you ask me about it?
GREEN. Well, I figured you knew what you were doing, and . . . .

Donald hesitates and looks at the ceiling, clearly uncomfortable.

GREEN (continuing). I was afraid that now that you know me better, you've decided that there is no point in trying to help me with people.
MCCRADY. You mean that you thought I had decided you were hopeless or something?
GREEN. I guess so.

Donald looks at his hands, obviously embarrassed.

McCrady. Are there things I've said or done that made you decide I thought you were hopeless?

Green. I guess just your attitude—you're always nice to me and encouraging me, like I'm pitiful or something. And I don't even think you like me.

> (Donald has just demonstrated the way his thinking and anxiety inhibit him with other people. He had tried to read my mind and had concluded something quite erroneous—that I thought he was hopeless—and then he was acting on that belief. As his therapist, I can help him see what he does, which should set the stage for beginning to deal with his social anxiety. I also think I should be fairly careful of Donald's feelings; my sense is that he can be hurt easily and doesn't recover from it very well. So my task is to help him see the irrational nature of his thinking and also to support him. There is an awkward aspect of this conversation, because I don't feel close to Donald in the way I do with some clients, and I don't want to give him false feedback about my personal feelings.)

McCrady. Let's go back a few sessions, Donald, to when you filled out those questionnaires about social situations. I remember that you told me you felt as though they were written just for you—they described your feelings so well.

Green. Uh-huh.

Donald isn't even looking at me at this point.

McCrady. I think what you've done with me is just what you described in the questionnaires. You started reading my mind, without any definite information, and came to some conclusions about how I was thinking and feeling without even checking it out with me. It sounds as though you've been making yourself miserable about something that's not even true!

Green. So I guess it's my fault?

McCrady. No, not really your fault. You've gotten into this pattern of expecting the worst from other people and avoiding dealing with them, so you don't have to hear what you're afraid they're going to say. It seems like a pattern you learned a long time ago—neither of your parents seemed to express their feelings to other people much at all. So I'm not trying to *blame* you, but I do want you to see how your thinking puts you into these unhappy situations. If you start to become aware of how you do this, then you can make a choice to learn to think differently.

GREEN. I don't know if that's possible.

MCCRADY. It's difficult, but something that I think you have the ability to do. You've made a lot of progress already, and with difficult problems. There's no reason you should be unable to change.

GREEN. Well, I don't know.

MCCRADY. To me, you still seem to be kind of uncomfortable and unhappy.

GREEN. I guess so.

MCCRADY. I can't read *your* mind, either, but is it because I haven't said anything about my feelings about you?

GREEN (looks away). Um.

MCCRADY. Well, let me try to answer you. I like working with you—you have a lot of courage, you've talked about things that obviously are hard or embarrassing for you to bring up, and you've really worked hard to make changes. I don't feel as though I know you real well, but my sense is that you have a lot of warm feelings and creative thoughts kind of locked up inside you. I'd like to help you be able to share more of yourself with me and with other people.

Donald sits up a bit straighter and finally looks at me again.

GREEN. You really feel that way about me?

MCCRADY. Absolutely.

GREEN. I can't believe that you actually like me. You've got so much going for you, and I'm such a blob.

MCCRADY. You're doing it again—thinking negatively about yourself. Let's begin to look at how you get your thinking into these negative cycles.
(This has been a very uncomfortable conversation for both of us, but I think it will be critical in helping Donald begin to deal with his problems with people.)

For the remainder of Session 13 and part of Session 14, we discuss the concept of cognitive distortions. I give Donald a copy of Burns's (1980) list of these distortions (see Figure 5.7). We start by looking at the list and trying to identify which types of distortions Donald used when he decided that I think he is hopeless, interpersonally. He says that he was (1) "disqualifying the positive" by focusing on one aspect of my behavior that he thought was negative but ignoring the positive aspects of my interactions with him, (2) "jumping to conclusions" by making an interpretation of my thinking without asking me about it ("mind reading"), and (3) engaging in "emotional reasoning" in that he felt hopeless and concluded that therefore it was true that he was hopeless.

After discussing these cognitive distortions that Donald has about our interaction, I give him as homework the task of identifying the distortions he experiences when he gets to work each day. He is to write these down on the back of his daily Self-Recording Form.

---

1. **All-or-nothing thinking.** Seeing things in black-and-white categories.

2. **Overgeneralization.** Viewing a single negative event as a pattern of defeat.

3. **Mental filter.** Picking a single negative detail and dwelling on it exclusively.

4. **Disqualifying the positive.** Rejecting positive experiences by insisting that they "don't count."

5. **Jumping to conclusions.** Making negative interpretations of equivocal events.
   a. *Mind reading.* Arbitrarily concluding that someone dislikes you.
   b. *The fortune teller error.* Anticipating that you will not succeed.

6. **Magnification (catastrophizing) or minimization.** Exaggerating the importance of things or inappropriately minimizing your good features and others' faults.

7. **Emotional reasoning.** Assuming that your negative feelings are correct.

8. **Should statements.** Motivating yourself with shoulds and shouldn'ts, musts and oughts.

9. **Labeling and mislabeling.** Attaching negative labels to yourself.

10. **Personalization.** Seeing yourself as the cause of events which in reality are not your fault.

FIGURE 5.7   Definitions of cognitive distortions. (Adapted from D.D. Burns's *Feeling Good: The New Mood Therapy* (New York: William Morrow, 1980.)

Session 14 is also our tenth treatment session, when our Initial Treatment Contract expires. I bring that up with Donald, and we review the goals we had set at the beginning of therapy. Donald and I agree that he has met his first goal, being on time for work, and that he does feel better when he takes his daily walks. It is clear that we have not made progress on the other two goals (carrying on brief conversations at work without excessive anxiety, and learning how to give directions). We decide to contract for an additional 15 sessions, with the following goals for Donald:

1. To be able to carry on brief conversations with people at work without becoming excessively anxious.
2. To be able to give directions to people at work, when appropriate.
3. To be more comfortable in the weekly engineers' meeting.
4. To get involved in some activity or situation outside of work where he could meet people.
5. To develop skills to carry on conversations with people without excessive anxiety.
6. To decrease negative and distorted thinking about people's opinions of him, and to increase his positive thinking about social interactions.

I ask Donald about his fear of barking dogs, and he again says that he does not want to bother with that. I also ask him if he has begun to imagine any catastrophes, but none were concerning him at that time.

Sessions 15–19

In the next five sessions, we do intensive work on Donald's cognitive distortions. His daily log of thoughts at work is helpful in describing in more detail the ways he makes himself uncomfortable. I teach him a simple technique to deal with this kind of thinking. First, he is to use his discomfort as a signal that he is probably thinking in a distorted way. Second, he is to identify what he is thinking. Third, he is to assign the thought to one or more of Burns's categories. Fourth, he is to generate an alternative thought that will allow him to feel more comfortable. We first use this technique, writing down each of the steps, on situations that had occurred during the past week. As homework, he is to use the same technique at the end of the day to analyze one situation that has made him uncomfortable during the day. Finally, he is to use this technique at least once a day.

Cognitive restructuring is difficult for Donald, and he is only partially successful. I estimate that his anxiety is so high that it inhibits his ability to use cognitive skills. Therefore, in Session 18, I introduce him to progressive relaxation. I have Donald close his eyes and sit back in the chair, and then I give him systematic instructions to tense and then relax different muscle groups in his body. I include instructions on breathing techniques to facilitate relaxation. The relaxation instructions take about 20 minutes, and Donald is able to relax fairly well. His discomfort with evaluation inhibits his relaxation somewhat, because he worries about what I think of how he is doing, but this is not a major factor. I assign the homework of practicing relaxation twice a day. We repeat the relaxation process during Session 19, and he is to continue to practice it at home.

Sessions 20–24

These sessions represent a period of successful work with Donald. He learns the relaxation technique well and begins to apply it at work. Once he is able to relax more, he can use some of the cognitive-restructuring techniques that he was less successful with previously.

We then construct a hierarchy of increasingly difficult interpersonal situations. These include brief conversations with Miss Donahue, sitting with other people at lunch, talking to people in the halls and at the company picnic, giving directions to people who work under him, and meeting new people. We role-play a number of these situations so that I can begin to get an idea of how he handles them, and then we practice how to handle the least difficult situation—the conversations with Miss Donahue.

When we role-play a situation, we first discuss what he could say, and then I pretend to be Donald and Donald pretends to be the other person, to give him a model of how to handle the situation. Then he tries out the behavior himself, with me taking the role of the other person. I then give him feedback about how he does, and he tries again. As homework, he is to rehearse each situation at home three times (to his mirror) and then try it out at work. By the end of Session 24, he is able to chat briefly with Miss Donahue in the morning, without any particular discomfort, and is sitting with other people at lunch. We have begun some specific practice with assertiveness, to help him in giving directions to employees, but he has not yet tried this skill out.

Sessions 25–29

During these sessions we continue the role-playing and cognitive restructuring. Donald has begun to try to give instructions to foremen and has encountered a fair amount of negative feedback from them. Upset by these reactions, he has begun to feel hopeless again about being able to change. We discuss how he is thinking about the foremen's reactions, and we identify several types of distorted thinking. I emphasize that he cannot control how other people react, and therefore he will not always get the results he wants when he is assertive. He needs to focus more on how he feels when he does and does not speak out, rather than on whether or not others are cooperative. I also suggest that he has the right to feel angry at them for reacting negatively, because his instructions are not unfair or excessive. This restructuring seems to help him. However, he is late for work two days during this time period (see Figure 5.6).

We also begin to focus directly on the engineers' meeting. Initially, I had Donald practice his relaxation skills during the meeting and focus on his cognitive distortions. This decreased his anxiety somewhat, but he still spent much of the meeting dreading when he would be asked to speak. We finally decide to have him ask if he can give his report at the beginning of the meeting, and he rehearses his speaking about it with the chief engineer. When he finally is able to make this request, although with considerable anxiety, the chief engineer is quite receptive. Donald continues to experience some anxiety before he speaks, but he is able to relax after he has spoken and finds the rest of the meeting less uncomfortable.

Although Donald is making a good deal of progress at work, his social life continues to be limited to his weekly dinner with Jim and Mary. I bring up the idea that, in order to feel less lonely, he needs to take some risks to meet people in other settings. He feels very uncomfortable with the idea but continues to express his desire to have a "normal" life. Therefore we begin to brainstorm where he might be able to meet people. Donald quickly says that he does not want to go to bars, he does not know how to dance, and he is not athletic. I observe that he is engaging in pretty negative thinking again and ask him to try to think about things that he likes instead.

We use brainstorming techniques to identify possible activities or places where Donald might meet people. In brainstorming, the client is encouraged to think of a range of ideas without censoring any ideas, and I write these down as we talk. Donald's final list includes: house tours, nature lectures, hiking club, adult education classes, volunteer work, Big Brothers, auto collectors clubs, square-dancing classes, chess clubs.

By Session 29, Donald has investigated some of these activities and decides to do some volunteer work at the local Boys' Club, where he can teach boys some of what he knows about auto repairs and restoration. I am concerned that this activity will not put him in contact with adults, and especially not with adult women, but since he is quite enthusiastic about the program, I do not want to discourage him.

We also review the treatment contract again, since we have completed 15 more sessions. Though Donald has met almost all of his goals, he still feels limited in carrying on conversations and is just beginning to involve himself in an outside activity. Therefore we contract for three more sessions to attempt to achieve these last two goals. I also decide to space these sessions at two-week intervals, to begin to prepare Donald for termination from treatment.

Sessions 30–32

Donald spends most of each of the last three sessions reporting on events at work and at the Boys' Club. We continue to discuss how to handle some work situations and talk about his volunteer work at the Boys' Club, which turns out to be extremely satisfying. His expertise with cars makes him an instant hit with the boys. He takes a car that he has purchased for restoration to the club, and they work on it together. A number of other adults, volunteers and staff, also are interested, and Donald begins to interact with them. Because they all want to help the boys, conversation with these adults seems easy for Donald.

At session 32, we review the progress Donald has made through treatment. He reports that he feels much better about himself and is enthusiastic when he gets up in the morning. He is getting to work on time and is interacting with the people at work. He has to deliberately use the relaxation and cognitive-restructuring techniques, especially in the engineers' meeting and with the foremen, and he occasionally falls into negative thinking. He is excited by his volunteer work. Though Donald still is living alone and has not made any progress toward meeting women or dating, he decides that he is ready to discontinue treatment and see how things go for a while. We schedule one more session to discuss termination. I give him the four major questionnaires that we had used at the beginning of treatment and ask him to complete them again as a way of formally evaluating his progress.

TERMINATION OF THE THERAPY

Termination in behavior therapy is designed to maximize the ability of clients to apply what they have learned and the probability that they will maintain the gains they have made in the therapy. Much of therapy can be considered preparation for termination, because it focuses on teaching a skill and then applying it in the client's real world. My intent in terminating therapy is to help my clients consolidate what they have learned and to improve their ability to continue to use these skills. As a guide for termination, I use the relapse prevention model first proposed by Marlatt and Gordon (1985) as a way to deal with addictive behaviors. This termination process includes several specific elements.

1. Instead of abruptly ending the treatment, I spread out the last few sessions so the client has more opportunity to apply what he or she has learned, as contact with me becomes less frequent.

2. I schedule some follow-up sessions after the end of the regular therapy. These sessions are sometimes called "booster" sessions, but I prefer to think of them as a way to review and consolidate progress and to identify any new problems before they become major or continuing problems.

3. I help the client identify the major changes that have been made and what the client considers most important to maintaining these changes.

4. I make a formal evaluation of the client's progress by reviewing the data collected during treatment and readministering any formal assessment devices.

For Donald, the last session of his regular treatment is Session 23.

McCrady. Last week you said you felt ready to stop treatment.
Green. Well, yes. I feel much better, and I think I can use what you've taught me. I don't want to keep depending on you every time I have a problem.
McCrady. I agree that you've made tremendous changes. I think you've really used therapy well—bringing up problems, trying out the techniques we've worked on here, talking about things that are pretty uncomfortable to discuss.
Green. I'm going to miss seeing you.
McCrady. I do appreciate that, Donald, and one thing I like to do is to schedule a couple of follow-up sessions to see how you're doing and if there is anything else you want to discuss. Usually my clients find these follow-ups helpful, but I must admit that I have a selfish reason to schedule them as well—I want to see what happens with you later.
Green. I like that idea a lot. When will I see you again?
McCrady. Let's schedule our first follow-up for a month from now. If all is going well, I'll see you next in three more months, and then six months after that.

GREEN. OK.

MCCRADY. For the rest of the session today, I'd like to spend some time discussing what you think of the therapy, what things were most helpful, and what you think is most important for you to do to keep the positive changes going.

GREEN. Well, this was very different from what I expected. As I said before, I thought that I'd lie on a couch and talk a lot, and you wouldn't say much. I guess I was surprised when I saw you, because you're not only a woman but you look pretty young. But I like how you work—everything made a lot of sense to me, and I felt like you respected me. I mean, I did get embarrassed, but then I always do—or at least, I always used to!

MCCRADY. I hope that's a thing of the past!

GREEN. Well, maybe not completely, but it is a lot better.

MCCRADY. It sounds as though you like the approach we took. Of all the things we did, which ones seem most important to you now?

GREEN. I liked the role-playing a lot. Sometimes when I'm getting uncomfortable now I can picture you in my mind, asking me how I could handle the problem, and then I see us role-playing and that helps. I don't use the relaxation stuff too much now, but it's nice to know how to use it. I like the walking—it gives me a lot of energy and starts the day out better. And I guess the cognitive distortions list is helpful, although I still feel pretty foolish when I use it and see what I'm doing to myself.

MCCRADY. So, some of the specific techniques, like the cognitive restructuring and role-playing, are helpful and you still use them, at least in your imagination, but others aren't so important now.

GREEN. That's right.

MCCRADY. Do you find self-recording helpful?

GREEN. Not so much now, but it sure helped you figure out what was wrong at the start.

MCCRADY. I like to think that it helped *us* figure that out! Anything else we did that was important to you?

GREEN. Not really. You did help me a lot, though. I feel better about myself in general now—I just have more confidence about things, and I haven't thought about any catastrophes at all.

MCCRADY. I think that's another sign of the progress you've made. Now let's look at your latest answers on the questionnaires, to see what they can tell us.

Donald hands me the four questionnaires, and I score them. His score on the Beck Depression Inventory is down to a 2. On the Fear of Negative Evaluation Scale he scores 15, which is just at the mean for that scale, and on the Social Avoidance and Distress Scale he scores 14, still somewhat above the mean but much improved from his initial score. On the Gambrill and Richey Assertiveness Inventory, he rates his discomfort as lower in most situations but still describes himself as unlikely to be assertive in several circumstances. Overall, the questionnaires reflect progress for Donald, though some discomfort and difficulty with social situations persist.

McCrady. It seems that the way you've answered these questionnaires goes along with the way you've been feeling—much better, even though you still get uncomfortable or uncertain of yourself.
Green. That's what I thought when I was filling them out.
McCrady. One other thing I'd like to do today—let's see if we can make a list of things that would be warning signs that your old problems might be coming back. Can you think of any specific occurrences that should tell you things are going wrong?
Green. If I started being late for work again, that would be one bad sign. And if I stopped going to help at the Boys' Club, that would be another.
McCrady (writing these down). Anything else you can think of?
Green. I'm not sure.
McCrady. What about if you started getting into a lot of negative thinking again?
Green. That absolutely would be a bad sign.
McCrady. OK, then, I'll put that on the list. What about any of your patterns of behavior at work—like eating alone, or doing work rather than assigning it to the foremen?
Green. I guess those wouldn't be very good signs either. You might as well add them to the list.
McCrady. OK. And, how about the daily walks—are they important enough to put down here?
Green. Yes, I didn't think of them, but I can't imagine not taking them.
McCrady. OK, then, do you think this list is complete enough now?
Green. Yes, I think so.
McCrady (handing him the list). Think of this as a list of warning signals —if any of them starts happening, you need to take immediate action.
Green. What do you mean?

McCrady. Let's talk about that. The first immediate action would be just to notice that one of these things is happening, and then you would need to ask yourself why it is happening. Then you can remember the skills you've learned in therapy and see which ones will help you get back on track. Let's try an example. Say you cut back on the number of hours you are spending at the Boys' Club.

Green. I wouldn't even want to think about that, but OK.

McCrady. I wouldn't either—you seem to be enjoying it so much. But let's just pretend for a minute.

Green. OK.

McCrady. What might be some reasons for you to cut back on your time at the club?

Green. I'd probably start thinking that someone there didn't like me—you know, like those catastrophes I used to imagine.

McCrady. OK, how could you go about handling that kind of thinking?

Green. I'd have to figure out if it was true or not, or if I was using one of those distortions in thinking again.

McCrady. Sounds like a good plan, but what if it doesn't work?

Green. Could I call you?

McCrady. Sure, that's always a possibility. Anything else you could do?

Green. I'm not sure.

McCrady. What about trying to talk to the other person to see if you're mind reading or not?

Green. That would be pretty hard for me to do, but it's an idea.

McCrady. The most important thing is to take the approach that it's a problem you want to solve, rather than just accepting that things are going wrong. You can try a lot of different ways of handling it.

Green. Kind of like therapy, huh?

McCrady. Right.

Green (looking uncomfortable again). Look, I want to thank you for helping me. I, uh, brought you a present. It's not much, but I just wanted to thank you.

Donald hands me a pair of earrings shaped like small roses. They are congruent with my taste and style and quite attractive. It is a thoughtful gift which really touches me. That he is able to thank me so directly also is an indicator of how far he has come in therapy.

McCrady. The earrings are beautiful. Thank you. I really have enjoyed working with you.

We confirm the appointment for our first follow-up session in a month, and then we say good-bye.

Follow-Up

Donald had a total of three follow-up sessions with me over the next year. During that time, some positive things continued to happen in his life. A group of volunteers and staff at the Boys' Club began to socialize together—going out for dinner occasionally, or chaperoning Saturday-night dances for the boys and getting together before or after them. Donald became particularly friendly with one of the female volunteers who also was somewhat shy, so he felt comfortable around her. The last time I saw him, they had begun to date. Donald was anxious about dating, since he never had done so before, and he was extremely anxious about displaying physical affection or having a sexual relationship. He did not want to return to therapy, however, because he knew that she was equally inexperienced, and, he thought, "Things will work out." My sense was that he was embarrassed talking with me about sex, and he seemed a bit uncomfortable telling me about his affection for this woman. We agreed that he'd call me if there were any problems, but I did not hear from him again. ∎

CRITIQUE OF DONALD GREEN'S TREATMENT BY BEHAVIOR THERAPY

by G. Terence Wilson

The case report of the treatment of Donald Green by Barbara McCrady provides a representative and informative description of the classical practice of behavior therapy. The report highlights several distinctive features of behavior therapy: the therapist-client relationship, clinical assessment, and multifaceted treatment.

Therapist-Client Relationship

McCrady wisely took pains to develop a good therapeutic relationship with Donald. A good therapist-client relationship is a necessary but insufficient ingredient of effective behavior therapy in complex cases such as his. This is one of the commonalities that behavior therapy shares with other systems of psychological therapy, although there are distinctive features about the way in which behavior therapists relate to their clients.

McCrady deliberately tried to make Donald feel like a cooperative partner in the task of helping him change his behavior. She explained the reasons for asking him to record his daily activities and thoughts, and she was careful to check that he understood this and other assessment and behavior-change strategies and that they made sense to him. Actively involving clients in the treatment plan and in the assignment of therapeutic activities between sessions (often called "homework assignments") is critical in ensuring that clients actually engage in them. Findings from experimental social psychology as well as clinical research show that clients are more likely to adhere to therapeutic instructions (they will resist less) when they are allowed to feel part of the behavior-change process and not simply given "doctor's orders."

Donald responded well to McCrady's various requests to keep records and practice treatment techniques. I attribute this in large part to McCrady's careful and sensitive handling of the therapeutic relationship. Recall that Donald entered into treatment with quite different expectations about what therapy would be like and what he would have to do ("lie on a couch and talk a lot"). Had these initially unspoken expectations about what therapy would be like gone unaddressed, it is likely that treatment would not have proceeded as smoothly. Clients do not always comply with therapeutic prescriptions as readily as Donald did. Behavior therapists frequently encounter resistance to behavior change on the part of their clients. Their conceptualization of resistance, and how they cope with it, has been detailed elsewhere (Lazarus & Fay, 1982; O'Leary & Wilson, 1987).

McCrady's style of inviting Donald's feedback about her understanding of his problems and how to treat them was vitally important in identifying some of his apparently typical self-defeating cognitive distortions. She uncovered how he engaged in "mind reading"—how he jumped to the inaccurate and dysfunctional conclusion that she really "didn't like him" and that she thought he was "hopeless." McCrady was able to use this information effectively in introducing the technique of cognitive restructuring. Here is a good example of a behavior therapist focusing on the in-session interaction between her and the client in order to provide the client with an important interpersonal learning experience.

The mind-reading example shows how behavior therapists work to have their clients see treatment as credible and relevant to their particular needs.

Developing trust in the therapist is another goal of treatment. To this end McCrady was open, direct, genuine, and selectively self-disclosing. She shared with Donald her true feeling about him in a way that was both genuine and emotionally supportive. She even shared some of her concerns about the probable effects of a treatment strategy she had adopted. Clients, as a whole, respond well to this therapeutic style and typically rate behavior therapists highly on dimensions of warmth and caring (O'Leary & Wilson, 1987).

Clinical Assessment

The case exemplified both the goals and methods of assessment in behavior therapy. The major goal is to identify the different factors that are currently causing the client's problems. Complex or relatively diffuse cases such as that presented by Donald Green are broken down into separate, albeit interconnected, parts. Notice that in arriving at her formulation of Donald's case, McCrady did not limit herself to a piecemeal analysis of specific behaviors. Rather, she focused on specific problems as well as a theme or common thread which she hypothesized to occur across different situations. She developed an integrated and clinically consistent analysis of Donald's problems. The focus was not only on his overt behavior but also on his thoughts and feelings. In other words, McCrady was concerned with understanding and then treating the "whole person."

Behavior therapists use a variety of assessment methods, as this case shows. A detailed clinical interview is fundamental, but it is complemented by self-recording by the client, role-playing, and the use of selected questionnaires. Assessment in behavior therapy is a continuous process in which the therapist constantly monitors the effects of treatment as a means of confirming the validity and utility of her formulation of the case. Hypotheses about the nature of a client's problems are tentatively framed and must be open to revision, based on response to intervention. Notice how McCrady constantly referred to Donald's self-recording to assess his progress and to identify pitfalls. This information provided specific guidelines for the strategies she used.

Behavior therapists typically do not rely on traditional personality tests for assessing clients and developing treatment strategies. These tests derive from personality trait theory and rest on the assumption that an individual's behavior is relatively consistent across different situations. Behavior therapists are more interested in assessing behavior in the context of specific situations. They select self-report questionnaires that measure relatively focal areas of clients' functioning. The assertiveness inventory and social anxiety scales McCrady used are examples of this emphasis on focal assessment within specific domains of functioning.

Multifaceted Treatment

Behavior therapists have at their disposal a wide range of different cognitive and behavioral treatment strategies. In part, the personal skill of the therapist rests in selecting appropriate methods and implementing them at the right time in therapy. McCrady's report illustrates the use of several of the most important, commonly used cognitive-behavioral techniques, such as self-monitoring, progressive relaxation training, cognitive restructuring, social skills and assertion training, and response prevention. Different techniques are usually required to overcome different dimensions of a client's problems. McCrady did not assume that one or two methods would necessarily have broad, generalized effects across all of Donald's problems. Rather, she tailored specific methods to each facet of his problems. However, it must be emphasized that behavior therapy is a way of thinking about clinical problems, rather than simply a collection of different treatment techniques. McCrady's selection and use of different techniques followed logically from her overall assessment of the interrelationships among specific facets of Donald's problems.

What is especially useful about the report is McCrady's discussion of her thinking behind choosing each technique and the specific effects she hoped to achieve. Notice that in selecting techniques McCrady took into consideration the degree to which they are supported by empirical evidence. A good example is the choice of response prevention to overcome Donald's obsessive-compulsive checking rituals. Obsessions and compulsions are among the most difficult of all clinical disorders to treat. Exposure plus response prevention is the only psychological method that has been shown to be effective in controlled clinical research (Steketee & Foa, 1985). More generally, it should be emphasized that all of the techniques employed by McCrady have been shown to be effective in one or another controlled clinical outcome study (O'Leary & Wilson, 1987).

The learning principles on which specific techniques are based are more important than the techniques themselves. Behavior therapists often have to improvise—to adapt particular techniques to the specific needs of individual clients. Therapeutic versatility of this sort requires an understanding of underlying principles of behavior change. McCrady provides a revealing example of therapeutic ingenuity in her use of exposure and response prevention. It was impractical for Donald to be supervised directly in his home. Instead of simply relying on instructions that he may well have found too anxiety-provoking and that he would not have followed properly, McCrady exposed Donald to a situation that elicited his checking compulsion in the kitchen of her building. This creative arrangement allowed her to monitor his progress in following through on what is an emotionally threatening task for most clients, at least initially.

McCrady's treatment approach exemplifies another key characteristic of cognitive-behavior therapy, namely, graduated behavior change. In the use of exposure and response prevention, for example, she constructed a hierarchy of situations ranging from the least to the most anxiety-eliciting.

The choice and sequencing of particular treatment techniques are a dynamic process in which there is a constant interplay between the therapist's judgment and the observed outcome. For example, shortly after introducing the technique of cognitive restructuring, in which she asked Donald to identify and then alter his distorted cognitions about social interactions, McCrady ran into difficulty. The technique proved only partially successful. Apparently, Donald was unable to adhere to her instructions about how to use cognitive restructuring. McCrady inferred that severe anxiety was responsible for this therapeutic impasse. To cope with the anxiety she then introduced progressive relaxation training, which reduced Donald's anxiety and facilitated his use of cognitive restructuring.

Alternative Treatment Formulations and Strategies

In my view, McCrady's formulation of the case and her selection of assessment and treatment strategies were well-founded. The picture one gets is of a seasoned and highly competent behavior therapist at work. Most important, the outcome was satisfactory. Donald showed marked improvement in different aspects of his functioning that had seriously interfered with his life and brought him to therapy. Moreover, this improvement was not short-lived. He continued to function well one year after treatment had ended. Donald's success is not surprising. The treatment-outcome literature shows that the types of problems he presented reliably respond well to cognitive-behavioral treatment. Nonetheless, as in any case report, it is possible to take alternative viewpoints and to speculate about how treatment might have been different.

It seems clear that Donald suffered from severe social anxiety and was lacking in assertiveness. His interpersonal functioning was significantly impaired, and he led a lonely life. McCrady included these deficits in her formulation of the case and began to address them systematically in Sessions 13 and 14. Some other behavior therapists might plausibly have tackled Donald's social anxiety and unassertiveness earlier in treatment, on the assumption that these problems were focal to the case. They seem related to his social isolation, his negative self-image, and his late arrival at work. The cognitive restructuring and role-playing strategies used by McCrady might have been implemented sooner.

At the end of treatment, Donald was still living alone and had not made any progress toward meeting women or dating. He chose to discontinue therapy at that point, although he did subsequently return for three follow-up sessions. It is unclear how readily McCrady accepted Donald's decision to end therapy, or whether the decision to end treatment reflected a mutual agreement between therapist and client. Some behavior therapists might consider treatment incomplete without greater progress in this important domain of interpersonal functioning. Lack of change or improvement in a critically important area such as heterosexual relationships would mean not only that his functioning was still limited but also that he would be more vulnerable to relapse or a recurrence of his problems in the future. There are several different treatment interventions behavior therapists might employ in such a case. One area of exploration would be Donald's apparent anxiety about sexual functioning. The therapist might probe Donald's knowledge and feelings about this more directly. It might be speculated that in part Donald's interpersonal anxiety and difficulties were motivated by an underlying fear of physical intimacy and sexual functioning. One of the strong suits of behavior therapy is its proven success in reducing sex-related anxiety and enhancing sexual adequacy and satisfaction. In this case, of course, Donald continued to improve after termination. The fact that during the one-year follow-up period he did begin to date a woman suggests that termination was not untimely.

■

REFERENCES

American Psychiatric Association (1987). *Diagnostic and statistical manual of mental disorders* (3rd ed., rev.). Washington, DC: American Psychiatric Association.

Barlow, D. H. (Ed.) (1985). *Clinical handbook of psychological disorders: A step-by-step treatment manual*. New York: Guilford Press.

Beck, A., Rush, A. J., Shaw, B. F., & Emery, G. (1979). *Cognitive therapy of depression*. New York: Guilford Press.

Burns, D. D. (1980). *Feeling good: The new mood therapy*. New York: William Morrow.

Gambrill, E. D., & Richey, C. A. (1975). An assertion inventory for use in assessment and research. *Behavior Therapy, 6,* 550–561.

Hollin, C. R., & Trower, (1988). Development and applications of social skills training: A review and critique. In M. Hersen, R. M. Eisler, & P. M. Miller (Eds.), *Progress in behavior modification*, Vol. 22. Newbury Park, CA: Sage Publications.

Lazarus, A. A., & Fay, A. (1982). Resistance or rationalization? A cognitive-behavioral perspective. In P. L. Wachtel (Ed.), *Resistance: Psychodynamic and behavioral approaches*, pp. 94–107.

McCrady, B. S., Longabaugh, R., Fink, E., Stout, R., Beattie, M., Ruggieri-Authelet, A., & McNeill, D. (1986). Cost effectiveness of alcoholism treatment in partial hospital versus inpatient settings after brief inpatient treatment: Twelve-month outcomes. *Journal of Consulting and Clinical Psychology, 54,* 708–713.

McCrady, B. S., Noel, N. E., Stout, R. L., Abrams, D. B., Fisher-Nelson, H., & Hay, W. (1986). Comparative effectiveness of three types of spouse involvement in outpatient behavioral alcoholism treatment. *Journal of Studies on Alcohol, 47,* 459–467.

Morey, L. (1988). Personality disorders in DSM-III and DSM-III-R: Convergence, coverage and internal consistency. *American Journal of Psychiatry, 145,* 573–577.

O'Leary, K. D., & Wilson, G. T. (1987). *Behavior therapy: Application and outcome* (2nd ed.). Englewood Cliffs, NJ: Prentice-Hall.

Steketee, G., & Foa, E. (1985). Obsessive-compulsive disorders. In: D. H. Barlow (Ed.), *Clinical handbook of psychological disorders: A step-by-step treatment manual*. New York: Guilford Press.

Turkat, E. D., & Maisto, S. A. (1985). Personality disorders: Application of the experimental method to the formulation and modification of personality disorders. In: D. H. Barlow (Ed.), *Clinical handbook of psychological disorders. A step-by-step treatment manual*. New York: Guilford Press.

Watson, D., & Friend, R. (1969). Measurement of social-evaluative anxiety. *Journal of Consulting and Clinical Psychology, 33,* 448–457.

Wilson, G. T. (1989). Behavior therapy. In R. J. Corsini and D. Wedding, *Current psychotherapies*. Itasca, IL: F. E. Peacock, Publishers.

Eclectic therapy is a broad term that applies to any approach that freely uses theories and techniques from several diverse orientations to treatment. Eclectic therapists use the ideas of dynamic, humanistic, behavioral and cognitive systems, as well as many other theories to devise a plan for therapy. This approach is based on the assumption that different techniques should be applied to different problems. Thus, therapy should be individually adapted to the needs of each client.

An eclectic therapist may use a variety of customary techniques such as interviews, diagnostic tests, role-playing, and group therapy, as well as less common methods such as homework, imagery, and muscle relaxation. Eclectic therapists emphasize both the patient-therapist relationship and research-based, technical procedures as components in the change process.

National surveys show that, in practice, a majority of therapists now use an eclectic form of therapy. Some day, in all probability, all therapists will be eclectic, taking the best of what is available and using everything selectively for the benefit of the client.

At times, eclectic therapists appear to use techniques that derive from conceptually incompatible positions. However, they are often able to blend such methods successfully. The case report by Sol Garfield which follows nicely illustrates one of the several ways in which integration of diverse methods has been attempted.

Allen E. Bergin

Eclectic Therapy

SOMETHING ABOUT THE THERAPIST • *Sol Garfield*

My experience as a therapist may not be typical of most psychotherapists today, but it is not unique for individuals who received their training earlier. I was not trained as a psychotherapist, nor did I particularly desire to be one. My earliest career goal was to be a child psychologist working in a school setting. I definitely was interested in clinical child psychology, although such programs did not really exist then. Official clinical psychology programs did not come into existence until 1946, and those who finished their training before that time received training of various types, most of which did not compare with current clinical programs. Clinical psychology did exist as a small area of psychology while I was a graduate student at Northwestern University, from 1938 to 1942, but it was not listed as a specific area or program of study.

During my graduate years I shifted programs and emphases several times. Actually, there were few formal programs at Northwestern, and considerable flexibility was the rule. I became interested in educational psychology and psychology in general after I secured a master's degree in counseling in 1939. I assisted Paul Witty in the psycho-educational clinic the following year and then became a research assistant to A. R. Gilliland, the chairman of the psychology department. I had previously read widely in areas related to clinical psychology, including C. M. Louttit's text on clinical psychology as well as the writings of Sigmund Freud and Alfred Adler. Of particular import was Gordon Allport's *Personality: A Psychological Interpretation;* I was impressed by its scholarship, wisdom, and ideographic emphasis. In addition to courses in experimental psychology, learning, statistics, test construction, and research, I took the first course on the Rorschach test given by Samuel Beck at Northwestern in 1941. I also participated in a seminar and externship with Phyllis Wittman, the chief psychologist at Elgin State Hospital; she came to the university once a week, and once a week I and five other graduate students visited the state hospital. At first this was an exciting experience. However, being in a large mental hospital with primarily psychotic patients, and having little significant involvement with the real activities of the hospital, soon dampened this euphoric state. None of the psychologists at the hospital was engaged in psychotherapeutic activities; their main work centered on diagnostic appraisals and research.

The training and experience I received in psychotherapy as a graduate student was therefore limited, to put it mildly. Clinical psychologists at that time were primarily involved with psychological tests and with research. In a survey of 111 psychologists employed in child guidance clinics, Louttit (1939) reported that the most frequent professional activity was psychometrics, and 86 percent of his sample engaged in it. By contrast, psychotherapy ranked sixth in terms of frequency of activity, and fewer than one-third of his sample engaged in it. Thus the situation with regard to clinical psychology and psychotherapy was drastically different from what it is today. However, my scientific and research training did influence my views of psychotherapy.

Professional Experience

After receiving my Ph.D. in 1942 I was inducted into the Army and eventually assigned as a psychological examiner at the Philadelphia Induction Station. From there I went to the Quartermaster Officer Candidate School, was commissioned a second lieutenant, and was assigned as chief psychologist to the station hospital at the Aberdeen Proving Ground in Maryland. Here I became deeply involved in all the clinical activities associated with the neuropsychiatry service. I read everything available in the hospital library and bought and borrowed books on psychotherapy, psychoanalysis, and psychiatry. I developed a very close relationship with Major Irwin Schatz, the chief psychiatrist, and learned a great deal about psychopathology from him.

The 14 months I served at Aberdeen were professionally stimulating and rewarding. I was well received by my colleagues on the medical staff, almost none of whom had ever worked with a psychologist. I was appointed director of group psychotherapy and also performed most of the individual psychotherapy. Despite my limited training, I was comparatively well informed and was looked up to by the young psychiatrist and the other two psychologists on our service, neither of whom had had a great deal of clinical training. For example, Colonel Henry Brosin, a well-known analyst, assigned three psychiatrists and me to another installation to screen soldiers for Eisenhower's headquarters. In the four days I was there, I was asked by the psychiatrists to discuss psychotherapy and psychoanalytic theory during free periods. As one of my friends remarked, "In the land of the blind, the one-eyed is king."

There is little question that my experiences at Aberdeen had a great impact and crystallized my view of myself as a competent clinical psychologist. This was more my reference point than that of psychotherapist, although I had developed a strong interest in therapy. I also worked in a variety of ways with both inpatients and outpatients. I did initial intake interviews, made rounds, lectured to the medical staff, participated in discharge boards, and acted as week-end neuropsychiatry officer of the day. During the last few months of 1945, when the war was technically over, we were getting few admissions. Dr. Schatz invited me to see every case with him, and we would discuss cases together—a wonderful learning opportunity.

Although I received little formal training in psychotherapy during this period, I was engaged in practicing psychotherapy and received what I regarded as worthwhile professional experience. I compared this experience in therapy with my reading and tried to evaluate the therapy I was conducting. On this basis I developed some initial skepticism about psychoanalytically oriented psychotherapy. I also noted that there was practically no research on dynamic psychotherapy, a situation which has not changed significantly in the past 40 years.

Upon being discharged from the Army, I accepted a position as chief psychologist in a 350-bed Veterans' Administration psychiatric hospital. My duties involved individual and group psychotherapy as well as diagnostic testing and research. The clinical director of the hospital sometimes asked me how my cases were getting along, but I did not receive much in the way of formal supervision. I found my work challenging, even though psychotherapy with primarily psychotic patients usually did not lead to great progress.

My next position was as director of clinical psychology training at the University of Connecticut. Although I had a large teaching load, I established a psychological clinic there, and in addition to teaching a course in psychotherapy I saw some clients myself. Needless to say, these cases were quite different from those I had worked with at the VA hospital. I could see some real changes take place and could clinically test specific therapeutic techniques. In teaching psychotherapy I combined features of dynamic therapies with client-centered psychotherapy—similar to developments that became popular in the 1970s (Marmor, 1971; Wachtel, 1977). It seemed to me at that time (and it still does) that neither approach by itself met the needs of most clients. I experimented using nondirective therapy, primarily with a couple of clients, and decided that it was not adequate. I greatly angered one client by my exclusive, nondirective role, and thereafter I dropped it.

After two years at Connecticut, I accepted a position in 1949 as chief psychologist at the VA Mental Hygiene Clinic in Milwaukee. In this setting psychotherapy became my primary activity, and my interest in it deepened. I became acquainted with the phenomenon of premature termination, something rarely mentioned in the books I had read. I also was impressed with the disparity between the dominant psychodynamic theories and the daily realities of the therapy and patient behavior in the outpatient clinic. Although the major emphasis in the clinic was on intensive psychoanalytically oriented psychotherapy, my first study of the psychotherapy conducted there indicated that the median length of such "intensive" therapy was six sessions! (Garfield & Kurz, 1952) There was little interest among my colleagues in doing research on psychotherapy; their attitude was that since positive results were obvious, why bother? In my two years at Milwaukee, my experience with service-connected psychiatric disorders convinced me that traditional psychodynamic methods were neither appropriate nor effective. Some patients clearly saw little sense in our treatment efforts; they wanted and expected the therapist to take a more active, directive role. Although such a view conflicted with the traditional passive role of the therapist, it seemed reasonable to me—and it has become accepted today as the therapist's role in most forms of brief psychotherapy. I also concluded that it is important to check out patients' expectations about therapy and to orient them to the therapy to follow.

Then, in 1951, I was appointed regional director of psychology training for the VA in Chicago, and I continued to see a small number of patients regularly at the VA Clinic in that city. In my work there I had interactions with a number of therapists: client-centered therapists from the University of Chicago, psychoanalytically oriented therapists trained at the Chicago Institute of Psychoanalysis, some Sullivanians, and a few Adlerians. I received supervision for a while from an advanced analytic candidate at the Chicago Institute of Psychoanalysis, and over a period of several years I attended the outstanding lecture and interview series at the VA Hospital at Downey, Illinois, chaired by Jules Masserman, an analyst and professor of psychiatry at Northwestern University. Among those I remember seeing in this series were Karen Horney, Karl Menninger, and, especially, Frieda Fromm-Reichman, who conveyed an outstanding degree of therapeutic warmth and genuine interest in patients. Although I did not agree with all she said, she impressed me with her personality and therapeutic skills. This had some impact, I believe, in my later view that what the therapist says is only important in terms of how it is perceived and accepted by the patient.

In 1957 I accepted a position as professor and chief of medical psychology at the Nebraska Psychiatric Institute, University of Nebraska, remaining there for six years. Then, in 1963, I accepted a position as principal research scientist at the Missouri Institute of Psychiatry, to conduct research on psychotherapy. However, this didn't work out, and from 1964 to 1970 I was professor and director of the clinical psychology program at Teachers College, Columbia University. I held a similar position at Washington University, St. Louis, from 1970 to 1978, when I gave up directing the clinical program and was appointed editor of the *Journal of Consulting and Clinical Psychology*. I continued as professor of psychology, teaching mainly graduate courses in psychotherapy, until 1986, when I was appointed professor emeritus, my present title. My most recent book is *The Practice of Brief Psychotherapy* (1989), an eclectic treatment.

Views on Psychotherapy

In the six years I was at Chicago with the VA, I wrote my first book, *Introductory Clinical Psychology* (originally published 1951), in which I more or less formulated my views on psychotherapy, on the basis of both my reading and my experiences. Earlier I had been stimulated by a brief article by Saul Rosenzweig (1936), which suggested a few common features shared by different approaches to psychotherapy, and by the book on medical psychotherapy by Maurice Levine (1948), whose discussion of a number of so-called supportive techniques I found particularly interesting. During my stay in Chicago I also renewed my friendship with Ralph Heine, then a staff psychologist at the Chicago VA Clinic, who had conducted a study comparing the responses of patients receiving psychoanalytic therapy, client-centered therapy, and Adlerian therapy. These patients generally underwent comparable changes in similar ways. Heine's (1953) work appeared to give strong support to the idea that there are commonalities or common factors within the different psychotherapies, and these are of some consequence in securing patient change.

By this time, the basic core of my views about psychotherapy had been developed, even though I have since tried to be receptive to new ideas, particularly when they are supported by empirical evidence. However, there were two other important influences on my views and formulation of psychotherapy. Probably the person in the field I have respected most is Jerome D. Frank. In many ways, he has been a model for me. He was a pioneer in psychotherapy research, and his work on the placebo response and on pretherapy training, among other areas, was stimulating and creative. His classic book *Persuasion and Healing* (1961) had a profound influence, as did his paper on therapeutic factors in psychotherapy. I was impressed by the manner in which he discussed and evaluated issues in psychotherapy and also by the fact that he did not try to establish a particular school of psychotherapy. Moreover, my views seemed quite similar to his.

The other individual who particularly influenced my views is Allen E. Bergin, my co-editor for the *Handbook of Psychotherapy and Behavior Change* (1986). We were colleagues in the clinical psychology program at Teachers College, Columbia, and although he was the junior faculty member there I was impressed with his intelligence, scholarship, and emphasis on empirical research. His openness to new ideas and respect for the empirical reinforced my own commitment to these values. He gave the first course on behavior therapy at Teachers College when the prevailing atmosphere was largely psychoanalytic and rather critical of behavioral views. This in no way made him a dogmatic behaviorist, however; his guide has always been empirical data.

These diverse influences have helped make me an empirically oriented, eclectic psychologist and psychotherapist. Although I was intrigued by Freud's creative and original ideas about personality and psychotherapy early in my career, I did not find traditional psychoanalytic views or procedures to be helpful in working with patients in the Army or the VA. My years at the Nebraska Psychiatric Institute also did not lead me to change my views in this respect. Furthermore, the lack of any empirical support for this type of therapy was disquieting. In contrast, client-centered therapy was distinguished in the 1940s and 1950s by its research efforts. I can recall going to A.P.A. meetings during those years and noting that most of the research on psychotherapy reported was presented by followers of Carl Rogers. I did not find client-centered therapy to be completely adequate when used exclusively, however.

Consequently, my attempts at psychotherapy have been primarily eclectic. I made use of some psychodynamic theories in evaluating the patient's motivation for therapy, I tried to adhere to the Rogerian emphasis on genuineness and empathy, and in later years I used cognitive and behavioral procedures. The major guiding views of my attempts at psychotherapy, however, have definitely been based on common factors in psychotherapy as described in my book *Psychotherapy: An Eclectic Approach* (1980).

To explain what I mean by common factors, start with the proposition that all individuals who seek therapy do so because they are unhappy, in pain, and demoralized. Making a voluntary decision to seek therapy is an important step which may facilitate the patient's desire to collaborate with the therapist. If the patient makes an appointment under pressure from others, the desire to collaborate may be questionable. Since the patient has certain expectations and possibly some misconceptions, the therapist must clarify these expectations and orient the patient to the particular therapy to be used. Ideally, this will lessen the chances for disappointment. How the therapist is perceived during the initial session also is of great significance. If the therapist is viewed as an interested, caring, and competent person, the chances for continuation of the therapy and a positive outcome are increased. These conditions hold for *all* forms of therapy and point to common therapeutic variables. The most basic factor, however, is the development of a positive therapeutic relationship between the client and the therapist.

There are potentially additional common factors. Most orientations in psychotherapy have their own theoretical views of what is wrong with the patient, and they generally provide some type of explanation to the patient. Analysts provide one type of "insight," Adlerians another, and cognitive therapists a different type. Obviously, these diverse formulations cannot all be correct or "true," but apparently the activity of providing some explanation to the patient can be therapeutic. This is particularly true if the explanation, interpretation, or rationale provided by the therapist is accepted by the patient. After all, the therapist is a socially sanctioned healer and mental health expert, and the fact that he or she seems to know what is wrong with the patient and is willing to help is a positive event. Ambiguity and uncertainty tend to increase anxiety and self-concern, and the therapist's explanatory statements have the potential effect of reducing negative affects and increasing the patient's hope of getting better.

In most forms of therapy, also, the patient talks about the things that cause discomfort, and as these painful matters are discussed over time with an understanding therapist, they become less troublesome. This is a process of desensitization. Some patients with feelings of guilt or anxiety may be greatly helped by verbalizing them and having them accepted by the therapist, with no criticism. In such cases, the process is one of emotional release or catharsis, which occurs in practically any form of therapy.

Many therapists use procedures such as suggestions, information, and encouragement which are not generally considered significant to the orientations they follow (see Klein, Dittman, Parloff, & Gill, 1969). Nevertheless, such variables may play a positive role in patient improvement. In addition, the passage of time and positive events occurring in the life of the patient can have a significant impact on the eventual outcome. Moreover, what therapists do in their therapy may differ from what they say they do.

Such views of the therapeutic process and the common factors in it have led me to take an eclectic approach which utilizes procedures from various approaches to psychotherapy and in which some of the variables are viewed in a unique way. Although I have emphasized common factors, I recognize that there are specific procedures or techniques that are particularly effective with certain disorders. I also maintain that the patient's perception of his or her world is what we must deal with and try to modify, and in this process we must deal with behavior, not just talk. We have the opportunity to observe not only the patient's behavior in the therapy situation but other symptoms such as shyness and social avoidance that can only be modified by having the patient try out new behaviors successfully.

The Setting for Therapy

The preceding account of my training, experience, and views of the psychotherapeutic process should provide some understanding of how these views have developed or been acquired. I have worked in a number of settings, probably more than most therapists, and have had a moderate diversity of experience. In addition to my work in a military general hospital and VA psychiatric hospitals and outpatient psychiatric clinics, I have worked in the psychiatry department and psychiatric institute of a medical school, directed three university clinical psychology programs, taught psychotherapy courses and practica, and supervised doctoral clinical students in psychotherapy as well as staff psychologists and psychiatric residents. For one year, I was a full-time researcher at a psychiatric institute.

I have worked in psychotherapy with a variety of patients, although in the past 30 years I have not worked with seriously disturbed, psychotic individuals. Since 1964 I have been a full-time university professor and have carried only a small number of clients at any time. Most of my cases have been mildly to moderately disturbed and my therapy has been rather brief, usually 8 to 20 sessions. Anxiety of different types, depression, social relationships, and marital difficulties have been the problems I have seen most frequently. With marital problems, I always have worked with the couple.

At Washington University, I practice psychotherapy on a part-time basis while functioning primarily as a professor. My referrals come frequently from out-of-town psychologists who have referred clients moving to the St. Louis area. I have seen these clients in my university office or in one of the offices of the Psychological Service Center at the university, located in the building housing the psychology department.

THE THERAPY FOR DONALD GREEN

Session 2

As I made some notes on my initial interview with Donald Green, I could see that there would be more to consider than his immediate reason for seeking therapy. Clearly, his inability to get up in the morning, despite all the procedures he has worked out, is not going to be a simple symptomatic problem or one that can be easily treated. This problem is now three years old and apparently getting worse. In addition, Donald has led a rather isolated existence; with one exception, he essentially has had no meaningful interactions with either men or women. In fact, he even appears to have no vices. He does, however, own up to feeling lonely and depressed. He refers to several panic states, a fear of dogs barking, and at times feeling worthless. Many concerns and problems make this a potentially complex case.

During the first interview I responded positively and sympathetically to Donald as a person living a life that appears to be lacking in normal experiences and satisfactions. Nevertheless, I was uncertain about how much positive change could be secured by means of psychotherapy. Since I did not come to any hard-and-fast conclusions, beyond those mentioned, I had agreed to a second session before reaching a definite decision about providing therapy. I wonder if it would be worthwhile to have a neurological checkup, although the list of the client's difficulties clearly suggests that the problems are psychological in nature, and the sleeping-late problem certainly does not appear to resemble narcolepsy. This is something I can check out later with Donald's physician and follow up if necessary. Apparently, however, his physician did conduct some tests and found no physical factors to account for this problem, so perhaps no additional physical examinations will be required.

My major goals for the second interview are to evaluate the potential for change by means of psychotherapy, to judge Donald's motivation for collaborating with me, and to see if a feasible plan for psychotherapy can be formulated. Although the symptomatic picture presented seems quite serious, Donald is intelligent, appears to recognize the psychological nature of his difficulties, and seems willing to try to do something about them. As far as I can tell, he responded to me in a positive manner in our initial session. My main task now is to determine what changes are possible and what procedures can be employed most effectively. The second interview thus is an important one.

Donald is on time for the interview and seems less anxious and tense than he had been during our first session. He says he felt better once he knew he would be coming to see me, adding that he realizes he has problems and needs help. I acknowledge this statement in a positive way by telling him that his recognition of this situation and his desire to secure therapy are positive first steps. In the meantime, there are a number of matters we need to discuss and clarify before we can come to a definite decision about future therapy.

First, I point out that he mentioned a number of things that were causing him discomfort and concern. Whether we could resolve all of the difficulties is uncertain, but it is best to start with the most troubling ones or those that might be the most responsive to therapy.

GARFIELD. In terms of how you now feel about things, what would you like us to work with first?

GREEN. Well, Doc, getting up late was the reason I came here, and I guess that would still be No. 1. My supervisor has been pretty sympathetic, but he will be leaving in a few months, and I would like to avoid that problem with the new one. My terrible fears also bother me a lot, and I would sure like to get rid of them.

GARFIELD. OK, we'll do out best to help you try to overcome these problems. But in whatever we try and whatever we do, you'll have to be an active partner and collaborator. If I make a suggestion or we agree on some program, it will be up to you to carry it out and do your share as best you can. Is this clear?

GREEN. Well, I don't know what you have in mind, but I certainly want to do whatever is required to help myself. I've suffered for some time, and I do want to get better.

(I bring up the matter of the client's collaboration at this point for two reasons. I want to assess his motivation for therapy, since, despite his difficulties, he had not sought therapy on his own until his work supervisor and his physician suggested it recently. I also want to emphasize that his participation and cooperation in therapy are essential for any real progress to be made.)

GARFIELD. Fine. Now let's take a look at your difficulty in getting up in the morning and getting to work on time. As I recall, you said that this all started about three years ago, sudden-like.

GREEN (nodding his head). That's right.

GARFIELD. I'd like you to think back to when this first started and tell me whatever you can remember about it.

GREEN. Well, Doc, I don't know if there was anything in particular that seemed to start it. At least I can't think of any one thing that happened.

GARFIELD. Did you have any particular reaction to being late for work the first time it happened?

GREEN. Now that you mention it, I was quite upset. I began to worry about what was happening to me. Apart from being embarrassed at showing up late for work, I wondered if something was happening to me.

GARFIELD. Something like losing control or feeling something unhealthy psychologically was occurring?

GREEN. Yes. Something like that. I always had feelings of concern about myself. Even though I did well at school and was successful on my job, I knew I wasn't really like most other people. Besides being a loner, I had nightmares and feelings of panic that I knew weren't right. Also, as I told you last time, I have been lonely and depressed many times. I thought there was probably something wrong with me, but I tried to put such thoughts out of my mind. Working on my job and working on my cars helped—it did help in a way, but I always had these self-doubts.

GARFIELD. So you did have concerns and doubts about yourself for some time, and even thought about counseling, if I remember correctly from our interview last week.

GREEN. M-hm, m-hm, that's right.

GARFIELD. However, apparently you were able to get along in some fashion without having to seek psychological help from some shrink. But, in the last three years, things have become more stressful because of the work situation, and now you want to do something about it.

(*I word my statement in this way to indicate that although Donald had experienced considerable discomfort for some time, he had been able to make some kind of adjustment until the additional stress of the last few years. I am trying to indicate that despite his problems, he also has some personal strengths. My statement also mentions again his present motivation to participate in therapy.*)

GREEN. That's essentially it.

GARFIELD. Well, let's go back to when the oversleeping problem began. You say that you can't seem to recall any particular thing that seemed to be associated with it, but it upset you a great deal. What seemed to take place in the weeks that followed? How did you respond to this?

GREEN. Well, as I said, I was quite upset. I would worry quite a bit about being late for work. Sometimes this would keep me from getting to sleep at night, along with my fantasies about possible catastrophes. I wouldn't fall asleep for a long time, and then I would get up late. So I started in with the clocks, having three in separate places—and when this didn't seem to work, I asked my neighbor to call and also had the paperboy wake me up. They must think I'm a bit of a looney, but I was really getting sort of desperate.

GARFIELD. Desperate?

GREEN. As if things might get even worse—and then what would I do?

GARFIELD. So you were really tense and worried, but you kept all these feelings bottled up inside yourself and didn't discuss them with anyone.

GREEN. That's right. I was afraid to tell anyone about the mess I was in or they might think I was a real mental case. There was really no one I could talk to anyway—I've never talked about myself to Jim and Mary, and I would be afraid to tell them. It might ruin my relationship with them.

GARFIELD. I can see now that you've had a pretty rough time for several years, but things have become even more difficult the last few years—and now you do want to do something about it. Keeping all your worries and fears inside you and not being able to talk about them or bring them out in the open with someone just increases your discomfort and worry. Being able to discuss these things freely and openly in therapy—that is, being able to ventilate your feelings—should at least make you feel a little better.

However, there may be other fears and anxieties that we also need to talk about as we proceed. For many years now you have kept a great deal to yourself and have kept all your fears, thoughts, and feelings bottled up. It will be helpful for you to share such matters with me. In addition, we will try to plan certain activities that may be of help in terms of reducing your anxieties and fears and may even help you to be a happier person. Does this sound sensible to you?

GREEN. Yes it does. I have kept everything inside and tried to go about my business even though I felt terrible much of the time—and I do feel better talking about these things with you. You seem to understand what I've gone through, and I'm awfully glad that I finally decided to see you. I guess I was really afraid to see someone—I was scared that they might say I was cracking up altogether. That just added to my worries. Now I want to try to get rid of them if possible.

GARFIELD. Good. I'm glad that your response is positive, and I think we can work quite well together. Now, before we end our session today, there are a few items I want to mention. First, psychotherapy is not a magical process, and I cannot guarantee that all your problems will disappear. They are not really simple problems. Nevertheless, I can reassure you that you are probably not cracking up or becoming crazy. I am willing to see you once a week for perhaps 20 or so sessions, but we can reassess this schedule after we have had a few more. I will expect you to be on time for your appointments, and our sessions will last for 50 minutes. During these sessions I hope you will tell me about any thoughts or feelings or behaviors that bother you. I am here to try to help you, not to judge you. Also, if at any time something in therapy or something else I do bothers you, please mention it or ask me about it. I will ask you from time to time to do certain things during the week, and your cooperation in this will be important in terms of the progress you will make. Now, is there anything you would like to ask me about what I've told you, or anything else?

GREEN. I think I understand everything you've said. As I said earlier, I want to do whatever I can to help myself. I'm very pleased that you don't think I was going nuts; that's a big relief. What kinds of things will you be wanting me to do?

GARFIELD. Well, for this week, I want you to keep a diary listing such things as when you get up the first time, when you get up for good, when you get to work, when you go to sleep, and what you do during your spare time. You can keep this in any form you prefer. Be sure to include any fears, anxieties, and the like you may have and the cause of them if it is apparent. In other words, keep a list of events in your daily life and the feelings you have and bring it to our next meeting. It may help us get a picture of what is going on in your life. Is that clear?

GREEN. I think so. It may be hard to find time for it in the morning, but I'll do my best.

GARFIELD. Good. I'll see you, then, at the same time next week.

> (In the last section of this interview, in addition to asking for certain information, I have tried to encourage Donald to bring forth and share his feelings with me. I regard this as important for several reasons. Troubled individuals frequently harbor fears and self-doubts that they are reluctant to reveal to anyone. Lacking in self-esteem, they cannot risk the possible disapproval from others that such self-disclosure might produce. This type of dynamic is even more likely to be present in a lonely and isolated individual, as Donald Green appears to be. The opportunity for him to share his concerns, to ventilate and express his emotions, and to have them accepted in an understanding, empathic, and noncritical manner is potentially therapeutic.
>
> I am able to bring out Donald's fears of a serious mental breakdown and to reassure him that this is not a likely possibility. Besides the relief he secures from this interaction, he is also being reinforced for revealing his thoughts and feelings to the therapist. As a result, he is likely to be open and cooperative in his work in therapy.)

Session 3

Donald enters my office carrying a couple of sheets of paper in his hand, appearing more relaxed than in the preceding interviews. Right at the start he mentions that he has done his homework, and I acknowledge this and ask him how things had gone during the week. Although he was late to work more often than not and was upset at hearing a dog bark in his neighborhood, he states that he seemed to feel less worried than he had in the past. He again says that being reassured he is not "cracking up" made him feel much better. Since there is nothing else he wants to tell me at this time, I go on to examine his list of the week's activities which I requested in the last session.

There does not appear to be any clear pattern concerning his time of going to bed and time of getting to work or any obvious relationship between these variables and any others. However, there are a few small possibilities that at least seem worth trying. Occasionally Donald notes that after drinking coffee in the evening he had trouble falling asleep. He not only tossed around in bed but also tended to dwell on some of the negative features of his life, and this made falling asleep even more difficult. I suggest that he avoid taking any caffeine at night, and if he has trouble falling asleep after ten minutes he should get up and leave the bedroom. (These are some procedures reported to be moderately effective by Lacks, 1987.) After a time doing something else, he can go back to bed when he feels sleepy and try again to fall asleep.

We then discuss his involved procedures for getting up in the morning. He agrees that it is an unusual scheme and that it makes him feel inadequate. I respond to his statement about his feelings of inadequacy; I feel this area is worth pursuing.

GARFIELD. Feeling inadequate is something you have mentioned before in relation to your being lonely, being late for work, and not having any friends. It is an uncomfortable feeling, one many people have had at some time in their lives. However, you have felt this way for some time, and I wonder if the problem of getting up in the morning is related to such feelings.

GREEN. Well, it could be. It's embarrassing and a real worry, and if I could get over it I'd feel a heck of a lot better.

GARFIELD. Here's what I think might be an important part of that feeling. In a sense, after coming to work late a few times, you panicked—you overreacted, and instead of relying on one alarm clock, as most people do, you went overboard and now, as it were, you really have five alarms or wakeups, yet this has not helped. As the last few years have gone by, I imagine this has made you feel even more inadequate. Is that correct?

GREEN. Yes, it really has. The others at work really must be wondering what is wrong with me.

GARFIELD. I think part of the problem is that in some ways you have felt that you have lost control, at least over that part of your life. Instead of being able to get up for work on your own, you have relied on others, but it hasn't worked. Something like that is bound to affect your self-confidence.

GREEN (nodding). Yes, it certainly has—and it's made me very tense, too. When I went to bed I'd be worrying about how things would work out in the morning. I certainly didn't want to be late all the time.

GARFIELD. One way to try to change the situation is to get back your control over your own life—be able, among other things, to get up when you want to and not have to feel like you never know what's going to happen. Being able to get to work on time is just one aspect of this, but it's an important aspect—so let's try to do something about it, OK?

GREEN. I'm certainly willing to try anything.

GARFIELD. Let's start with the idea that your present system for getting up doesn't work. It doesn't get you to work on time, and it's helping to make you a nervous wreck. Right?

GREEN. Hmm, hmm.

GARFIELD. Therefore, is there any reason to continue it?

GREEN. Well—technically no, but then what would I do? I don't want to be late for work.

GARFIELD. True, but you currently are being late for work, so why keep relying on a faulty procedure?

GREEN. I know it doesn't make sense, but I...I can't rely on just one clock—I'd be late for sure.

GARFIELD. Aren't you late "for sure" most of the time anyway? It seems you've gotten yourself caught in a procedure or ritual you developed to help you with a problem, but it hasn't worked and it's time to discard it and try something else—something that probably can't be any worse, and may actually be a lot better. Do you see what I mean?

GREEN. Yeah, I guess I do, but....

GARFIELD. But, you're not sure, and I can understand that. You've been relying on a lot of props for a long time, regardless of how they worked, and I'm saying, "Let's do away with them all—in one big swoop." And, you're wondering what's going to happen.

GREEN. Yes, I am.

GARFIELD. All right, maybe it's time now to discuss what we might plan to do in place of what you've been doing the past few years. Since I know that this has been upsetting you and has caused considerable stress, I want to discuss everything with you and have it clearly understood. I also want you to let me know how you feel about anything I suggest. You are the person involved, and your active cooperation is absolutely necessary. I'll do my best, and you'll have to try to do your best, too. Agreed?

GREEN. Yes. What you say does make sense, and I'll try my best.

GARFIELD. Good. What I have in mind is for you to start out by telling your neighbor not to call you in the morning and to tell the paperboy to just leave the paper without ringing your bell. I realize that my suggesting this probably is increasing your anxiety now, but that's understandable and you'll gradually get over it. It is important, however, to face the situation squarely and to do something to change it. I also suggest that you use only two alarm clocks. Now what's your response to what I've suggested so far?

GREEN. It's scary, but as you pointed out, my system hasn't worked out. I'll give it a try.

GARFIELD. Very good. It will be important also to change your pattern of behavior when you first get out of bed. Apparently, after you turn off the alarm clock or answer the phone and the door, you go back to sleep most of the time. This, obviously, nullifies all of your efforts to get up, and so we have to do something to keep you from going back to bed or falling asleep again. Let's see what we can think of that might keep you from going back to sleep. Can you think of anything that would be worth trying?

GREEN. Well, once I get up I'd have to try to stay out of the bedroom and also off the couch, that's for sure. I've tried before but I'll have to try harder. It's almost like I didn't want to go to work, yet I like my job—hmm.

GARFIELD. That may be worth discussing, perhaps next time. However, since we just have a few minutes left, let's concentrate on what you might do to stay awake.

GREEN. I suppose I could have the alarm clock in the kitchen and when I go to turn it off, I could put on the radio and start the coffee. I could also shut the bedroom door and soak my head in cold water for a while until I feel fully awake. I don't know. What do you think?

GARFIELD. That seems like a good start. Maybe there are one or two additional things we might try.

In the last few minutes of the session we settle on a tentative program that Donald will try to put into practice. In addition to the actions he has suggested, we also agree that he could go get the morning newspaper, take some deep breaths of fresh air, and perhaps look at the front page or the sports section to help him become more fully awake. He also decides to use only one alarm clock. He is encouraged to work hard on the program. As before, he will keep a record of his activities.

> *(Donald is serious about collaborating in therapy, which might have been predicted on the basis of his personality and past history. Although his diary does not convey anything of great significance, it signifies that he is taking his assignment seriously. In this session I made the suggestion about avoiding caffeine, etc., to indicate my attempts to help, and it conceivably might help a bit. I focused on two items that I think are important, his feelings of inadequacy and his being unable to control his life. I tried to be empathic and to encourage him to be free*

> in expressing any negative or depressive affects. Finally, I discussed with him the failure of his current attempts at coping with the late-at-work problem and attempted to get him involved in some new attempts to overcome it.
>
> The idea of giving up his current props was anxiety-provoking, but he went along with it and participated in the planning of substitute procedures. I think it wise to have him participate in this process and not have it all come from me. Although I might have speculated with Donald about some of the psychological reasons accounting for his difficulty, I have decided it is more effective to try to get some positive change in his behavior if at all possible.)

Session 4

Donald again brings the notations on his feelings and activities that he had made during the week. He says he was afraid of what would happen, but he had notified his neighbor and the paperboy to discontinue calling or waiting for him until further notice. He seems less tense and worried than previously, and I expect (and hope) that he has been successful in making some inroads on handling his problem.

While Donald has not been completely successful, he has made progress. He has been on time for work three of the five days during the past week and is exuberant about this degree of success. I am pleasantly surprised and praise him for his determination and ability to stick to our program, even though I know it makes great demands on him. I also caution him that he still has to work hard on it, and there most likely will be some setbacks along the way. Nevertheless, I say, he has shown clearly that he has the ability to work on his problems, to overcome them to a significant degree, and to regain control over his own life. He agrees with these comments, and I again tell him I am pleased with his efforts.

After a brief discussion of the two mornings he was late during the past week and of some modifications that might improve our success rate, I turn to a discussion of Donald's loneliness and his isolated style of life.

> (Although there are still some other more-specific symptoms, Donald's nonrewarding life-style seems to be a central problem. Furthermore, since progress is being made on the most acute problem, it seems worthwhile to shift our focus at this time.)

GARFIELD. Perhaps now we might discuss your feelings of loneliness. During our first session you mentioned that you had been wanting to talk to someone because you felt your life was empty and you had no real friends. This should be a good time to talk about these things.

GREEN. It's true that I have thought about this for awhile. My life has been empty, and I want to be like other people. I envy men with their families and the fact that they lead normal lives. Sometimes I think of joining some type of club or going to parties for singles, but I never get up enough courage to go. I've always been very shy, particularly with girls. I've daydreamed about them—not just sex, but having a girlfriend and doing things together—but this was a fantasy and not reality.

GARFIELD. It was what you wanted, but you didn't attempt to do anything about it.

GREEN. That's right. I just was too shy, too unsure of myself. I was afraid that girls wouldn't like me, I wasn't very good-looking, and I was short.

I encourage Donald to verbalize his doubts and negative feelings about his self, since he has had little opportunity in the past to talk about himself and to express his feelings. He refers to his early life, the few interactions and the lack of any real relationship with his father, and the absence of any real show of affection from either parent. He sees his older sister as very sociable but also disobedient and "wild." He, on the other hand, was the good child—obedient, hardworking, good in school, and retiring. I point out that although he may have been genetically more withdrawing and less assertive than his sister, it is quite likely that his experiences as a child and an adolescent accentuated these personality patterns. Thus his more or less "good" but isolated pattern of living kept him from making new contacts with others, and this solidified the pattern even more. However, this does not mean he can never change. As with the sleep problem, it is possible to change, but it will not come automatically or easily. He will have to work at it and attempt to do things that he has tended to avoid in the past.

I tell Donald that he has probably focused on the negative aspects of himself and, for the most part, minimized his positive features. I ask him to list the personal qualities he has that most people would value positively, and he says he is good at his job, a hard worker, and honest and conscientious. I point out that the industrial psychologist also found him to be neat-appearing and friendly. He agrees that he does have some good qualities, but he is not sure that these are the ones that attract people or that are particularly valued.

As this discussion continues, with considerable interest on Donald's part, I emphasize that the problem is not so much that others do not value his positive personal qualities as that he never really gives people a chance to know what kind of a person he is. In actuality he keeps people away from him, both physically and psychologically. Even with his only friends, Jim and Mary, he hardly ever talks about personal matters or, apparently, expresses any interest in their personal lives. Yet when Donald was worried about not paying his income tax and confided in Jim, his friend immediately came to his aid. Thus he is keeping himself away from others and is not being open with them. Donald agrees with the points I am making but tries to explain why it is difficult for him to interact socially with others.

GREEN. I've always been pretty much of a loner. I don't feel comfortable around other people and envy those who know how to get along. I even have trouble correcting foremen who do not supervise the workers effectively.

GARFIELD. I understand your feelings of discomfort in such situations, and I know they make you feel somewhat inadequate. It is like a vicious circle. You are ill at ease and anxious in interacting socially with others, and these feelings also make you depreciate yourself, and this in turn keeps you from further interactions with others. These feelings and negative self-thoughts even lead to feelings of depression at times, particularly when you compare yourself to others.

Donald nods affirmatively at this description.

GREEN. That seems to fit me, all right.

GARFIELD. It is important for you to try to understand your feelings and how they influence your behavior and well-being. If we didn't understand to some degree how we function, we might be unduly troubled about the events of our lives and believe that there is little chance for change. Acknowledging and trying to understand these factors, therefore, is an important first step. However, the really important thing is to try to make some changes in life-style so that there are more positives and fewer negatives. This clearly is the more difficult task, but changes can be made, as you have already demonstrated. That's all for now; we will continue next time from this point.

> (Although I am not at all sure that Donald's improvement in getting to work on time is going to be permanent, in this session I decided to accept the current success, praise and reinforce his positive performance,

and discuss what I feel is his most significant problem, which is also the one most difficult to secure significant change in. This clearly is his isolated life-style. Also, since his past opportunities to really relate on a close level with another person and discuss his own thoughts and feelings have been severely limited, I think the opportunity to do so might have some therapeutic value. At the same time I realize, as I mentioned to Donald, that this is just a preliminary step, and behavioral change along with a changed self-view has to take place. This is the obvious goal. Depending on how things go in the week ahead, I will try to offer suggestions toward achieving it.)

Session 5

Donald opens the session by stating that the preceding week had gone fairly well. He is having less of a problem getting up in the morning, although he was late once because he stayed up later than usual the evening he visited his friends, Jim and Mary. Donald says that since our last session he has thought quite a bit about what I said concerning his way of life. He can see how he has avoided opportunities for contact with others, and, particularly in the case of Jim and Mary, has seemed to veer away from talking about anything of a truly personal nature. He says that at first he felt a little depressed about this, but this feeling has begun to dissipate. He feels that now he is trying to do something about it, and perhaps things will be better.

GREEN. I don't know why, but my mood changed and I suddenly felt more hopeful about myself. On my way over to have dinner with Jim and Mary I picked up a good bottle of wine. Whether that influenced me or not, I was more talkative than usual and asked them some rather personal questions. I also talked more about myself and even mentioned that I was now in therapy. It seemed good to share these things with them, and they appeared interested in what I had to say. When I got home, later than usual, I was rather keyed up and had trouble falling asleep. As a result I wasn't watching what I was doing in the morning and fell back to sleep for a short while. I was late that morning, but not by much, and I wasn't really upset by it.

GARFIELD. Well, that sounds good. It seems that you not only thought seriously about what we discussed last time, but you actually started to do something about it on your own. You didn't wait for me to tell you what to do. That's great.

> (*What I am doing here is probably quite obvious. I'm trying to reinforce with praise the behavior the client is describing. His taking some initiative in modifying his behavior in this instance is quite important and should be reinforced.*)

GREEN. Yes, and I felt happier than I have in a long time. But I'm still by myself most of the time. Something else that bothers me: At work one day, I really felt like bawling out one of the foremen and I almost did, but then I chickened out. I wish I could be different.

GARFIELD. So another thing we might consider working on is being able to assert yourself and to say what you want to when necessary.

GREEN. Yes—that has bothered me for a long time.

GARFIELD. All right; let's see what we can try to do about that.

For the rest of this session we discuss the kinds of feelings Donald has when he feels an urge to correct a foreman or ask someone to do something over. Not only is such behavior exceedingly difficult because it is completely out of his behavioral repertoire, but he is painfully sensitive to how the other person might feel toward him for behaving that way. In our discussion it becomes evident that Donald wants the foreman (as well as all others) to view him positively. He is afraid that any criticisms or corrections he offers will make others respond to him negatively. This fear of disapproval appears to have an important role in his nonassertive behavior.

We first examine his expectations about how different individuals might perceive him and how they might view certain changed behaviors on his part. At first Donald tends to be overly general in this analysis and says only that others would take offense or wouldn't like him. By asking him to clarify and be more specific in his appraisals, I have him deal with the problem on a more realistic level. His expectation of a negative response from others is a general belief underlying his restrictive behavior, but he gradually is able to see that this expectation is causing him to react to every situation in an identical manner, and this is an inadequate way to respond. He can see, for example, that he could ask a foreman to perform a task in a specified way, but it would be wiser not to react the same way toward his supervisor.

I focus on how Donald's expectations and perceptions influence his behavior, a process that occurs in everyone. He shows real interest in what we are talking about, is an active participant in the discussion, and seems to accept the ideas that are brought forth.

GARFIELD. Where our expectations and the beliefs associated with them are not quite accurate, we tend to make things more difficult for ourselves. When we overgeneralize about how people respond to us or how they might respond, we do not use our powers to discriminate one situation from another. Everything is seen as black or white, and we do not notice the various shades of gray.

Well, Donald, we have had quite a discussion today about some things that I believe are quite important. Has it all made sense to you?

GREEN. Yes, it has. I'm beginning to understand more about myself and why I've acted the way I have. I'm hoping that understanding this will help me change in some ways, and I won't be so fearful or insecure.

GARFIELD. I hope so, too. Keep up the good work. Next time we can discuss some things you might do that could be helpful.

>*(I have spent a good deal of this hour focusing on the importance of Donald's expectations, cognitions, and related feelings. This may seem to have been a very didactic session, or even a seminar, at times, but I felt it was worth doing, and at the end I have the feeling it has been useful. Although I am not officially a cognitive psychologist, I do believe that perceptions and cognitions can influence our behavior and affects. One objective of therapy, therefore, is to bring about a change in the client's cognitions. I considered it more effective and beneficial to try to deal with these aspects before dealing more directly with attempts at changing Donald's behavior. If perceptions and cognitions can be modified in terms of a more realistic view of one's self and one's environment, the odds favor possible changes in behavior and personal satisfaction.)*

Session 6

Donald begins this session by saying he has had a busy week at work, where he is trying to complete a difficult project. On the whole, the work has proceeded well, and there are no serious problems with it. He then says he has thought quite a bit about our session last week, and he can now see how his own feelings have led him to be a loner and kept him from expressing himself to others. He says this doesn't mean that his behavior will change much, but he is getting to understand himself better, and that is one of the things he has hoped to get out of therapy.

Getting to work on time is no longer a serious problem, and his supervisor has made some positive comments to him about this which made him feel good. Donald does mention an incident in which he experienced some feeling of panic. While driving home from work, he noticed a police car following him and became anxious, wondering if he had been speeding or missed a stop sign. But the police car turned into another street after a few blocks, and his anxiety lessened.

I listen attentively to Donald's remarks, nodding when appropriate and reflecting his feelings and thoughts.

GARFIELD. Good work, Donald! It seems you are collaborating very well with me in our therapeutic work. Now we might consider some activities or procedures that could be helpful in furthering your progress. Since one of your main problems is shyness or an inability to assert yourself, why don't we start with some activities in this area?
GREEN. Good, I'd like that.
GARFIELD. Your main contacts with people occur at work, so we might think of some things for you to do that are related to the time you spend on the job. There are two specific work situations in which interpersonal contacts occur or are possible: exchanges with foremen and technicians on production matters, and interactions with others during the lunch period.

As Donald indicated in his initial interview, he usually eats alone or brings his lunch. Here is an opportunity to interact with others that has not been utilized before, one he could try to make use of now. I ask him to describe the cafeteria setting so I have a clear picture of that daily situation, and I point out a few possibilities for interaction. At the most superficial level, he could try to say hello and greet everyone he knows. Donald agrees that although he hadn't done this in the past, it is something he could try. We discuss how he could approach people and say "Hello" or "Nice to see you" or some greeting of that kind. I then have him role-play the interaction with me as the other person. He is quite self-conscious about this at first and tends to avoid looking directly at me, but he gradually improves and seems to gain in self-confidence. As always, I acknowledge his successful performance with an approving remark, and I emphasize that he should greet others naturally and without exaggeration.

Next we talk about other types of activity that are more demanding. We agree that his social skills could be enhanced by eating with others at lunchtime and avoiding his solitary habits; this would indeed be a marked change in his behavior. We talk again about his feelings when he must take the initiative in interacting with others, a behavior that his long-standing pattern of shyness has made difficult and anxiety-laden.

GARFIELD. I appreciate your feelings about this; I know it won't be an easy task for you to perform. However, it is not impossible; it *can* be done, and others with similar difficulties have been able to improve their behavior in this respect. You know, the more a person engages in any behavior, the easier and more natural it becomes. Besides, I know that you have the personal qualities that are required for any successful performance—you are intelligent, hardworking, and conscientious.

GREEN (as his serious expression gives way to something of a smile). I guess there's no reason I can't try.

We then engage in some role-playing of the task of approaching others eating in the cafeteria and asking if he can join them. I sit at my desk representing a fellow worker having lunch, and he is to walk over and ask if he can join me or share the table. We practice this single activity first and rehearse it a number of times so his behavior appears more natural and less wooden and tense. We also discuss the various situations he might encounter. He might choose between tables with several people at them or tables where a single person was eating. There would be tables where he might know someone and tables where all the people were strangers. There would also be tables where most or all of the people would be women, which would present a different challenge than tables made up mostly of men. Donald expresses his feelings about these possibilities, and I tell him to start by selecting tables that he thinks he can approach most easily and then gradually try the more difficult ones.

Before closing the session, I bring up the matter of conversation while having lunch with others. Again, different combinations of table companions would present different possibilities or requirements. At a table with several people who know one another, the necessity for considerable conversation on Donald's part would be limited, but at a table with just one other person he would have to contribute to the conversation. We have little time to discuss this and the related matter of what topics Donald might bring into the conversation, so I ask him to make up a list of topics he might talk about with others and bear them in mind in his interactions, as well as to keep a record of his interactions. He is to bring both to our next session.

Session 7

Donald begins this session by saying that the past week was rather difficult for him, and he had been quite apprehensive about it, particularly in the early part of the week. The first day he purposely worked later than usual at lunchtime so he would have just a brief time to eat. Consequently, he just took the nearest empty table, but he did say hello to one of the employees in the cafeteria. The fact that he hadn't complied with my request bothered him, and after lunch he had some difficulty concentrating on his work.

This experience also was unsettling because Donald feels that it is very important for him to succeed. As he describes his thoughts and feelings, it seems as if the experience points up what he perceives as a choice point.

GREEN. Not doing what I should have done made me depressed for a while. After all, I've been making progress and getting along fairly well. I thought to myself: "Oh, oh, I'm slipping back instead of going forward. What's Dr. Garfield going to think? I've got to handle these things or I'll never change." I was really upset.
GARFIELD. You were really upset because you felt that all your wishes and hopes might go down the drain, but you also didn't want to disappoint me or have me think poorly of you.
GREEN. That's right, I had all these feelings and they pulled me down.

I give Donald the opportunity to fully express the feelings he experienced during this period and try to clarify how his thoughts influenced these feelings.

GARFIELD. You were preoccupied with thoughts of failure and impending doom as well as concerns about how I might view you. So you perceived one small setback as a sign of total failure and a bleak future. You know, if we perceive situations in a certain way, there is bound to be an accompanying feeling. Obviously, it is better to view the situation as a minor setback and then try to do better the next time.
GREEN. I agree, but it isn't always possible to think the way I should or to see things in a better light.
GARFIELD. Well, yes, but as we become more aware of what goes on inside our heads, we can change in our ability to do this. Your concern about how I might view you is understandable. We naturally want others to view us positively, and right now I am a particularly important person for you. It is good that my opinion matters to you, but the important thing is your progress and well-being, and this has to be your main concern.

During the remainder of the session, Donald recounts other events of the past week. It is evident that initiating social contacts and interactions is a difficult and trying experience for him. He makes some weak attempts at approaching others, but he also makes much stronger and more successful attempts at avoiding others. Not only is he very ill at ease when attempting to interact with others, but these feelings are augmented by fears that he will never be able to change and become more outgoing. I encourage Donald to express his feelings fully and try to communicate that I understand his feelings and concerns. I comment that this is really the first setback of any consequence, and it may have heightened his feelings of failure on the suggested homework assignments. He has been unusually successful in handling his problem of getting to work on time, and this may have given us a somewhat distorted expectation in the present situation. I emphasize that he has made some attempts at carrying out the suggested assignments, and that he was successful one lunch period when he sat down at a table with another person who works in his department. Thus I point out the positive as well as the negative aspects of his experience.

Our discussion seems to have a positive impact on Donald's mood and outlook. I tell him that I probably had assigned him more to do than was actually desirable, so I am going to modify my previous suggestions. He should continue to greet people as he meets them or passes them at work or elsewhere, since this is not a particular problem. At lunchtime, however, he should attempt to join only people he knows somewhat. We will see how this works out and will not try anything else for the time being. I suggest that he also continue his more extended personal conversations with Jim and Mary, since they seem to be going well.

Sessions 8–12

During the next five sessions our focus is on Donald's attempts to increase his social initiatives and interactions. Progress is slow, but there is progress. After a couple of weeks, Donald's apprehension about approaching people he knows to some extent gradually diminishes, but I decide it is not wise to push him too fast. It is not until the 11th interview that I suggest some additional activities. Once a week, he is to try to sit at a table with people he essentially does not know. By this time he is much more acquainted with what goes on in the cafeteria, what groups sit where, and similar details, so he can canvass the situation and plan what to do. I consider the possibility of using systematic desensitization but instead decide to have Donald role-play the situation with me as a stranger. We practice until his performance becomes almost natural. I point out that another positive development is that his talks with Jim and Mary are becoming increasingly personal.

When we meet for the 12th interview, Donald reports that the past week had progressed fairly well. Although he was tense, he had carried out the task of approaching a strange group, asking if he could join them, and introducing himself (as we had practiced), and he had made it through the meal without any real problems. He actually felt elated at having carried out this activity successfully. The other people had been friendly and had shown an interest in him. It appears this has been a positive experience, and I hope we have turned an important corner in the therapy.

Donald then brings up another thing that has changed for him at work.

GREEN. You know, my supervisor will be retiring in a couple of months, and I'll miss him. But I don't worry any longer about what the new supervisor will think about me.
GARFIELD. In fact, Donald, the supervisor's retirement does not have to mean that you are to have no further contact with him.

Donald gives me a quizzical look.

GARFIELD (continuing). If the supervisor will still live in town, you can maintain a relationship with him—have him over for a meal, go to a ball game together, or something like that.
GREEN. Well, yes, we could do things like that. The supervisor is actually younger than my friend Jim is.
GARFIELD. The same goes for Jim and Mary—you could consider doing other things with them than just having dinner together every Thursday.

As the session draws to a close, I again compliment Donald on his progress and tell him that he should try to increase his table contacts at lunchtime, but I do not specify any particular number of contacts. I feel that he has the ability to decide what he can do, and in the long run, of course, he will be the one who makes the decisions. I suggest, however, that he try to find some leisure activity he can engage in with some of the people he works with.

> *(Donald seems to be progressing reasonably well at this point. Apparently, I tried to go too fast and pushed him too hard earlier, but he seems to have recovered from that experience. He does not have any*

real concerns about the work situation now, appears to have a more intimate relationship with his friends, and has had a moderately important "success" experience this week. In terms of these developments, I made the first indirect reference to future termination by stating that in the long run he would be the one to make the decisions. It is interesting that he has made few references to panic reactions, although we have given them little direct attention.)

Sessions 13–16

Donald continues to show some progress in his social interactions. He reports that he generally eats lunch with others, and although he is not always at ease with all groups, he is comfortable with most of them. He particularly enjoys eating lunch with one group of workers, all males. He is still quite shy as far as women are concerned.

I encourage Donald to talk about his thoughts, fantasies, and feelings about women, including sexual emotions. This is not an easy topic for him to discuss freely, and at times he appears to be somewhat embarrassed. He does try to convey his views and feelings in this important area, and I attempt to be both encouraging and accepting. Among other items, we discuss his idealized view of his mother, the nonexistence of displays of affection in his family, the essentially absent but at times harsh father, the lack of support from his rebelling sister, the absence of any positive role models for him, and the teasing of a boyhood friend, in part because of his size. Donald recalls some of these experiences with real affect, which probably has some moderate cathartic effect.

The discussion about sex and masturbation is quite poignant. He has had yearnings and fantasies about relationships with women, tender as well as sexual, but except for one kiss with a barmaid, his actual activities have been limited to these fantasies. Donald's sexual fantasies are associated with masturbation. He does not have a great deal of guilt or shame about these activities; rather, they seem to accentuate his feelings of inadequacy. I primarily listen to Donald and reflect his feelings, although on occasion I have him clarify what he is trying to describe.

(Since Donald has never shared these important feelings and self-views with anyone else, I believe this is a constructive development. However, I do not intend to get involved with the sexual area per se. This has not been a specific goal of the therapy, and I feel that the broader goals of increasing social interaction and reducing feelings of inadequacy and isolation are more basic.)

During these sessions I also bring up the possibility of increasing the range of Donald's social interactions. I point out that beyond the social activities associated with his job, there are other possibilities that can be explored. Although he has not been a regular churchgoer, most churches offer opportunities for social participation and contact. There are groups that sponsor activities aimed specifically at single persons, and there are opportunities to participate in charity organizations and political groups. There are even organizations for individuals interested in old cars. I suggest he participate in one or two such groups and see how he fares. Donald indicates that taking the initiative on such matters still is not easy for him, but he could exert the effort.

In Sessions 15 and 16 I give Donald some simplified instructions for practicing relaxation. I tell him that being able to relax when he feels tense or panicky can help him get over such feelings. These procedures are useful at times in coping with stressful situations. Then I begin to prepare him for termination.

GARFIELD. You've made definite progress in some of the problems we discussed when therapy began, and you have a better understanding of yourself and your life experiences. I think we can now taper off our sessions and plan for eventual termination. You know, therapy should not go on forever; it should help you be able to handle your future life more effectively on your own.
GREEN. Yes, I know the therapy has to end at some point; in fact, I've been thinking about this recently.
GARFIELD. All right, then, let's meet again in two weeks instead of a week. We probably will consider termination in about four more sessions.

Sessions 17–19

Donald remarks at the beginning of Session 17 that at our regular time last week, he had thought about me and our sessions. Seeing me at that hour had become an accustomed event, and he was adjusting to the change. He has no real problems to bring up. He went to a movie with Jim and Mary and enjoyed it, and he plans to do more of this type of thing. He sent in for information on a cruise for single people that was advertised in the travel section of the newspaper. Frank, a man at work, had heard him talking about his hobby of working on old cars and asked if he could visit and observe some time. This pleased Donald, and he was going to invite Frank to come see his garage the following week. Since Donald is getting along without any undue difficulty, I schedule the next session for three weeks later and tell him that the remaining few sessions would be at this interval.

During the next two interviews, it is clear that our therapy is drawing to a close. There is more talk of the future in general and some specific plans and arrangements. It is evident that although Donald has not undergone any great personality transformation, he has changed in certain ways and is still changing slowly. He is more relaxed, speaks with more enthusiasm and less tension, and is more outgoing in his outlook on life. His periods of depression are less pronounced. He is finding out about opportunities to meet people, in a conscientious, cautious manner. He asks more questions, usually about relating to people, taking the initiative in calling others, and matters of this type. For example, he has seen an advertisement for dancing lessons and wants to know what I think about it. Instead of answering directly, I explore with him his feelings and how he would make his final judgment about this.

At the end of Session 19, I tell Donald that we will be having our last session in a month. We have accomplished pretty much what I hoped we might, and he has more than fulfilled his part of our joint endeavor. We will meet again in a month to tie up any loose ends, make some final evaluations, and say good-bye. Donald agrees and says he also is pleased, and he'll see me again in four weeks.

TERMINATION OF THE THERAPY

As always, Donald is on time for our last interview. When I ask him how he has been during the month, he says he has been doing OK. He has been working hard on a new project at work.

GREEN. I've been thinking about everything we've talked about here and what I've learned about myself and other people. It's hard to change your views and feelings, but I can see that some changes have taken place over the past several months. Although in most ways I'm still the same Donald Green, in other ways I'm, well, sort of different. I do mix with people more than before and I don't get down in the dumps the way I used to, which I guess is a real change. But I think the most important thing is that I feel better about myself. I can accept myself more—I don't feel that I am quite the creep I used to think I was. You know what I mean?

GARFIELD. Yes, I believe I do. In the past, for a variety of reasons—and we talked about them—you saw yourself as a person who didn't compare favorably with most people, one who was inadequate in certain ways. As a result, you undervalued yourself and overvalued others. Now you have learned to view yourself more positively. You're less self-critical, but you also have changed. You see things differently and that's a change . . . and you're doing things that previously you thought you would not be able to do.

GREEN. Yeah, that's right. Things have happened that I wasn't sure would ever happen. I must admit that I was plenty scared and concerned that either you'd say I was going to have a mental breakdown or that there was no hope for me. The fact that you agreed to see me and didn't treat me as if I were a truly crazy person really had a strong effect on me. I not only felt there was some possibility of being helped, but I really became very determined to do whatever I could to cooperate. Having always kept my feelings to myself and worried about them, I got a terrific lift from talking about them with you. The fact that you didn't seem startled or upset by what I was telling you somehow seemed to make everything less bad, less terrible. It's interesting how just talking about things that bother you can have such an effect.

GARFIELD. So, having the opportunity to express your concerns and fears did make you feel better.

GREEN. Yes, it certainly did.

GARFIELD. However, as you have learned, there's more to psychotherapy than just talk. There are also things you have to do, or to work on, even when they are very difficult for you to do.

GREEN. That's certainly true! At least it's been true in my case. Some of these things aren't easy to do, but I've learned that nothing comes easy in this world. You always have to work at it, but when you are able to do things that are difficult, you feel good about accomplishing such things—and the more you do them, well, they do get easier to do. I guess starting something is always the hardest part, particularly when you have real doubts or fears about your ability to pull it off. I was so shy that it was very hard for me to approach people and say anything to them. If you hadn't said I should do this—or try to do it—I don't think I would have ever tried.

Donald pauses, and I encourage him to continue.

GREEN (continuing). Well, as you pointed out, we had to do more than just talk about problems, and if I wanted to get away from being a complete loner the rest of my life, I had to work at it. I knew this was a chance I had to try to be different, and at this stage of the game I couldn't afford to pass it by—and I'm glad, really glad, I didn't.

GARFIELD. It's true that it is very difficult to engage in activities that make you feel anxious or inadequate, and a person often needs some sort of push or encouragement to get started. I think that's true for a lot of people. However, you worked at it and stuck with it, even when I pushed you too hard, and that's where your being conscientious paid off.

GREEN. That's right, and I feel good about that.

GARFIELD. And you should. . . . Now, is there anything else that occurred in the past four weeks that you would like to mention? Or are there any questions you would like to ask me?

GREEN. Yes, there are a couple of things I might mention. I've gotten to be friends with Frank, the guy from work who's also interested in fixing up cars, and he comes over some Saturdays and works with me or just talks. I've been to his home for dinner, and I plan to follow your suggestion and have him and his wife over for a cook-out. His wife is a very nice, friendly woman, and I like her. I still see Jim and Mary every week, too, and I really enjoy my evenings with them. Oh yes, one of the bowling teams at work is short of members and I've been asked to join them. I'm not a very good bowler and I was going to say no, but then I thought, "Why not? What have I got to lose?" I also thought you would agree that it is a good thing for me to do, and I'm going to join the team tomorrow.

GARFIELD. Donald, it does sound as if you're thinking things through and not just withdrawing from situations that you have felt uncomfortable with in the past. That's really a good way to react, and it shows that you are handling interpersonal or social situations much better than you did before. That's great. It's also important, of course, for you to continue to react that way, and from now on you will have to keep doing things like that and the other things we've talked about on your own—and there's no reason you can't. Therapy is like the initial push and the initial lesson. It gets you started in the right direction, and then you keep progressing on your own. . . as you have done.

With what you've learned from our discussion about how we view ourselves and others and how these views affect our feelings and behaviors, you should now be better able to evaluate your own experiences and cope with them. It's as if you reason with yourself and don't let small negative events get magnified out of proportion to their importance. And you've learned some relaxation procedures and used them a few times in stressful situations, so you should be able to use them again when necessary. In other words, even though we're ending our sessions, it doesn't mean that the therapy or the improvement in your life has to stop. It just means that you're going to be your own therapist now—instead of me.

GREEN. Well, I hope I can keep things going in the right direction. I know I need to improve in my relationships with women, but I'm not as ill at ease there as I used to be. Did I tell you I'm going on a cruise in a month and I'm looking forward to it? Now that I've learned a few dance steps I'll be less of a wallflower, I hope.

GARFIELD. I'm reasonably optimistic about how you will handle things in the future. You've made some progress on some pretty tough problems, and you were always able to keep from getting discouraged when the going was rough. That's a good sign. You've also been realistic in your expectations and haven't looked for any miraculous cures—so you haven't been disappointed.

GREEN. Hmm, hmn.

GARFIELD. As we've said before, there are always ups and downs in a person's life. Life doesn't always go smoothly, and usually there are some things we can't fully control. If we see these things realistically, we can accept them for what they are and not brood over them unnecessarily. If we expect everything to turn out perfectly, we usually are disappointed. Isn't that so?

GREEN. Yes, that's true . . . certainly in terms of how I used to feel about myself. In my daydreams, things could be wonderful and I could be a great guy, and then in real life things would look bleak and I'd see myself as a misfit, a real sad character. I don't daydream like that any more; I don't always expect life to be rosy, and I can accept things as they come much better. As I said, I feel I'm not such a terrible guy now and I try to handle my fears as best I can. I guess I have a different outlook on life, and that helps me.

GARFIELD. Hmm, hmn. It does. You still may get anxious or fearful; we haven't done away with all such feelings you could have. But now you can do your best to cope with these situations and not let them overpower you.

Well, perhaps we've talked enough about this. Is there anything you would like to bring up now before we come to the end of our last session?

GREEN. No, I can't think of anything right now—although I'll probably think of something after I leave. I think we have covered everything I had on my mind (pauses). You know, I understand myself better than when I first came here to see you. I can remember that I was very upset then and fearful about what was going to happen, what kind of a person you'd be, and if there was much hope for me. Things are rather different now, and I hope the worst is behind me.

GARFIELD. I believe it is.

GREEN. At least now I have fewer problems or things that bother me than I had when we started. I'm getting along OK at work, and I'm getting up with just one alarm clock (smiles). I feel better about myself, and I'm able to take things in my stride much better than I used to.

So, really, there isn't anything I should ask you about now. On the one hand, it seems I've been coming to see you for a long time, and on the other hand, the time has seemed to pass quickly. If things continue to go as they are now, I think I'll be able to manage all right. But if something unusual should happen or I have a problem I'd like to talk over with you, could I call you and arrange an appointment?

GARFIELD. Of course. I hope you won't ever have to call me because of any problem, but if something should come up in the future, by all means feel free to give me a call. You've been a very good person to work with, and I'm personally very pleased that things have turned out as well as they have. It reflects your cooperative attitude and determination to help yourself. I hope all will continue to go well for you and you'll continue to make progress.

GREEN. Thanks, Doc, I appreciate very much all that you've done to help me. Your interest in me has meant a great deal. Good-bye.

GARFIELD. Good-bye, Donald—all the best.

This was our last session and I responded positively to it. Donald pretty much determined the content of the session, offering some appraisal of whatever changes he had noted or experienced in himself. His statements reflected many of the discussions that went on during the therapy sessions, with emphasis on his changed self-perception and the changes in how he interacts with others and responds to the events of his life.

His self-appraisal seemed quite realistic to me. In most respects he still resembles the old Donald Green, but in some ways he is different, and the difference is in a positive direction. At least to me, his therapist, he is a happier person than he was when he entered therapy. He still gets anxious at times, but these intervals are relatively brief and nondebilitating. I did not directly attempt to treat what appeared to be occasional panic states because I gave a higher priority to other goals, and he has used the coping procedures he learned to reduce the negative effects of these incidents. The change secured in other areas has had a positive effect on these symptoms as well.

Although I initially rated the prospect for change through this therapy as limited, Donald surprised me. His earnestness, sincerity, and cooperation contributed to make the outcome somewhat better than anticipated. It also reaffirmed my belief that we must not be too rigid in our initial appraisals of potential clients. Our knowledge of psychopathology, personality, and psychotherapy is far from complete, and therefore an eclectic approach to clinical work seems the best to use. ∎

CRITIQUE OF DONALD GREEN'S TREATMENT WITH AN ECLECTIC APPROACH

by Allen E. Bergin

In using the phrase "an eclectic approach" rather than "the eclectic approach," Sol Garfield's case analysis reflects an important feature of the eclectic trend in psychotherapy. There are many ways to be "eclectic." Garfield's way represents one of the more common modes in that it utilizes cognitive, behavioral, and relationship therapy principles. It is also results-oriented and empirically based.

Garfield's approach does not rely on traditional, long-term dynamic therapy principles, although it borrows somewhat from brief dynamic therapies that focus on specific symptoms, aim for limited goals, and engender expectations of reasonably rapid change. Garfield has clearly been influenced by Franz Alexander, who pioneered efforts in the 1940s to make psychoanalysis an efficient procedure. Psychoanalytic influence is also evident in his occasional emphasis on the motivating and anxiety-reducing effects of self-understanding. This does not, however, place Garfield in the position of depending on the theory and technique of psychoanalysis as it applies to insight. Unlike many eclectics, he rejects complex dynamic constructs.

Garfield handles the therapy of Donald Green adroitly by shrewdly assessing a complex array of symptoms in terms of the "soft spots" in the pathology where change is both most probable and most likely to spread to other problem areas. The therapist uses technique and relationship skills effectively to stimulate an optimum amount of change in a brief time, with the assumption that the change process would continue after termination by virtue of the client's self-initiated efforts. Although the therapy is pictured as neatly fitting the symptomatology and the therapist's schema for change, more changes might have been possible if psychodynamic issues had been addressed more intensely.

Given the careful focus on major modifiable problems within the therapist's framework, the change process is conducted with precision, efficacy, and sensitivity. Still, the therapist is open to self-criticism and notes a common problem that occurs in focused, time-limited treatment: The patient can be pushed too hard and too fast at times. This can lead to discouragement and to resistance, thus undermining motivation and the therapeutic alliance. In this case, Garfield shows clearly how corrective measures can be employed in such situations. However, it is possible that even better measures could have been taken with greater effect had the therapist been slightly more open to psychodynamic considerations.

Eclectic therapy does not focus much on causation. Rather, it devotes effort to directing a concrete and specific change process centered around the presenting dysfunctions. Motivation and generalization of change are thought to be advanced by success in achieving small but quick improvements.

This theme is particularly evident in the therapist's choice to ignore Donald's panic attacks, as well as the origins and dynamics of his obsessional conduct. To dynamic therapists, this would result in superficial and possibly harmful therapy. Research findings to date tend to support Garfield's approach, but it should be noted that nearly all of the good-outcome research on such problems has been done by cognitively and behaviorally oriented scientists who approach treatment and research from their special perspective. Definitive findings are yet to be accumulated on the ramifications of dealing more directly with the pathodynamics of obsessive-compulsive disorders within an eclectic framework.

While assessment and diagnosis are not emphasized in Garfield's case report, they can and probably should be important to an eclectic approach. In more rigid and narrower approaches there is less need for diagnostic sophistication, because they tend to employ similar techniques with most cases. In an eclectic system, it is expected that diagnostic evaluation will result in differential treatments suited to particular patients and their arrays of symptoms, each of which may require a different intervention.

Psychological testing or more systematic behavioral assessment would have been appropriate in Donald's case. The therapist approaches this problem through interview questions, having Donald monitor his self-behaviors in a diary, and obtaining self-reports on new-behavior experiments between sessions. There are additional valid alternatives, however. One would be the simple expedient of obtaining more explicit observations of the client's behavior from co-workers and his few friends. A suggestion in this direction can be found in the industrial psychologist's report of the perceptions Donald's co-workers had of him. The therapist could have used a simple reporting device to show more clearly the negative changes in Donald that needed to be addressed. For instance, co-workers or supervisors might have been asked (with Donald's permission) to rate his degree of withdrawal or estimate the frequency (probably low) of his prosocial acts. This might have provided a better baseline for evaluating the seriousness of his isolation syndrome, which, without a lot of evidence, the therapist considers to be primary.

It might also have been helpful to see how Donald scored on some objective personality questionnaire relative to obsessive-compulsive disorders. Such normative data would provide better guidance with respect to the relative seriousness of this problem and its prognosis. Garfield makes this aspect of Donald's symptoms much easier to modify than might have been the case, particularly since severe disorders of this type do not respond well to any kind of treatment. It is also possible, however, that better assessment would have shown the obsessive-compulsive aspects of his syndrome to be less entrenched and more amenable to the kind of rapid modification illustrated here. In either case, a better understanding of Donald's diagnostic status would have been helpful, and it would have shown how an eclectic therapist makes intervention choices from an array of possibilities, based on careful assessment. In this respect, eclectic therapy parallels medical practice; in both, diverse treatments are prescribed on the basis of sophisticated diagnostic signs.

Nevertheless, Garfield does a nice job of showing how different methods of intervention can be matched to different problems in the same case. Given the pattern of inadequacy and social backwardness that undergirded the client's fears, phobias, and obsessions, Garfield wisely avoids the impulse to rush in and fix things immediately, an error to which neophyte brief-therapists are prone. Instead, he devotes time and energy to the client's self-image, motivation for treatment, and relationship with the therapist. This strategy would be characteristic of many eclectic therapists who value the "common factors" derived from traditional therapies.

This client has a whole world of feelings, memories, and perceptions bottled up inside him which Garfield genuinely and warmly invites him to share. Although the client's social fears at first inhibit him, he soon finds self-disclosure to be an emotional relief, and the therapist's relationship skills soothe his phobic reactivity. His tendency to withdraw from a deepening interaction is desensitized in this humane context, and he is reinforced for continued approach behavior.

At the same time, Garfield delivers to Donald a substantial series of messages of encouragement and support. These are very important in that they engender hope (Frank, 1961) and the beginnings of a new sense of self-efficacy (Bandura, 1986). The therapist bases these remarks, in part, on evidence already revealed about the patient's strengths. As Jerome Frank has pointed out, effective development of hope is always based on a measure of evidence.

These procedures help Donald overcome his fear of risking disapproval in a relationship and provide an opening wedge for experiments with new behaviors involving other persons. The sharing of self in a warm, noncritical relationship abets growth in other contexts. Herein we observe an adept application of traditional humanistic relationship therapy, principles of learning and generalization, and the role of persuasion in boosting morale and motivation.

Some therapists function this way virtually exclusively, but Garfield proceeds to demonstrate the value of going beyond the "common factors" of good therapy and using specific techniques. These include precisely applied cognitive and behavioral strategies, such as interpretation, persuasion, and cognitive restructuring. I use the term "interpretation" because it seems to fit the verbalizations of many cognitive therapists, and it suggests that the presumably new cognitive therapies have roots in traditional therapies. I add the term "persuasion" because I believe that Garfield and most modern cognitive therapists, unlike traditional therapists, use persuasion frequently to accelerate change. Their beliefs about change are similar to experimenters in the social psychology of communication, persuasion, and attitude change. The process is more directive than in ordinary verbal psychotherapy and geared more toward a change in perspective than to affect-laden insight.

Such reconstruing is based not on theories of unconscious processes but on a straightforward application of cognitive processes and social influence. Some eclectics, however, weave psychodynamics into the flow of change.

Rather than depending on dynamic formulations, Garfield leaps in with a sweeping interpretation that the client accepts. It isn't clear that a "real" client would do so, but in this fabricated dialogue an important point is illustrated. Garfield identifies a whole series of client complaints (embarrassment, panic, overreactivity, obsessive rituals, increasing inadequacy feelings, and heightened tension) as creating a major sense of loss of control. This is interpreted as the precipitating *thema* that sends Donald for help. In Bandura's terms, a dramatic loss of self-efficacy propels the patient's search. This is communicated to Donald, and he is persuaded that his various efforts at stemming this loss of control are not working and that he should give them up. All this is presented more rapidly than would likely occur in an actual case, but it makes the point. The therapist also provides considerable reassurance to back up his suggestions, and he reinforces the client's expectations for success in dropping the symptomatic pattern. This means Donald must give up the multiple alarm clocks, the paperboy's cueing, and the neighbor's alerting him that it is time to get up.

The widely used procedure of response prevention is thus applied with apparent success. The patient is able to manage a new level of self-regulation and is ecstatic over his progress. Stopping the symptomatic rituals yields feelings of control and an associated euphoria, instead of making him more anxious, as dynamic theories would predict. There is little speculation about causes here, but rather a devotion to direct and immediate change, showing again the behavioral slant to the therapist's eclecticism.

Practical attention is given to specific daily routines and stimulating the client to participate actively in designing a plan of action. For instance, Donald suggests how he might stay awake: "I suppose I could have the alarm clock in the kitchen and when I go to turn it off, I could put on the radio and start the coffee. I could also shut the bedroom door and soak my head in cold water. . . ." Garfield adds that they agree he could "go get the morning newspaper, take some deep breaths of fresh air, and perhaps look at the front page or the sports section." Thus Garfield directs and expects small changes in Donald's behavior, rather than spending much time on history-taking or analysis of the origins of symptoms. The immediate changes that flow from this become significant morale boosters and intensify Donald's motivation to try hard for larger effects. The therapist reinforces his initial successes with praise and encouragement to face more difficult challenges.

This style of intervention, which derives directly from behavior therapy, represents a distinctive contribution to the field. The resulting important shift in therapeutic thinking has been so successful that it is unlikely to ever be reversed. It is only one aspect of the repertoire of almost all eclectic therapists.

As Donald continues making progress in managing symptoms, Garfield makes another major interpretation of the situation. He judges a subset of the presenting complaints to represent a *life-style* pattern that "underlies" and abets the main symptoms. This pattern consists of shyness, isolation, introversion, inhibition, or a socially phobic and socially unskilled way of functioning. Garfield believes Donald's deficiencies in this area are fueling his fears and depression and preventing positive social rewards that would enhance growth and normality.

Garfield again uses persuasion and cognitive restructuring to ally Donald with him in a new course of action. He also uses the inspiration of hope and reinforcement of Donald's self-image or self-efficacy to motivate the new change efforts. He lists Donald's virtues and recounts evidence of positive feedback from other observers. He makes a major causal statement to the effect that Donald's life-style of inhibition is retarding growth and the expression of a wonderful potential that is already there, waiting to be actualized. Garfield becomes virtually Maslowian in endorsing Donald's possibilities. At the same time, he warns Donald against overgeneralizing about his defects and concluding that he is worthless, thus employing the correction of negative cognitive distortions. He encourages Donald to engage in some self-reflection and endorses the value of self-understanding. These techniques influence behavior and well-being and are an antidote for confusion, anxiety, and self-doubt. The insights thus obtained help to motivate and manage the course of changes in life-style patterns.

In order to effect changes in life-style, Donald is instructed to monitor his own social behavior in a variety of personal and work situations. His limitations are pointed out, but Garfield demonstrates alternative modes of conduct that should prove more satisfying. Donald practices these in the safety of the consulting relationship and then applies them in "homework" assignments. He begins to talk more openly, do things for others, assert himself, initiate conversations and new relationships, join groups, and otherwise follow the prescriptions, despite some setbacks.

As predicted, these new patterns, reinforced both clinically and naturally in the environment, reduce the presenting symptoms while also building a new repertoire of prosocial activity. Donald's new ability to be appropriately assertive (for example, in correcting a co-worker) provides concrete evidence to support the change in his mental stereotype of himself as inadequate and deserving of rejection and isolation.

The Problem of Psychodynamics

As an example of therapy that is successful in modifying a number of problems, Garfield's case report depicts one style of eclecticism rather well. At the same time, it leaves room for comment about dynamics. The most dramatic psychodynamic event occurs when Donald is pushed too hard by Garfield to perform behavioral assignments in social skills as homework. Garfield uses this episode to illustrate a common problem and adeptly shows how therapists should admit mistakes, back off, and adapt to the client's capacities. Nevertheless, the description omits a great deal that probably would occur in an actual case.

As a result of proximal failures in his efforts, Donald regresses significantly in his sense of self-efficacy and becomes preoccupied with fears about how the therapist perceives him. A significant transference occurs which might have been used to facilitate better change. Donald is clearly relating to the therapist in the same way he has to other figures in the past, especially authorities. Here is a great opportunity to draw him out and work through his feelings concerning power in relationships with superiors which probably have a long and deep history. Though his self-image is malleable under cognitive-behavioral and relationship therapy techniques, it is likely to be riding on a conflicted substrate that is never dealt with. The fact that elements of it arise so quickly in relation to the therapist reveals its probable potency and pathogenic nature. To have managed Donald's transference in a more traditional way might well have resulted in a deeper change, one that would resist future failures and distresses more adequately. It is possible that learnings from such a therapeutic experience could have aided the homework assignments, and a more thorough generalization of new responses might have been facilitated by having them occur in a core relationship. Such an analysis might also have made Donald's family history more comprehensible. Closing off such exploration may or may not prove problematic over the long term.

Donald's panic attacks, which were never addressed directly, could have had any of several origins. Garfield chooses to guess that they are closely connected with the other symptoms and would improve along with change in the targeted complaints. It is also possible, however, that these symptoms had more profound implications. It would have been possible to discern them by dynamic techniques, and this might have led to additional strategies for change or targets for change. The nagging questions persist: Will change continue in Donald's life, and were the panic and obsessive-compulsive aspects of his disorder adequately dealt with?

In this case report, termination with Donald Green goes smoothly. Sessions are gradually reduced in frequency, and short-term changes are reinforced and expanded upon in the overview of the case and discussion of future prospects. Donald is showing progressive interest in relations with women, although this important area of his life has not been explored. Indeed, sex and aggression are surprisingly absent from the case study. This underscores the relative absence of a psychodynamic emphasis in Garfield's eclecticism. Is it possible that anger and sex fears contributed to Donald's panics and obsessional states? If his fear of the therapist's disapproval had been analyzed, would anger have been found lurking beneath the phobic content? Were his social inhibitions based on fear of losing control in quite different ways from those suggested by Garfield?

The question of medication did not arise, but would assessment and prescription have had an appropriate place? Would psychotherapy have been facilitated by at least a modest drug regimen?

It is clear that the case could have been handled in a variety of ways, even among eclectics. The way it is outlined here seems appropriate and fits one style of multimodal intervention. A variety of methods were applied in specific ways that made sense. The use of relationship factors to facilitate implementation and effects of the specific procedures was exemplary. The inclusion of other common factors alluded to by Jerome Frank—such as dealing with morale, having a rationale for the change process, inspiring hope and confidence—was all to the good. Garfield has provided a viable outline of an eclectic system adapted to the status and potential of the client, Donald Green.

Describing an eclectic system is difficult; the approach is evolving, there is much diversity, and there has been little research on process and outcome. Putting together a variety of approaches creates conceptual and technical problems that are not as evident when describing a singular, coherent approach. Despite such difficulties, eclectics assume that patient welfare will be enhanced by applying a variety of efficacious methods, as opposed to the more comfortable, but more narrowly applicable, singular orientations.

■

REFERENCES

Adler, A. (1927). *The practice and theory of individual psychology.* New York: Harcourt.

Allport, G. W. (1937). *Personality: A psychological interpretation.* New York: Henry Holt.

Bandura, A. (1986). *Social foundations of thought and action: A social cognitive theory.* Englewood Cliffs, NJ: Prentice-Hall.

Beutler, L. E. (1983). *Eclectic psychotherapy: A systematic approach.* New York: Pergamon Press.

Frank, J. D. (1961). *Persuasion and healing.* Baltimore, MD: Johns Hopkins Press.

Freud, S. (1938). *A general introduction to psychoanalysis.* New York: Garden City Publishing.

Garfield, S. L. (1957). *Introductory clinical psychology.* New York: Macmillan.

Garfield, S. L. (1980). *Psychotherapy: An eclectic approach.* New York: John Wiley.

Garfield, S. L. (1989). *The Practice of Brief Psychotherapy.* New York: Pergamon Press.

Garfield, S. L., & Bergin, A. E. (1986). *Handbook of psychotherapy and behavior change.* (3rd ed). New York: John Wiley.

Garfield, S. L., & Kurz, M. (1952). Evaluation of treatment and related procedures in 1216 cases referred to a mental hygiene clinic. *Psychiatric Quarterly, 26,* 414–424.

Goldfried, M. R. (Ed.). (1982). *Converging themes in psychotherapy: Trends in psychodynamic, humanistic, and behavioral practice.* New York: Springer.

Heine, R. W. (1953). A comparison of patients' reports on psychotherapeutic experience with psychoanalytic, nondirective and Adlerian therapists. *American Journal of Psychotherapy, 7,* 16–23.

Klein, M. H., Dittman, A. T., Parloff, M. B., & Gill, M. M. (1969). Behavior therapy: Observations and reflections. *Journal of Consulting and Clinical Psychology, 33,* 259–266.

Lacks, P. (1987). *Behavioral treatment for persistent insomnia.* New York: Pergamon Press.

Lazarus, A. A. (1981). *The practice of multimodal therapy.* New York: McGraw-Hill.

Levine, M. (1948). *Psychotherapy in medical practice.* New York: Macmillan.

Louttit, C. M. (1936). *Clinical psychology.* New York: Harper & Brothers.

Louttit, C. M. (1939). The nature of clinical psychology. *Psychological Bulletin, 36,* 361–389.

Marmor, J. (1971). Dynamic psychotherapy and behavior therapy—Are they irreconcilable? *Archives of General Psychiatry, 24,* 22–28.

Norcross, J. C. (Ed.). (1987). *Casebook of eclectic psychotherapy.* New York: Brunner/Mazel.

Norcross, J. C. (Ed.). (1986). *Handbook of eclectic psychotherapy.* New York: Brunner/Mazel.

Prochaska, J. O., & DiClemente, C. C. (1984). *The transtheoretical approach: Crossing the traditional boundaries of therapy.* Homewood, IL: Dow Jones-Irwin.

Rosenzweig, S. (1936). Some implicit common factors in diverse methods of psychotherapy. *American Journal of Orthopsychiatry, 6,* 412–415.

Wachtel, P. L. (1977). *Psychoanalysis and behavior therapy.* New York: Basic Books.

FIVE THERAPISTS AND ONE CLIENT
Composition by Point West, Inc., Carol Stream, Illinois
Printed and bound by McNaughton & Gunn, Inc., Saline, Michigan
Designed by Willis Proudfoot, Mt. Prospect, Illinois
Production supervision by Robert H. Grigg, Chicago, Illinois
The text is set in ITC Berkeley Oldstyle